VOLUME THREE:

BROKEN CURSES

Volume Three: Broken Curses

Story by
SERENA VALENTINO

Art by
BREEHN BURNS

Introduction by
LANDRY WALKER

Guest Art by
PAUL CHIEN
RICK CORTEZ
ANTHONY GUARISCO
BILLY MARTINEZ
CRAB SCRAMBLY
JILL THOMPSON

Created by
SERENA VALENTINO &
TED NAIFEH

Cover design by
BREEHN BURNS &
CHRISTINA BECKERT

Editrix
JULIA DVORIN

Ink Assists by
PETER REPOVSKI

Published by SLG Publishing

President & Publisher
DAN VADO

Editrix-in-Chief
JENNIFER DE GUZMAN

Director of Sales
DEB MOSKYOK

GloomCookie Volume Three: Broken Curses
collects issues 13 – 17 of the SLG Publishing
series *GloomCookie*.

www.slavelabor.com
www.gloomcookie.com

Second Printing: November 2005
ISBN 0-943151-88-0

SLG Publishing
P.O. Box 26427
San Jose, CA 95159-6427

My Introduction to GloomCookie
by Landry Walker

I think that any good introduction to a book should contain some clever anecdote by the introducer that somehow illustrates the impact that said body of work has had on the aforementioned introducer. Unfortunately, I don't have one. I'm either not a clever anecdote kind of guy, or I would have been better off writing this sober, and not three hours before the deadline. Sorry about that, Serena.

That does not mean that I have absolutely nothing to relate, far from it. But most of what I want to talk about is Serena herself. See, I'm of the understanding that you:

A: Do not really give a rat's ass what I think.

B: Can read the book for yourself and get a perfectly clear understanding of it without needing any input from me.

C: Will be better served by being given some insight on the author of this work, thereby giving you a better understanding of the work itself.

The first thing I would like to address is the rumor of Serena's inherent evilness. What you should know without me having to tell you is that all rumors have at least some basis in truth. Have no doubt, Serena is pure evil. Oh, she hides it well, what with her charming smiles and offers of coffee. But given time, anyone can see through the ruse. She is evil, in its most pure and unadulterated form. She has powerful mind-control abilities that make her smile impossible to resist and force you to give her bags of presents. This is not something that the human will can oppose. This is the force of nature that can only be described as Serena's Ultra-Powered-Hypno-Vision. Whatever you do, do not look her directly in the eye. If you do, all will be lost.

The second thing you should know is that Serena is freakishly honest. Don't get me wrong, I'm sure she is capable of lying; it's just that she has no need. Her honesty is so disarming that it will leave a person dazed, disoriented. That's when she moves in for the kill. To be honest, I'm not sure what the kill part is. I haven't figured out that part, yet. Unfortunately, by the time I do, it will likely be too late for me. Why? Because that's the kill part. I'm sure my last thoughts on this earth will be something like "Gaaakkkk!!! Serena's one weakness is…" And then I will die. Curse you, Serena! Curse you for inflicting this horrible possible future upon me!!

Sigh.

If you think I'm just ranting, you are probably right. In all honesty, I do that a lot. The reality of it is, when it comes to the subject of Serena Valentino, I'm dead jealous. I would give my left nut to be half the writer that she is. She's prolific and frighteningly imaginative. She has a shrewd practical side that is totally at odds with her oh-so-squishy persona. Her characters are a clever blend of the people around her and the voices in her own head. Each one resonates in a unique way, and the stories continually surprise me with the twists and turns they take. The end result is a cast of characters that you feel at home with. At least in a sort of creepy, somewhat deranged way, the characters feel real. There's a comfort to be found in seeing the Lex and the others (including the oh-so-sexy Chrys, but I suppose this is neither the time or the place for my personal fetishes) drinking coffee and discussing the sometimes outrageous elements of their lives in an almost gossipy way. You feel as if the events transpiring in their lives are events you can relate to. Even if they involve such things as….

But I digress. You can figure these things out for yourself. Read the book. Do you want me to spoil it for you? Of course you don't.

And of course, there is the beautiful artwork of Breehn John Burns. This is a more difficult subject for me to write an introduction on, having only met Breehn once. My first impression was that he was very nice. This almost certainly means he is hiding something. So Breehn, when you read this, understand that I'm on to you. I'll be watching.

Anyway, I have to say this: I don't envy Breehn. Being the third artist to work on to a popular title must have been difficult. Not in the artwork itself. As anyone can plainly see just by glancing at this book, Breehn quickly proved himself to be more than up to the task. What I would imagine would be hard is having to constantly be (for better or for worse) compared by the readers to the previous artists. The fact is that the look Breehn brings to *GloomCookie* is unique; an expressiveness to the individual characters that is charming (a perfect example of this is found in the look on the face of a little boy dressed as a werewolf. I want that image as a sticker), and a rhythm to his sequentials that do exactly what good sequentials are supposed to do. They flow naturally, allowing the readers to lose themselves in the dialogue. Again, you can see all this for yourself, and I highly doubt that you need me to point these things out for you. But just in case there are one or two people out there who would miss these subtle intricacies of the art, I felt that I had to force you into awareness with my words.

So read the third installment of *GloomCookie*. Enjoy it. Appreciate it. Seriously. If you don't, Serena might use her Ultra-Powered-Hypno-Vision on you. And it hurts. A lot.

Landry Walker is the mostly harmless writer and co-creator of Little Gloomy *and* X-Ray Comics, *both published by SLG.*

Lovingly dedicated to
my husband Eric
& my sister Jesse
–Serena

To my family and friends
for their unconditional
love and support.
–Breehn

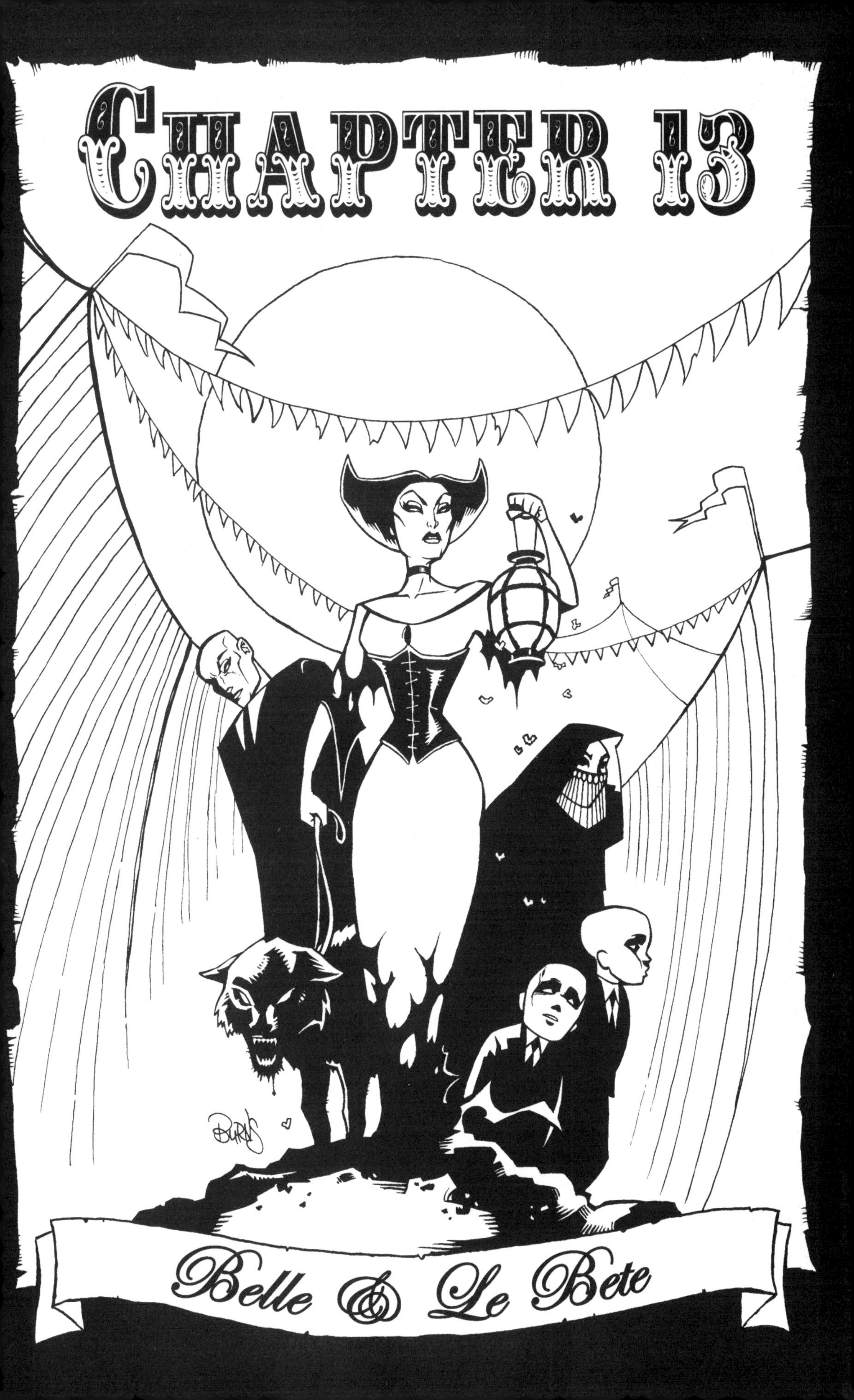
CHAPTER 13
BURNS
Belle & Le Bete

Breaking The Curse

Part II

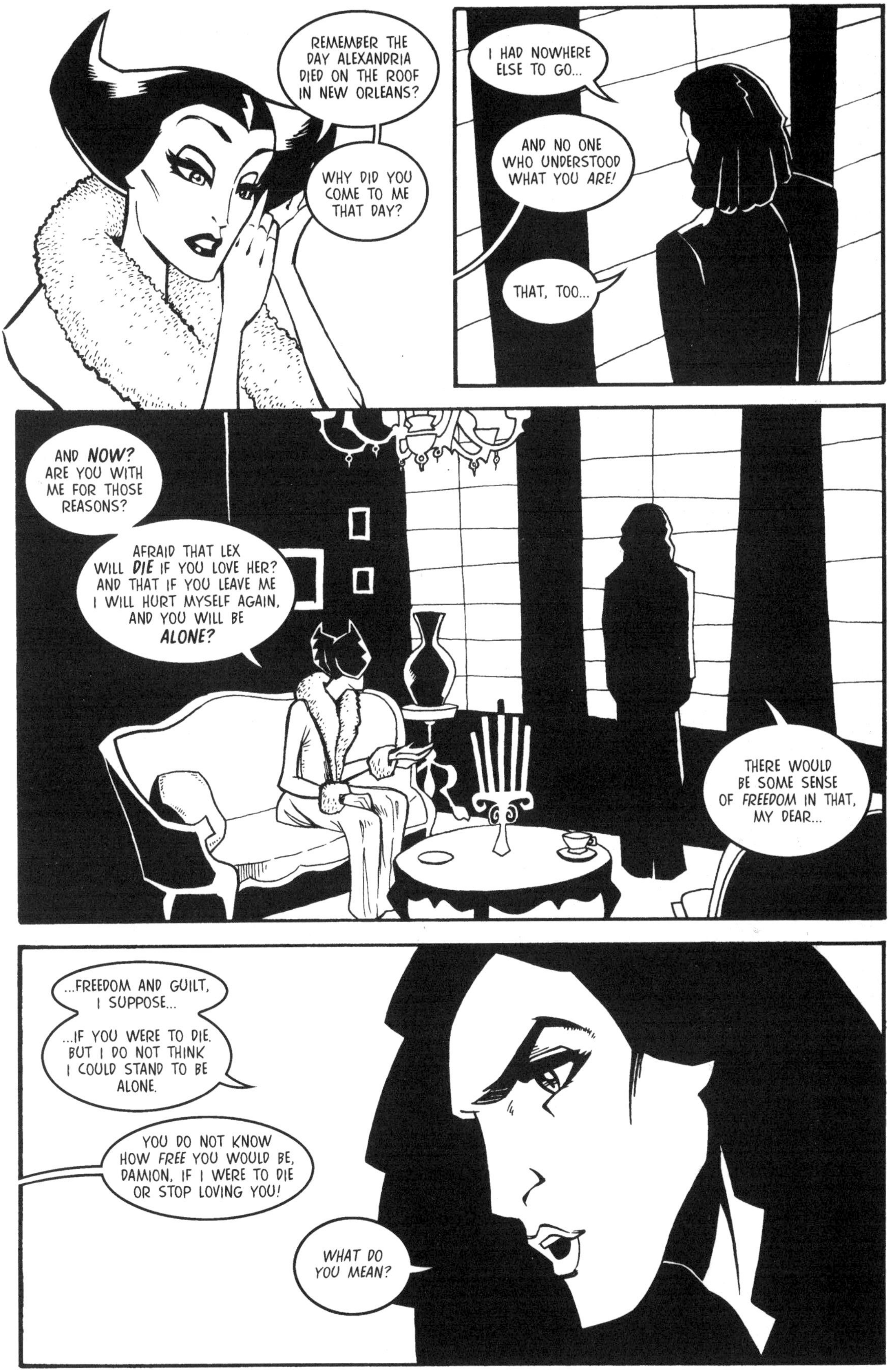
REMEMBER THE DAY ALEXANDRIA DIED ON THE ROOF IN NEW ORLEANS?
WHY DID YOU COME TO ME THAT DAY?
I HAD NOWHERE ELSE TO GO...
AND NO ONE WHO UNDERSTOOD WHAT YOU *ARE!*
THAT, TOO...
AND **NOW?** ARE YOU WITH ME FOR THOSE REASONS?
AFRAID THAT LEX WILL ***DIE*** IF YOU LOVE HER? AND THAT IF YOU LEAVE ME I WILL HURT MYSELF AGAIN, AND YOU WILL BE ***ALONE?***
THERE WOULD BE SOME SENSE OF *FREEDOM* IN THAT, MY DEAR...
...FREEDOM AND GUILT, I SUPPOSE...
...IF YOU WERE TO DIE. BUT I DO NOT THINK I COULD STAND TO BE ALONE.
YOU DO NOT KNOW HOW *FREE* YOU WOULD BE, DAMION, IF I WERE TO DIE OR STOP LOVING YOU!
WHAT DO YOU MEAN?

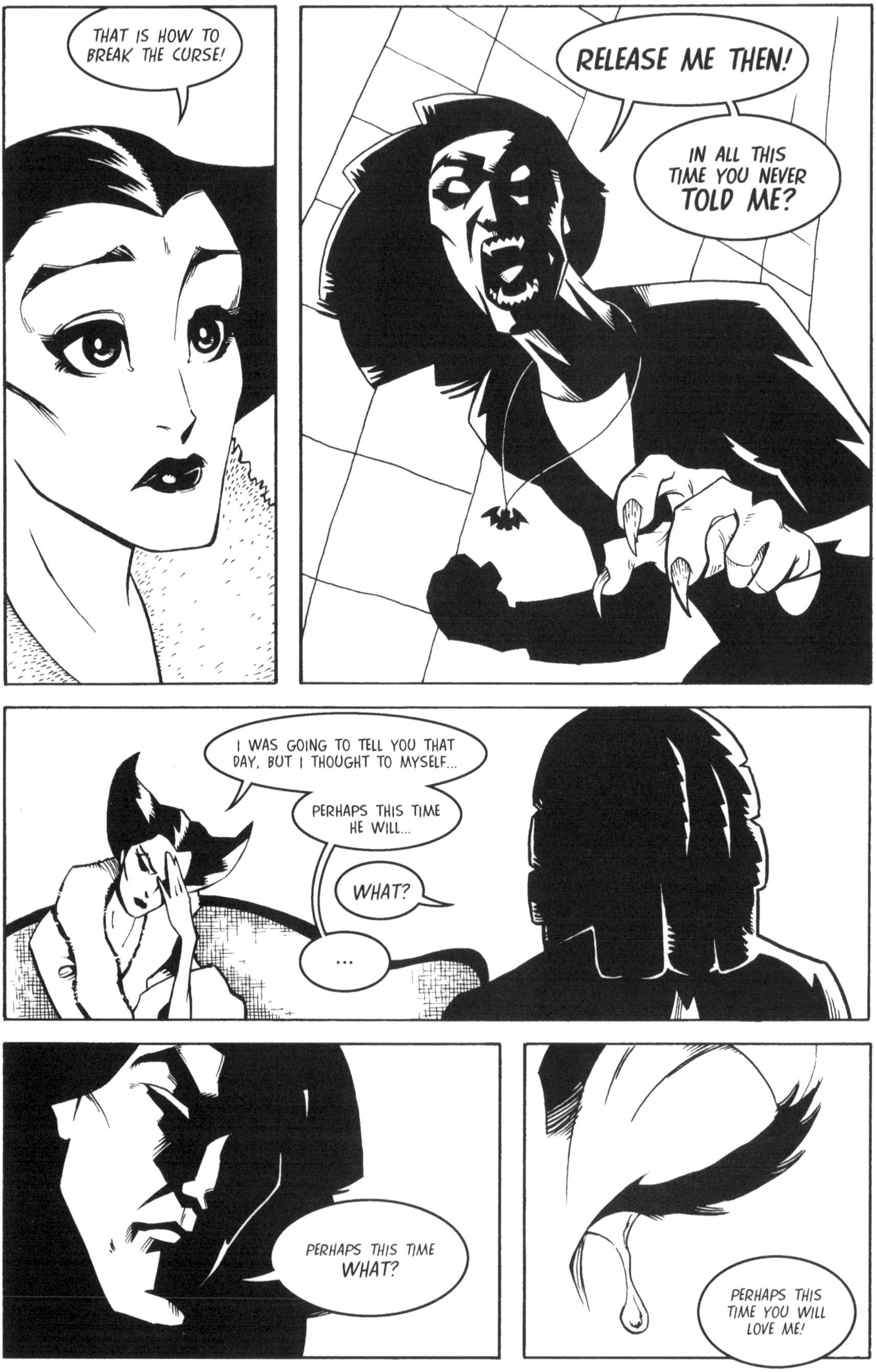
THAT IS HOW TO BREAK THE CURSE!
RELEASE ME THEN!
IN ALL THIS TIME YOU NEVER TOLD ME?
I WAS GOING TO TELL YOU THAT DAY, BUT I THOUGHT TO MYSELF...
PERHAPS THIS TIME HE WILL...
WHAT?
...
PERHAPS THIS TIME WHAT?
PERHAPS THIS TIME YOU WILL LOVE ME!

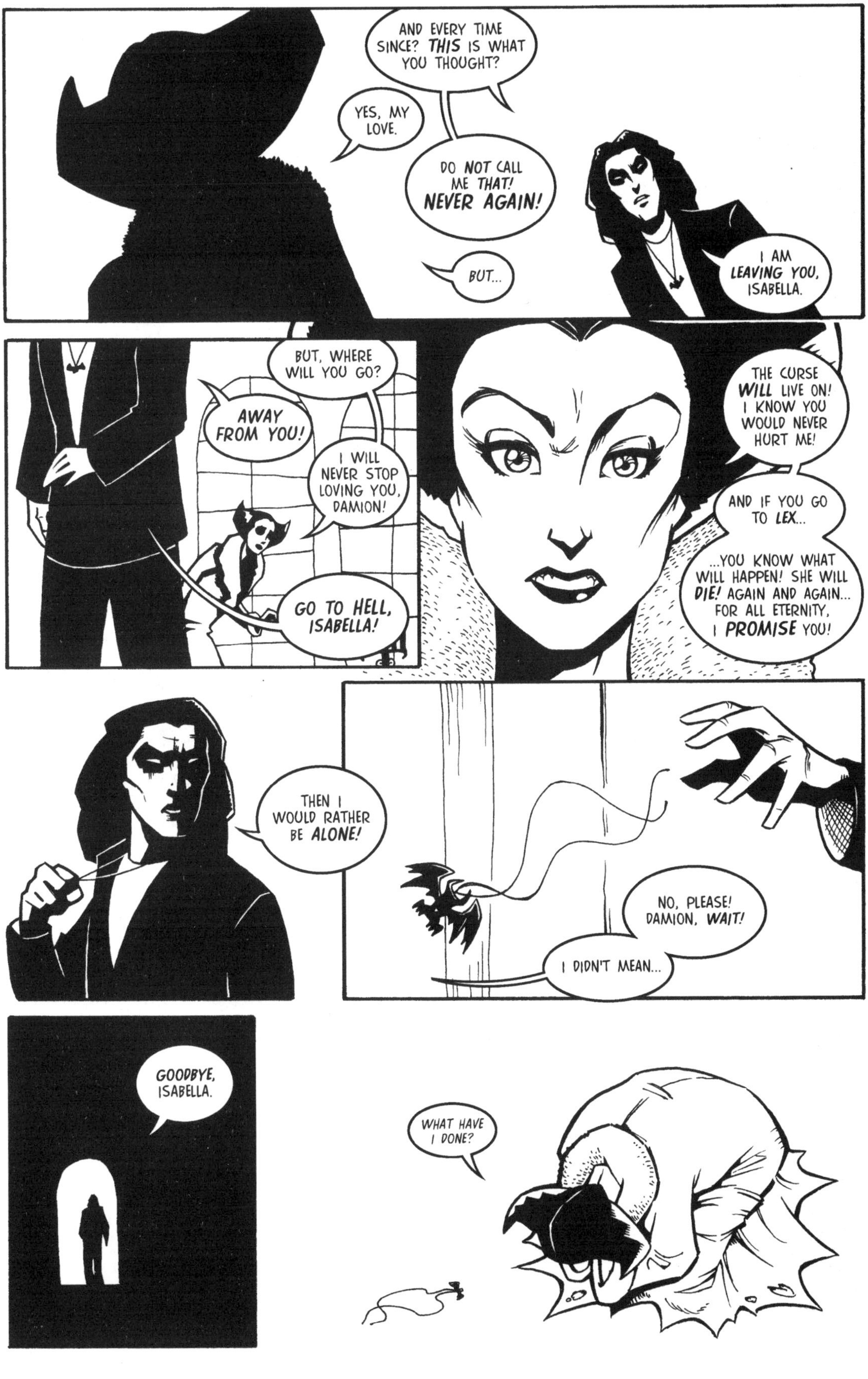
AND EVERY TIME SINCE? THIS IS WHAT YOU THOUGHT?
YES, MY LOVE.
DO NOT CALL ME THAT! NEVER AGAIN!
BUT...
I AM LEAVING YOU, ISABELLA.
BUT, WHERE WILL YOU GO?
AWAY FROM YOU!
I WILL NEVER STOP LOVING YOU, DAMION!
GO TO HELL, ISABELLA!
THE CURSE WILL LIVE ON! I KNOW YOU WOULD NEVER HURT ME!
AND IF YOU GO TO LEX...
...YOU KNOW WHAT WILL HAPPEN! SHE WILL DIE! AGAIN AND AGAIN... FOR ALL ETERNITY, I PROMISE YOU!
THEN I WOULD RATHER BE ALONE!
NO, PLEASE! DAMION, WAIT!
I DIDN'T MEAN...
GOODBYE, ISABELLA.
WHAT HAVE I DONE?

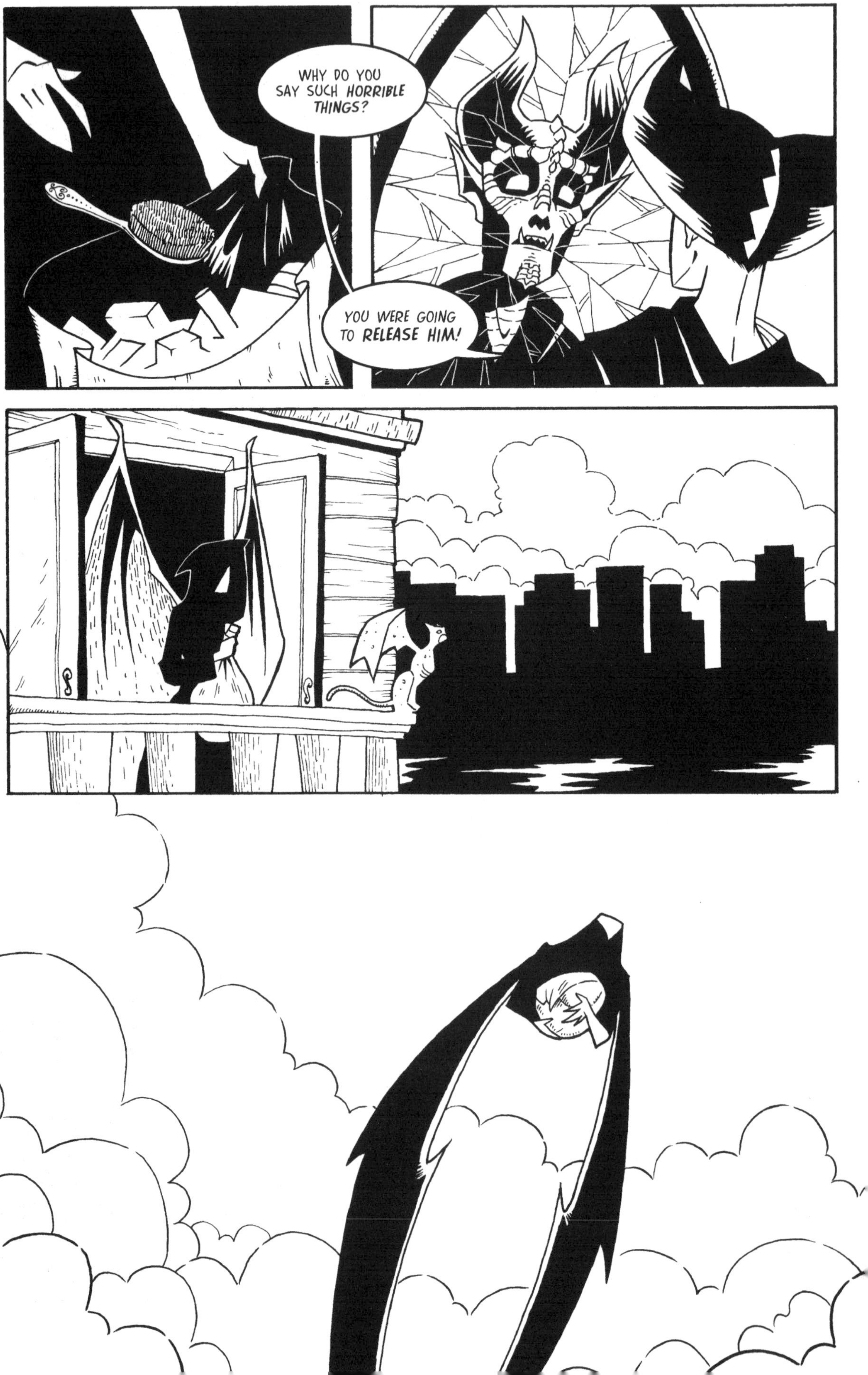
WHY DO YOU SAY SUCH HORRIBLE THINGS?
YOU WERE GOING TO RELEASE HIM!

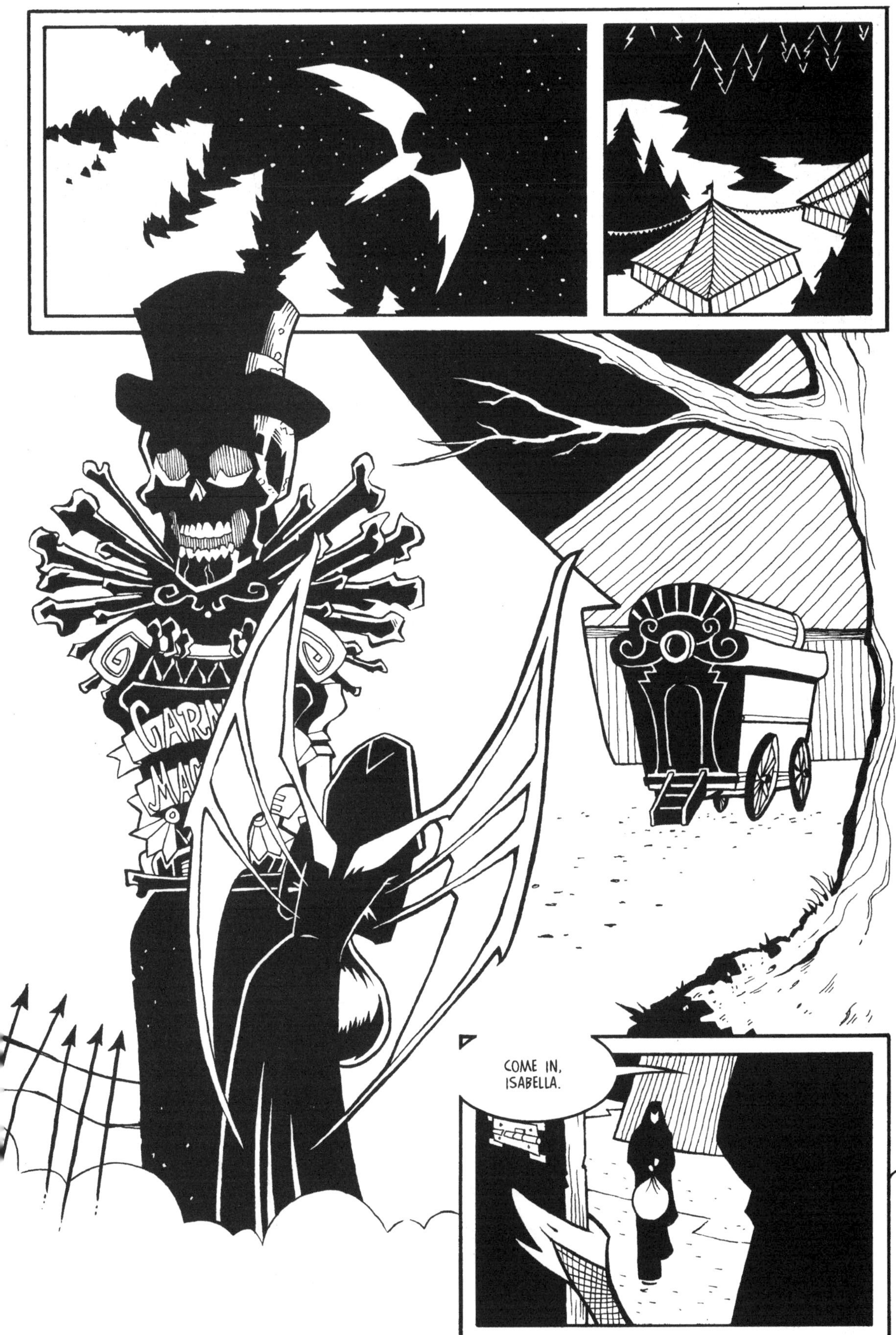
COME IN, ISABELLA.

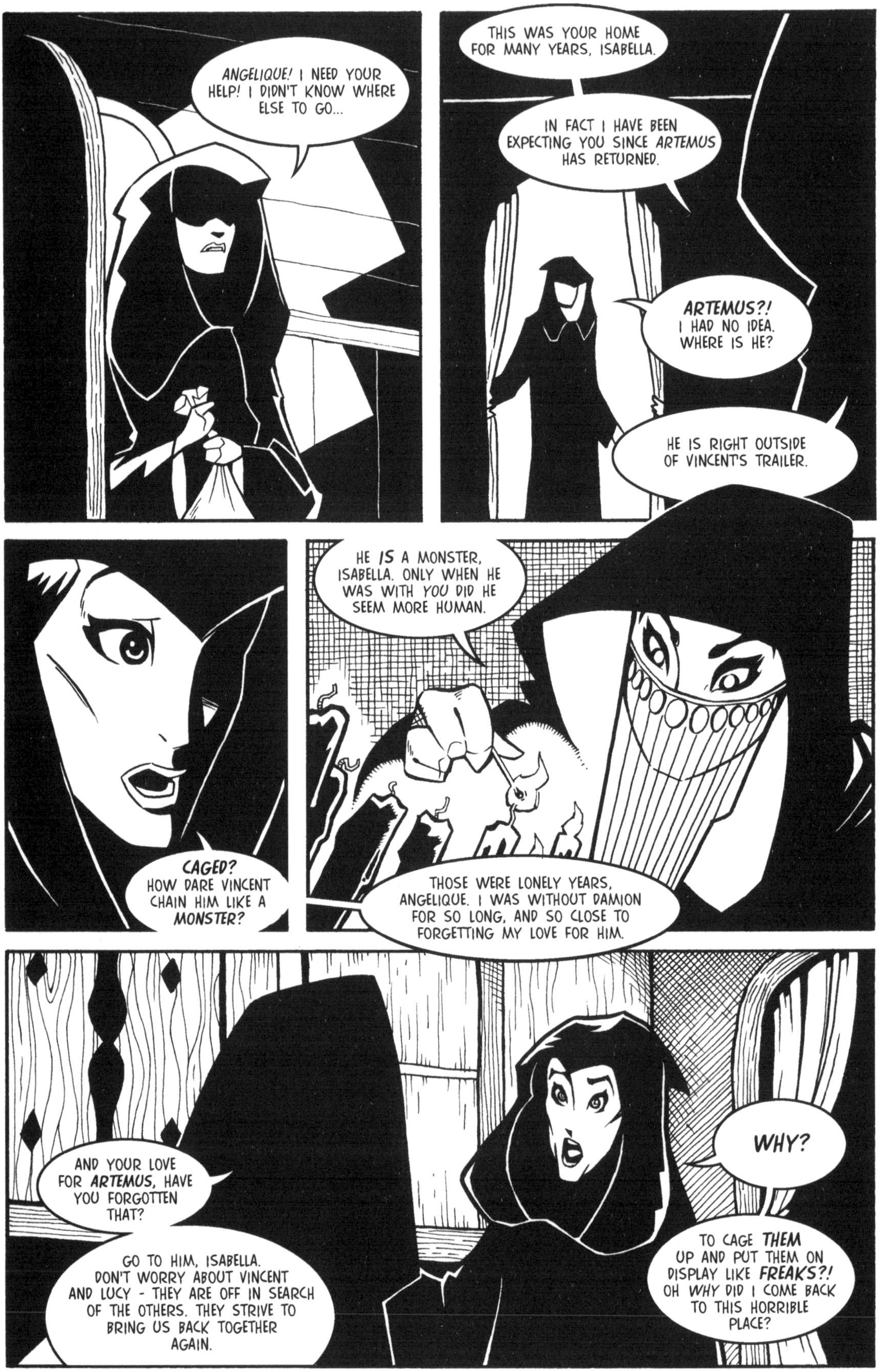
ANGELIQUE! I NEED YOUR HELP! I DIDN'T KNOW WHERE ELSE TO GO...
THIS WAS YOUR HOME FOR MANY YEARS, ISABELLA.
IN FACT I HAVE BEEN EXPECTING YOU SINCE ARTEMUS HAS RETURNED.
ARTEMUS?! I HAD NO IDEA. WHERE IS HE?
HE IS RIGHT OUTSIDE OF VINCENT'S TRAILER.
CAGED? HOW DARE VINCENT CHAIN HIM LIKE A MONSTER?
HE IS A MONSTER, ISABELLA. ONLY WHEN HE WAS WITH YOU DID HE SEEM MORE HUMAN.
THOSE WERE LONELY YEARS, ANGELIQUE. I WAS WITHOUT DAMION FOR SO LONG, AND SO CLOSE TO FORGETTING MY LOVE FOR HIM.
AND YOUR LOVE FOR ARTEMUS, HAVE YOU FORGOTTEN THAT?
GO TO HIM, ISABELLA. DON'T WORRY ABOUT VINCENT AND LUCY - THEY ARE OFF IN SEARCH OF THE OTHERS. THEY STRIVE TO BRING US BACK TOGETHER AGAIN.
WHY?
TO CAGE THEM UP AND PUT THEM ON DISPLAY LIKE FREAKS?! OH WHY DID I COME BACK TO THIS HORRIBLE PLACE?

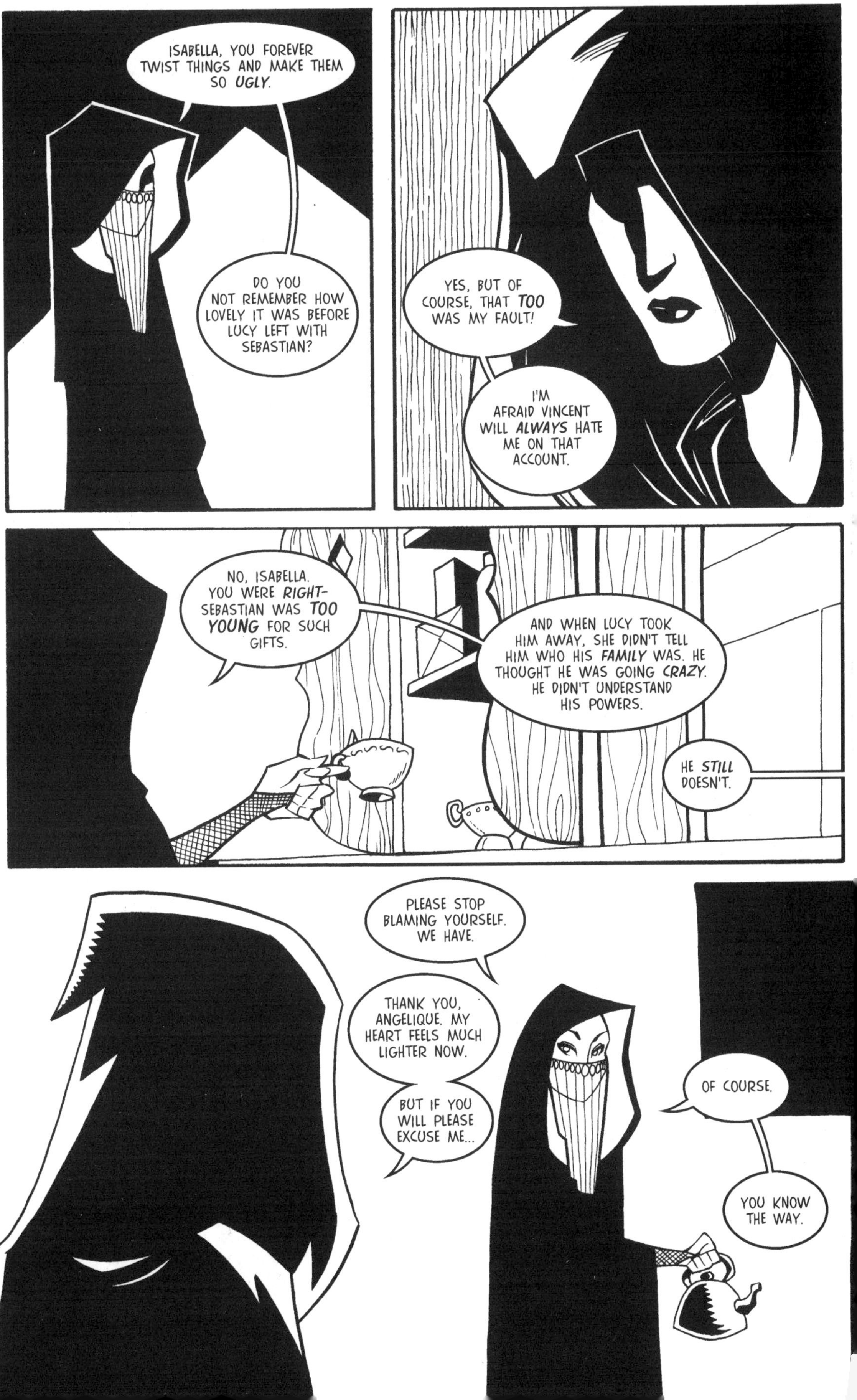
ISABELLA, YOU FOREVER TWIST THINGS AND MAKE THEM SO UGLY.
DO YOU NOT REMEMBER HOW LOVELY IT WAS BEFORE LUCY LEFT WITH SEBASTIAN?
YES, BUT OF COURSE, THAT TOO WAS MY FAULT!
I'M AFRAID VINCENT WILL ALWAYS HATE ME ON THAT ACCOUNT.
NO, ISABELLA. YOU WERE RIGHT- SEBASTIAN WAS TOO YOUNG FOR SUCH GIFTS.
AND WHEN LUCY TOOK HIM AWAY, SHE DIDN'T TELL HIM WHO HIS FAMILY WAS. HE THOUGHT HE WAS GOING CRAZY. HE DIDN'T UNDERSTAND HIS POWERS.
HE STILL DOESN'T.
PLEASE STOP BLAMING YOURSELF. WE HAVE.
THANK YOU, ANGELIQUE. MY HEART FEELS MUCH LIGHTER NOW.
BUT IF YOU WILL PLEASE EXCUSE ME...
OF COURSE.
YOU KNOW THE WAY.

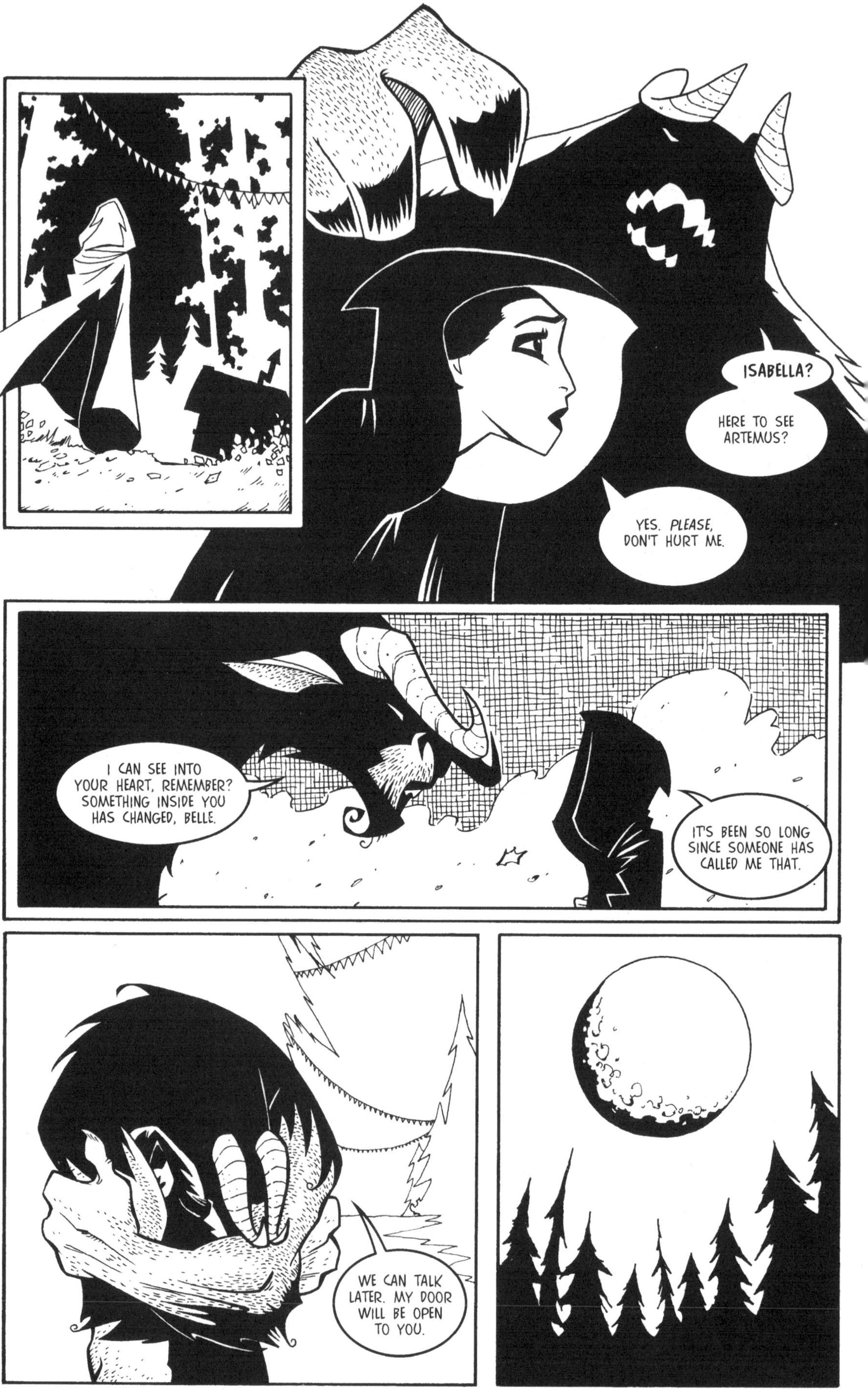
ISABELLA?
HERE TO SEE ARTEMUS?
YES. *PLEASE*, DON'T HURT ME.
I CAN SEE INTO YOUR HEART, REMEMBER? SOMETHING INSIDE YOU HAS CHANGED, BELLE.
IT'S BEEN SO LONG SINCE SOMEONE HAS CALLED ME THAT.
WE CAN TALK LATER. MY DOOR WILL BE OPEN TO YOU.

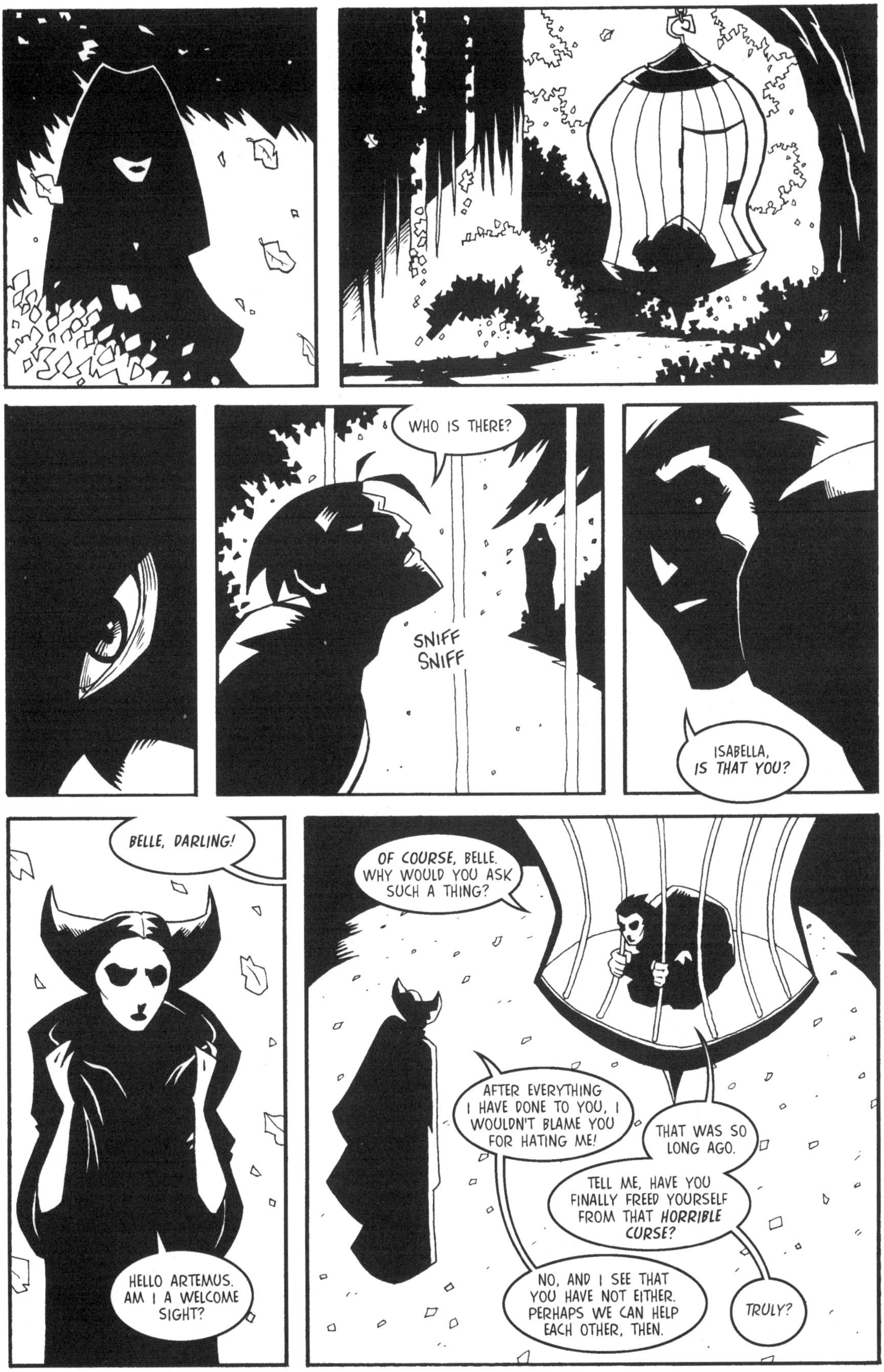
WHO IS THERE?
SNIFF SNIFF
ISABELLA, IS THAT YOU?
BELLE, DARLING!
HELLO ARTEMUS. AM I A WELCOME SIGHT?
OF COURSE, BELLE. WHY WOULD YOU ASK SUCH A THING?
AFTER EVERYTHING I HAVE DONE TO YOU, I WOULDN'T BLAME YOU FOR HATING ME!
THAT WAS SO LONG AGO.
TELL ME, HAVE YOU FINALLY FREED YOURSELF FROM THAT HORRIBLE CURSE?
NO, AND I SEE THAT YOU HAVE NOT EITHER. PERHAPS WE CAN HELP EACH OTHER, THEN.
TRULY?

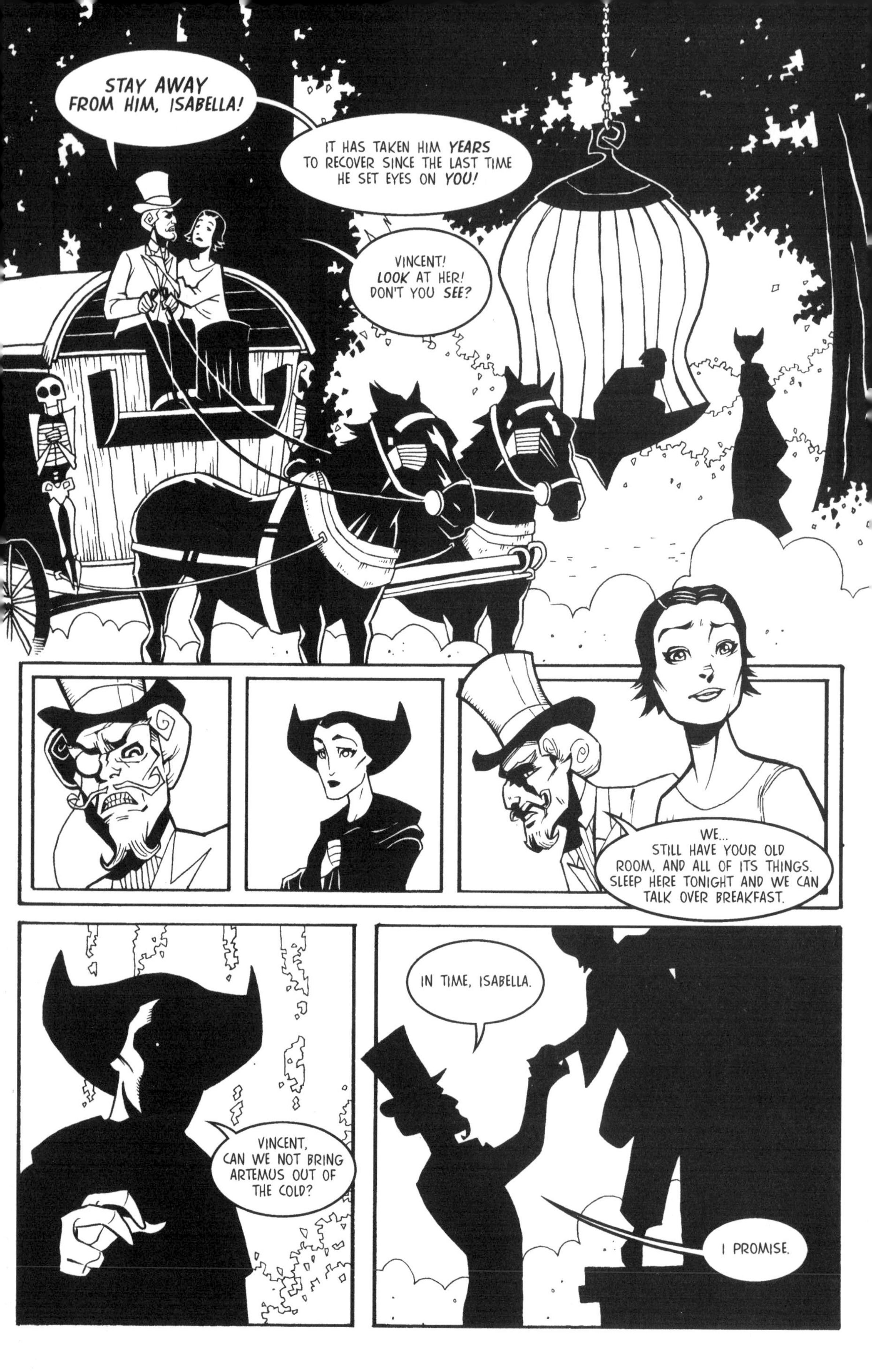
STAY AWAY FROM HIM, ISABELLA!
IT HAS TAKEN HIM YEARS TO RECOVER SINCE THE LAST TIME HE SET EYES ON YOU!
VINCENT! LOOK AT HER! DON'T YOU SEE?
WE... STILL HAVE YOUR OLD ROOM, AND ALL OF ITS THINGS. SLEEP HERE TONIGHT AND WE CAN TALK OVER BREAKFAST.
VINCENT, CAN WE NOT BRING ARTEMUS OUT OF THE COLD?
IN TIME, ISABELLA.
I PROMISE.

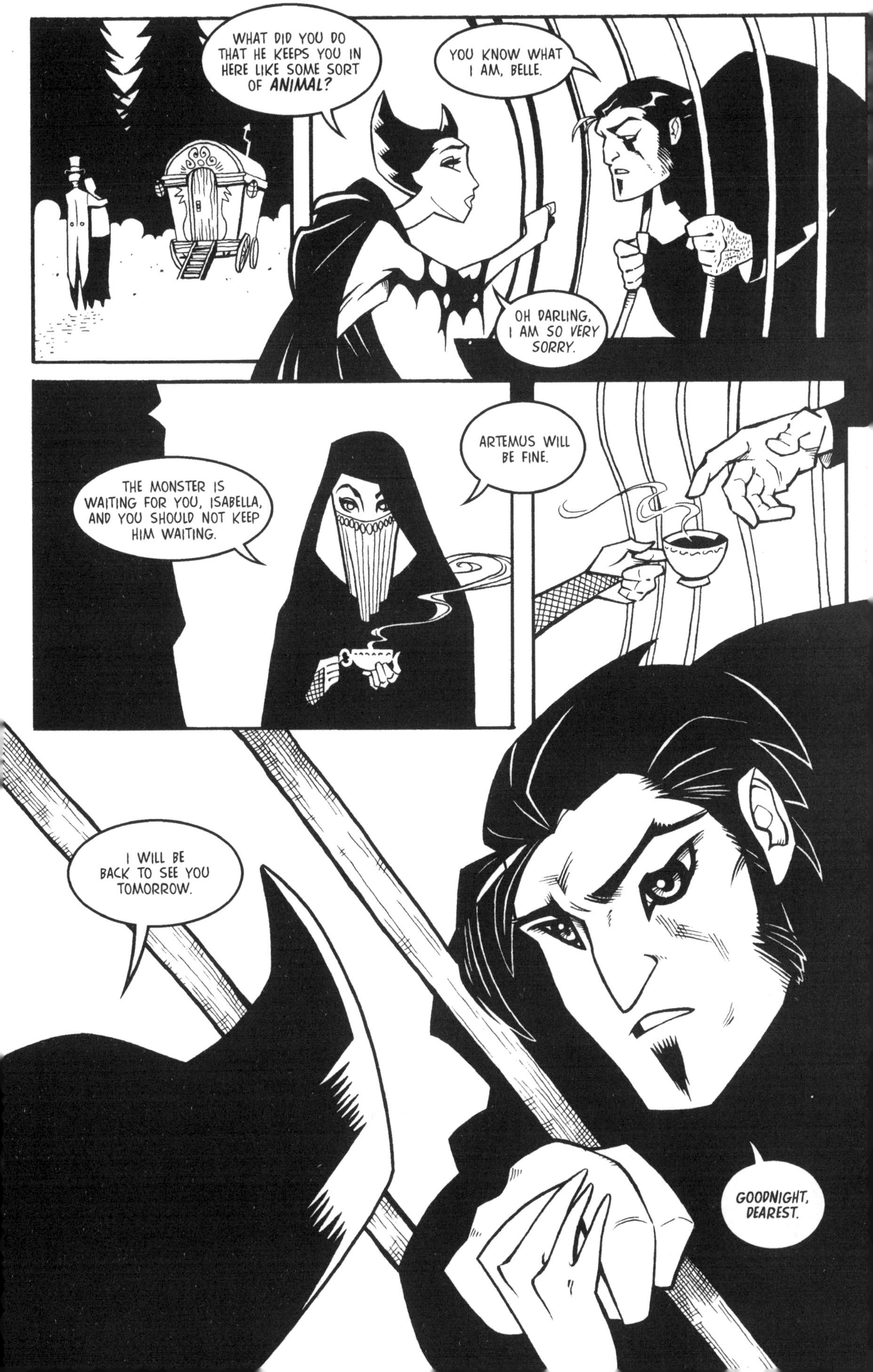
WHAT DID YOU DO THAT HE KEEPS YOU IN HERE LIKE SOME SORT OF ANIMAL?
YOU KNOW WHAT I AM, BELLE.
OH DARLING, I AM SO VERY SORRY.
THE MONSTER IS WAITING FOR YOU, ISABELLA, AND YOU SHOULD NOT KEEP HIM WAITING.
ARTEMUS WILL BE FINE.
I WILL BE BACK TO SEE YOU TOMORROW.
GOODNIGHT, DEAREST.

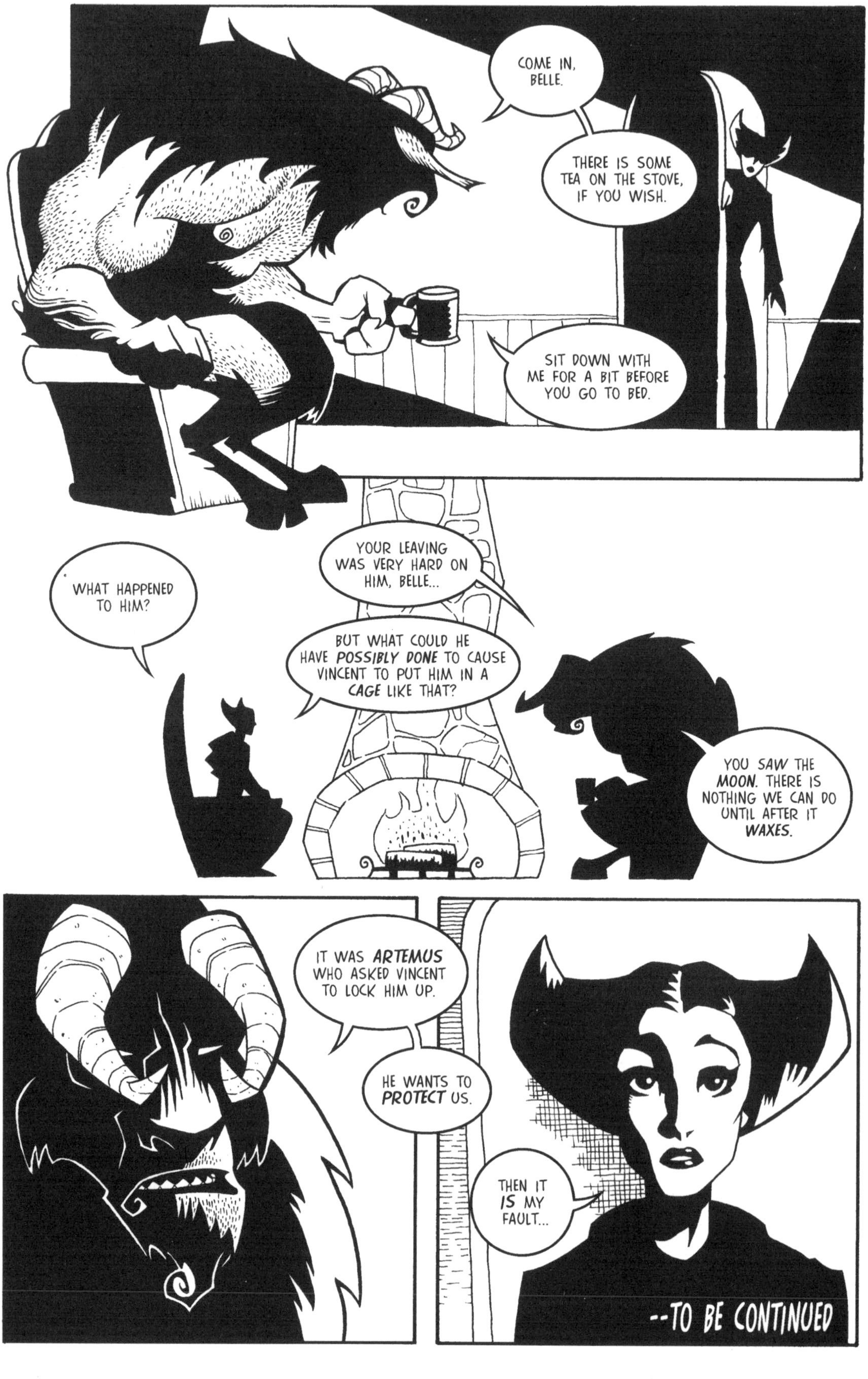
COME IN, BELLE.
THERE IS SOME TEA ON THE STOVE, IF YOU WISH.
SIT DOWN WITH ME FOR A BIT BEFORE YOU GO TO BED.
WHAT HAPPENED TO HIM?
YOUR LEAVING WAS VERY HARD ON HIM, BELLE...
BUT WHAT COULD HE HAVE *POSSIBLY DONE* TO CAUSE VINCENT TO PUT HIM IN A *CAGE* LIKE THAT?
YOU *SAW* THE *MOON*. THERE IS NOTHING WE CAN DO UNTIL AFTER IT *WAXES*.
IT WAS *ARTEMUS* WHO ASKED VINCENT TO LOCK HIM UP.
HE WANTS TO *PROTECT* US.
THEN IT *IS* MY FAULT...
--TO BE CONTINUED

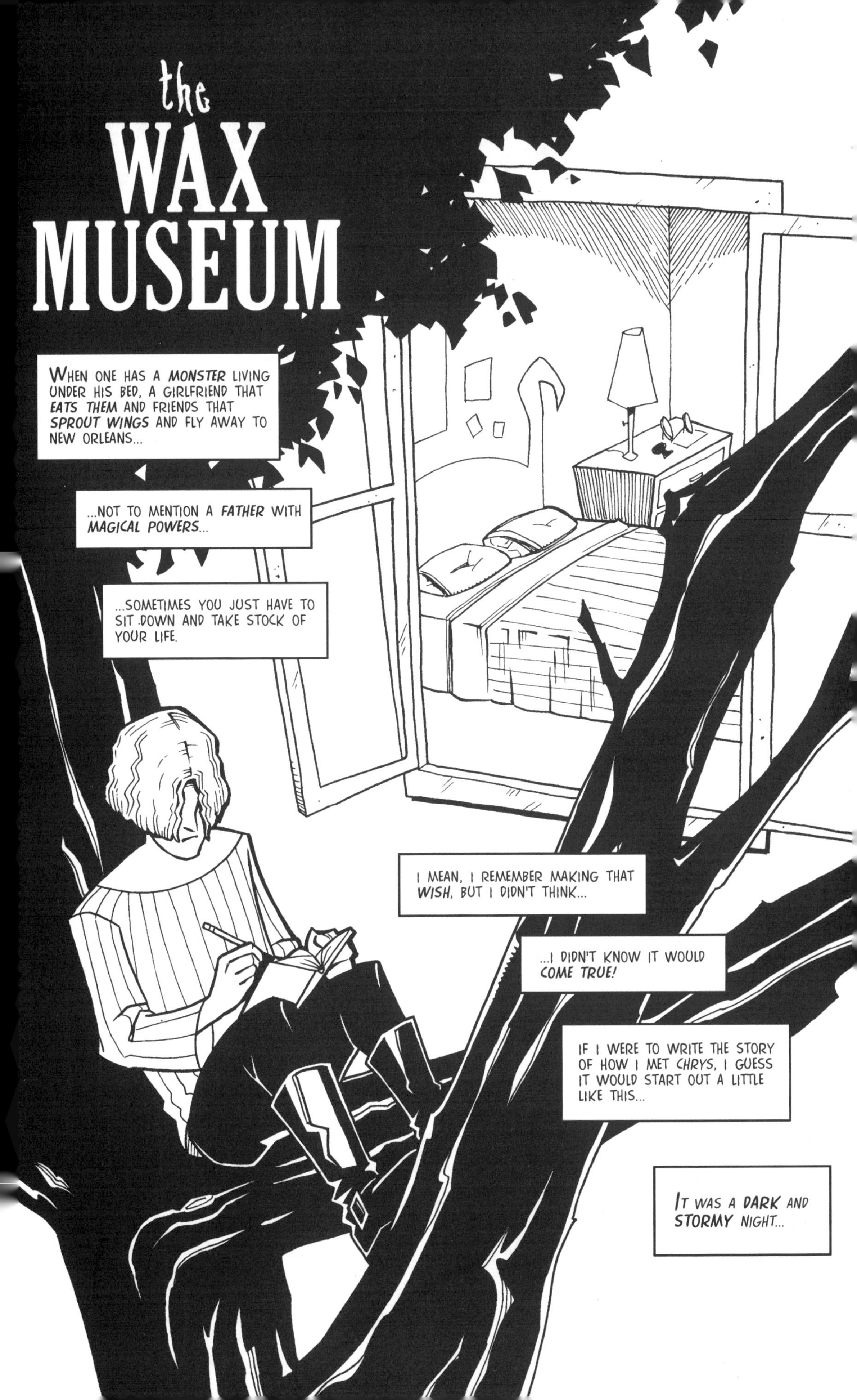
the WAX MUSEUM
WHEN ONE HAS A MONSTER LIVING UNDER HIS BED, A GIRLFRIEND THAT EATS THEM AND FRIENDS THAT SPROUT WINGS AND FLY AWAY TO NEW ORLEANS...
...NOT TO MENTION A FATHER WITH MAGICAL POWERS...
...SOMETIMES YOU JUST HAVE TO SIT DOWN AND TAKE STOCK OF YOUR LIFE.
I MEAN, I REMEMBER MAKING THAT WISH, BUT I DIDN'T THINK...
...I DIDN'T KNOW IT WOULD COME TRUE!
IF I WERE TO WRITE THE STORY OF HOW I MET CHRYS, I GUESS IT WOULD START OUT A LITTLE LIKE THIS...
IT WAS A DARK AND STORMY NIGHT...

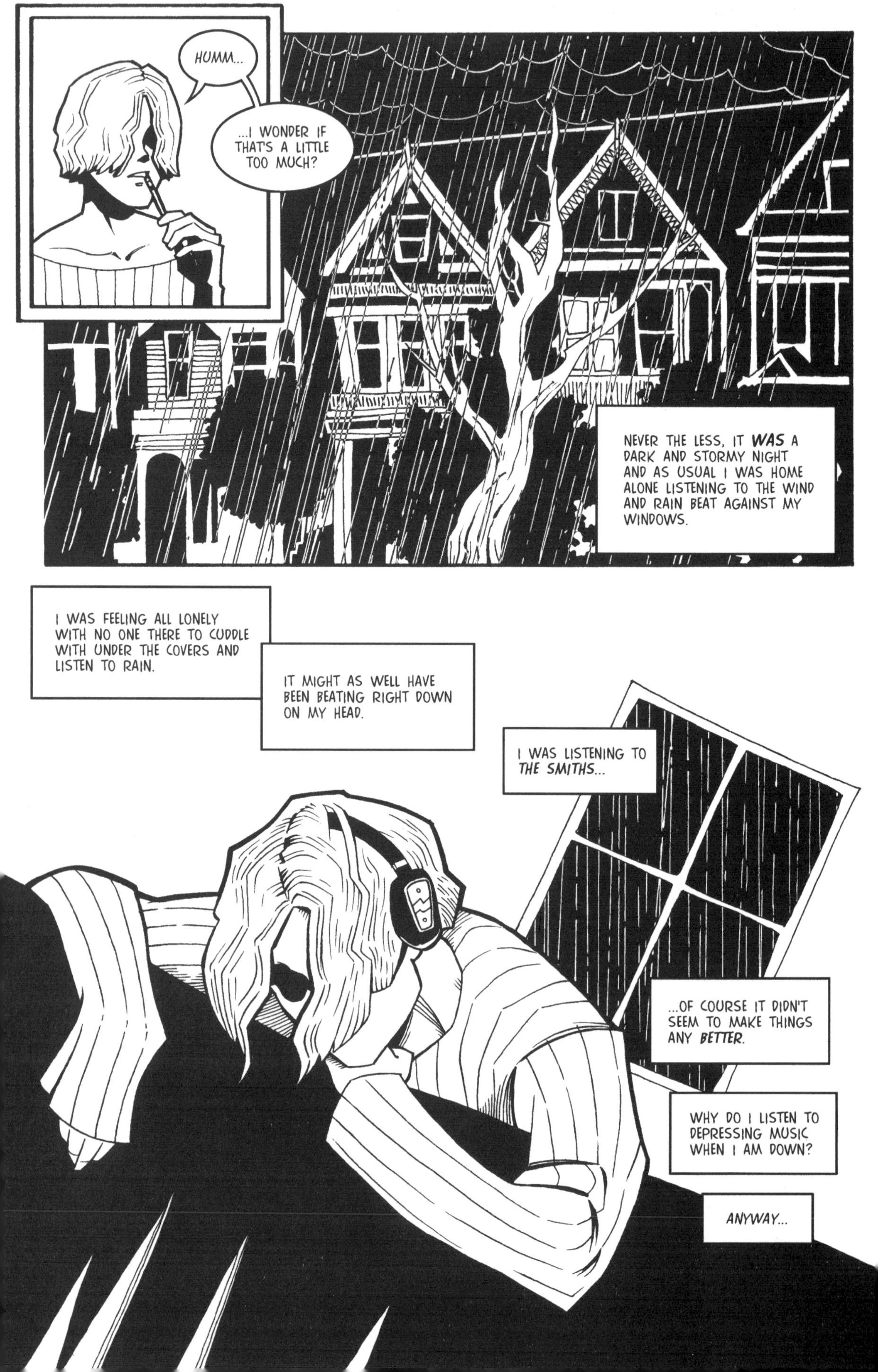
HUMM...
...I WONDER IF THAT'S A LITTLE TOO MUCH?
NEVER THE LESS, IT WAS A DARK AND STORMY NIGHT AND AS USUAL I WAS HOME ALONE LISTENING TO THE WIND AND RAIN BEAT AGAINST MY WINDOWS.
I WAS FEELING ALL LONELY WITH NO ONE THERE TO CUDDLE WITH UNDER THE COVERS AND LISTEN TO RAIN.
IT MIGHT AS WELL HAVE BEEN BEATING RIGHT DOWN ON MY HEAD.
I WAS LISTENING TO THE SMITHS...
...OF COURSE IT DIDN'T SEEM TO MAKE THINGS ANY BETTER.
WHY DO I LISTEN TO DEPRESSING MUSIC WHEN I AM DOWN?
ANYWAY...

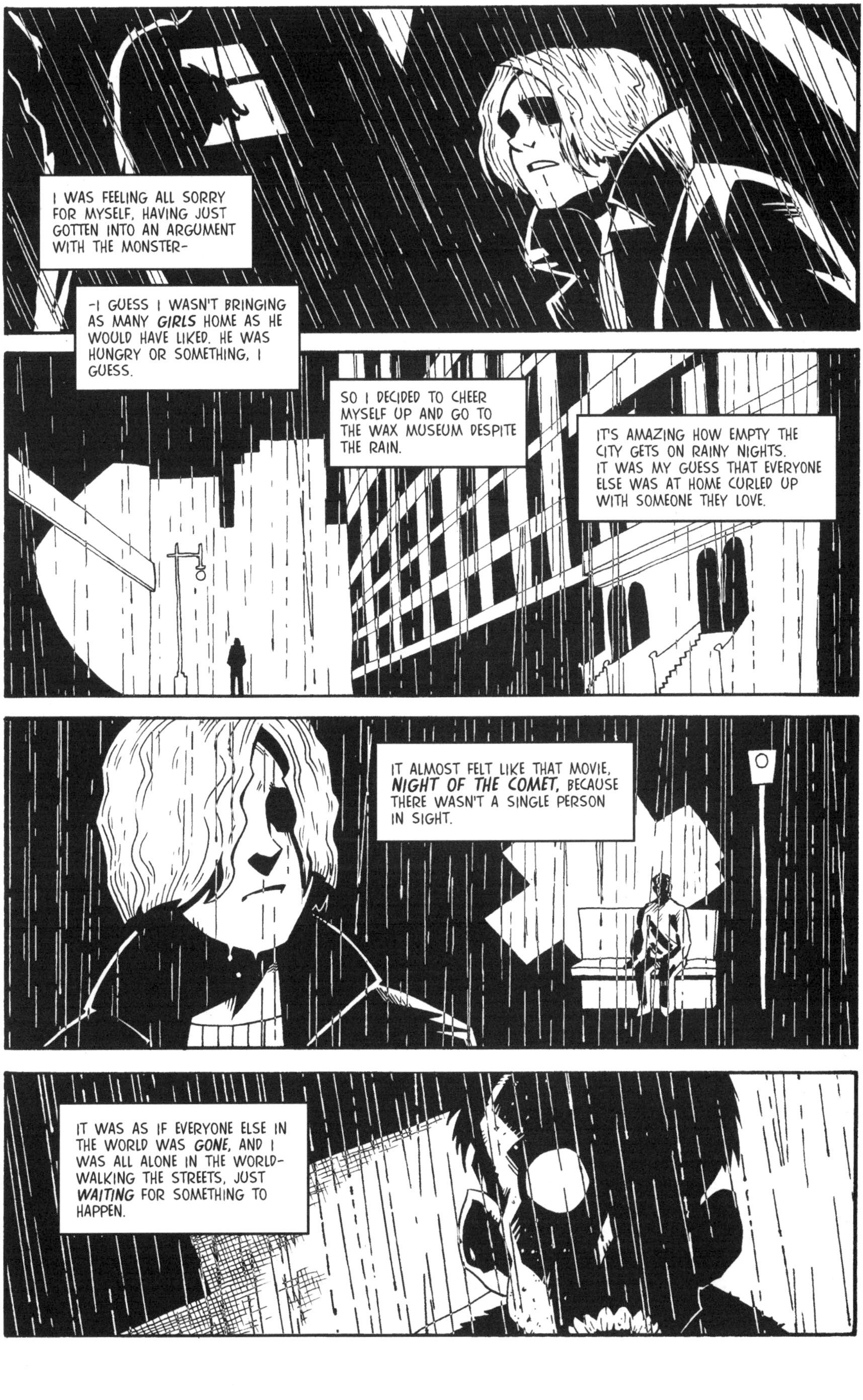
I WAS FEELING ALL SORRY FOR MYSELF, HAVING JUST GOTTEN INTO AN ARGUMENT WITH THE MONSTER-
-I GUESS I WASN'T BRINGING AS MANY *GIRLS* HOME AS HE WOULD HAVE LIKED. HE WAS HUNGRY OR SOMETHING, I GUESS.
SO I DECIDED TO CHEER MYSELF UP AND GO TO THE WAX MUSEUM DESPITE THE RAIN.
IT'S AMAZING HOW EMPTY THE CITY GETS ON RAINY NIGHTS. IT WAS MY GUESS THAT EVERYONE ELSE WAS AT HOME CURLED UP WITH SOMEONE THEY LOVE.
IT ALMOST FELT LIKE THAT MOVIE, ***NIGHT OF THE COMET,*** BECAUSE THERE WASN'T A SINGLE PERSON IN SIGHT.
IT WAS AS IF EVERYONE ELSE IN THE WORLD WAS *GONE,* AND I WAS ALL ALONE IN THE WORLD-WALKING THE STREETS, JUST *WAITING* FOR SOMETHING TO HAPPEN.

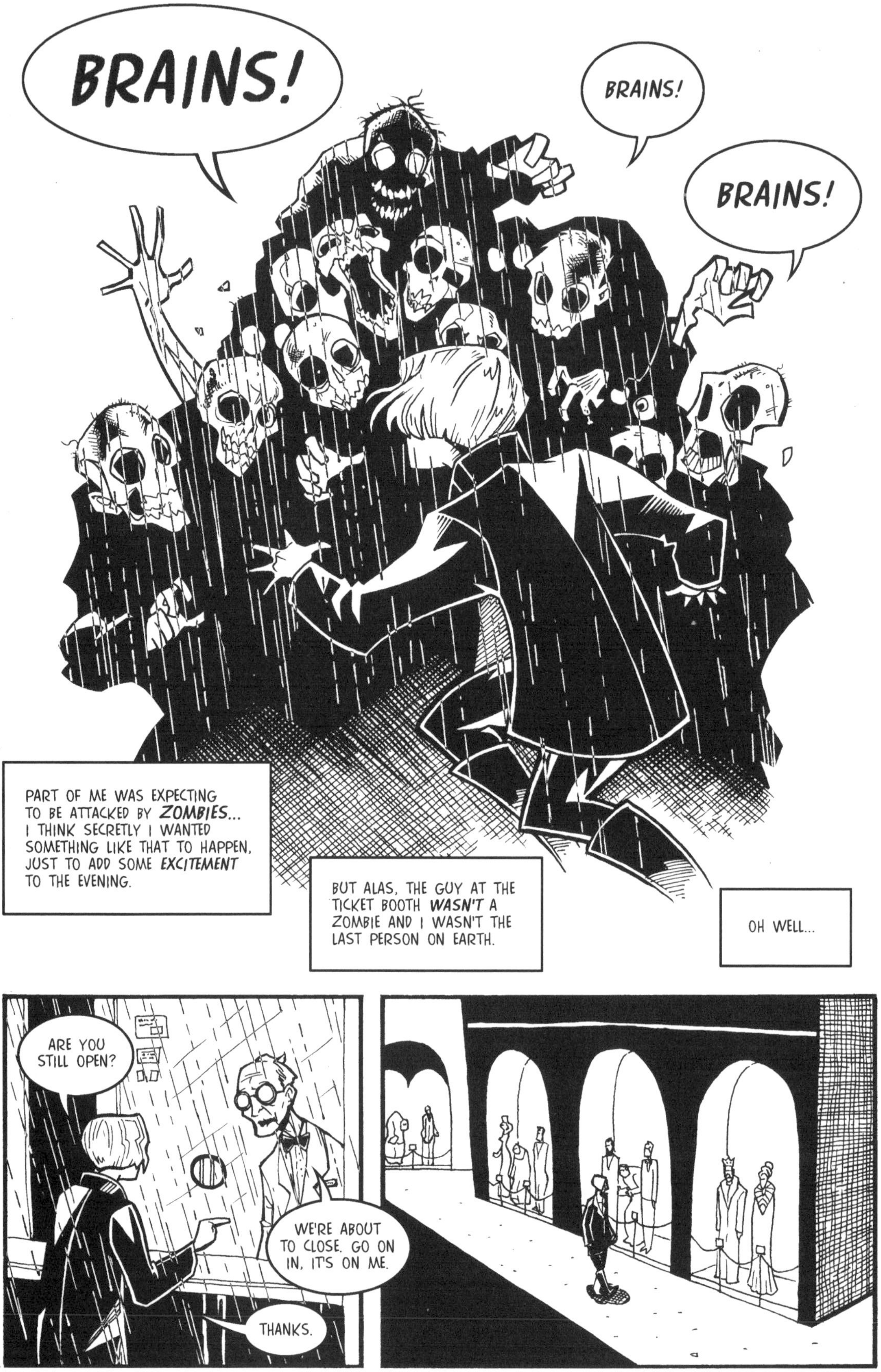
BRAINS!
BRAINS!
BRAINS!
PART OF ME WAS EXPECTING TO BE ATTACKED BY ZOMBIES... I THINK SECRETLY I WANTED SOMETHING LIKE THAT TO HAPPEN, JUST TO ADD SOME EXCITEMENT TO THE EVENING.
BUT ALAS, THE GUY AT THE TICKET BOOTH WASN'T A ZOMBIE AND I WASN'T THE LAST PERSON ON EARTH.
OH WELL...
ARE YOU STILL OPEN?
WE'RE ABOUT TO CLOSE. GO ON IN, IT'S ON ME.
THANKS.

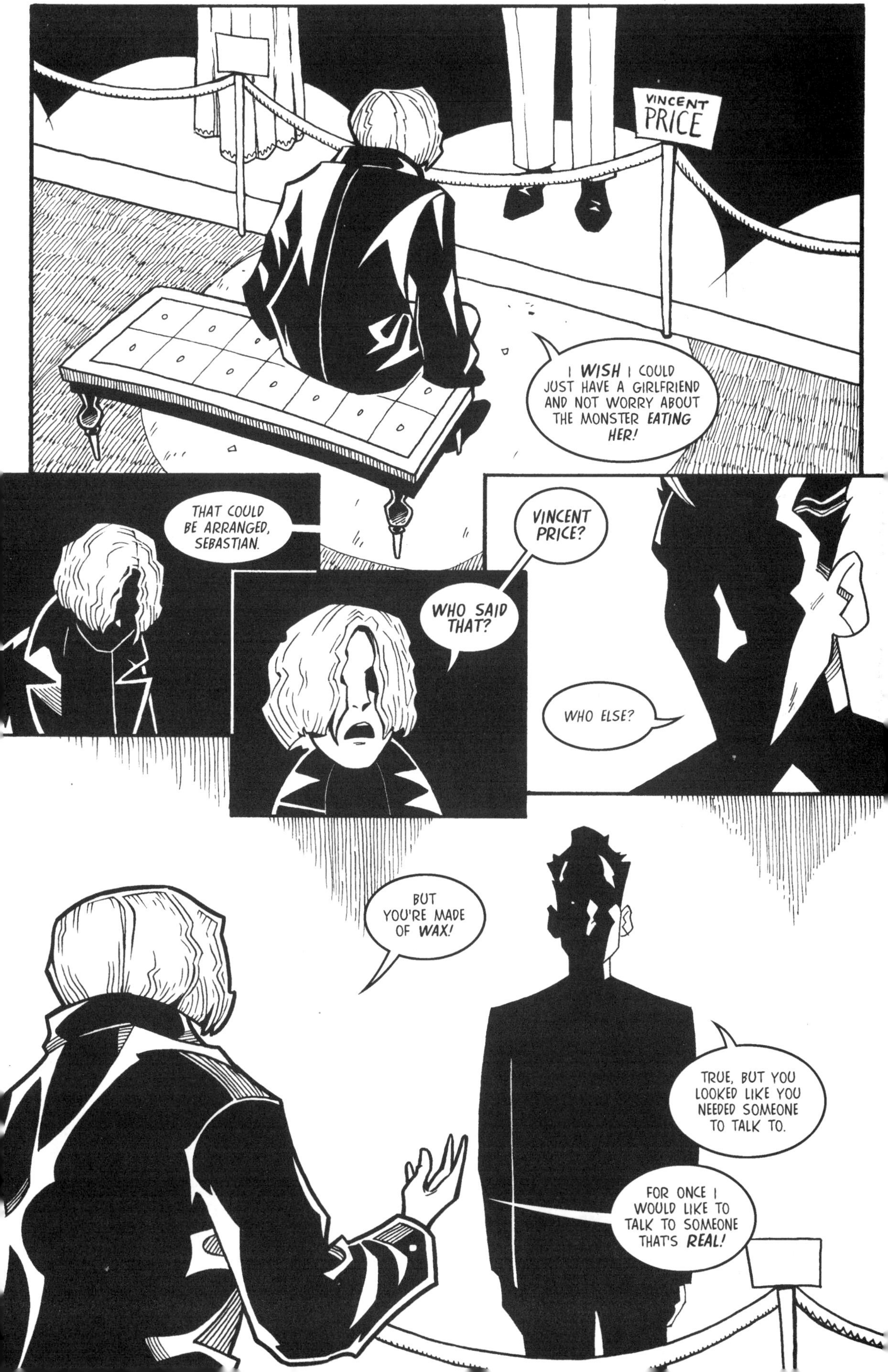
VINCENT PRICE
I WISH I COULD JUST HAVE A GIRLFRIEND AND NOT WORRY ABOUT THE MONSTER EATING HER!
THAT COULD BE ARRANGED, SEBASTIAN.
WHO SAID THAT?
VINCENT PRICE?
WHO ELSE?
BUT YOU'RE MADE OF WAX!
TRUE, BUT YOU LOOKED LIKE YOU NEEDED SOMEONE TO TALK TO.
FOR ONCE I WOULD LIKE TO TALK TO SOMEONE THAT'S REAL!

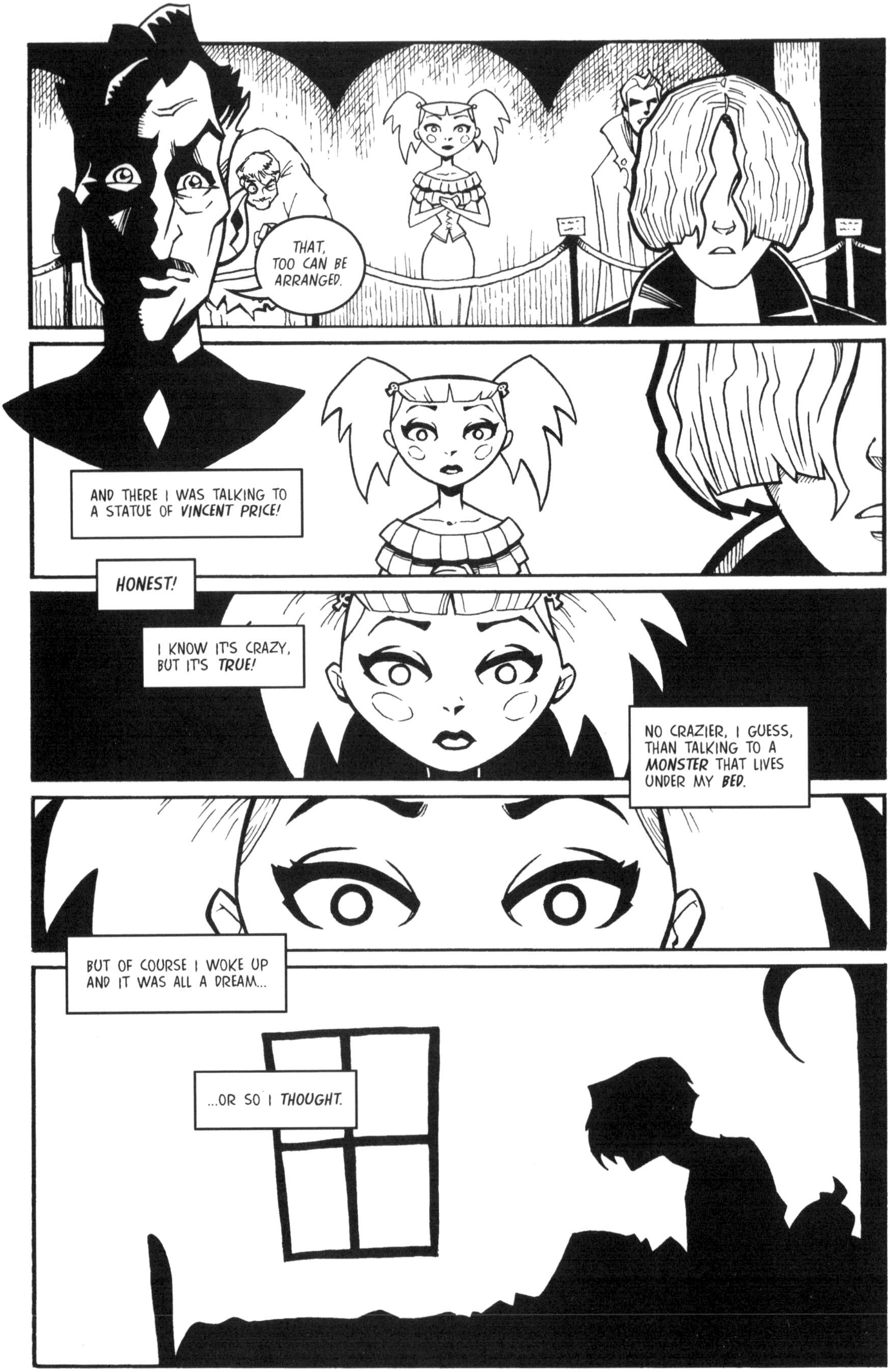
THAT, TOO CAN BE ARRANGED.
AND THERE I WAS TALKING TO A STATUE OF VINCENT PRICE!
HONEST!
I KNOW IT'S CRAZY, BUT IT'S TRUE!
NO CRAZIER, I GUESS, THAN TALKING TO A MONSTER THAT LIVES UNDER MY BED.
BUT OF COURSE I WOKE UP AND IT WAS ALL A DREAM...
...OR SO I THOUGHT.

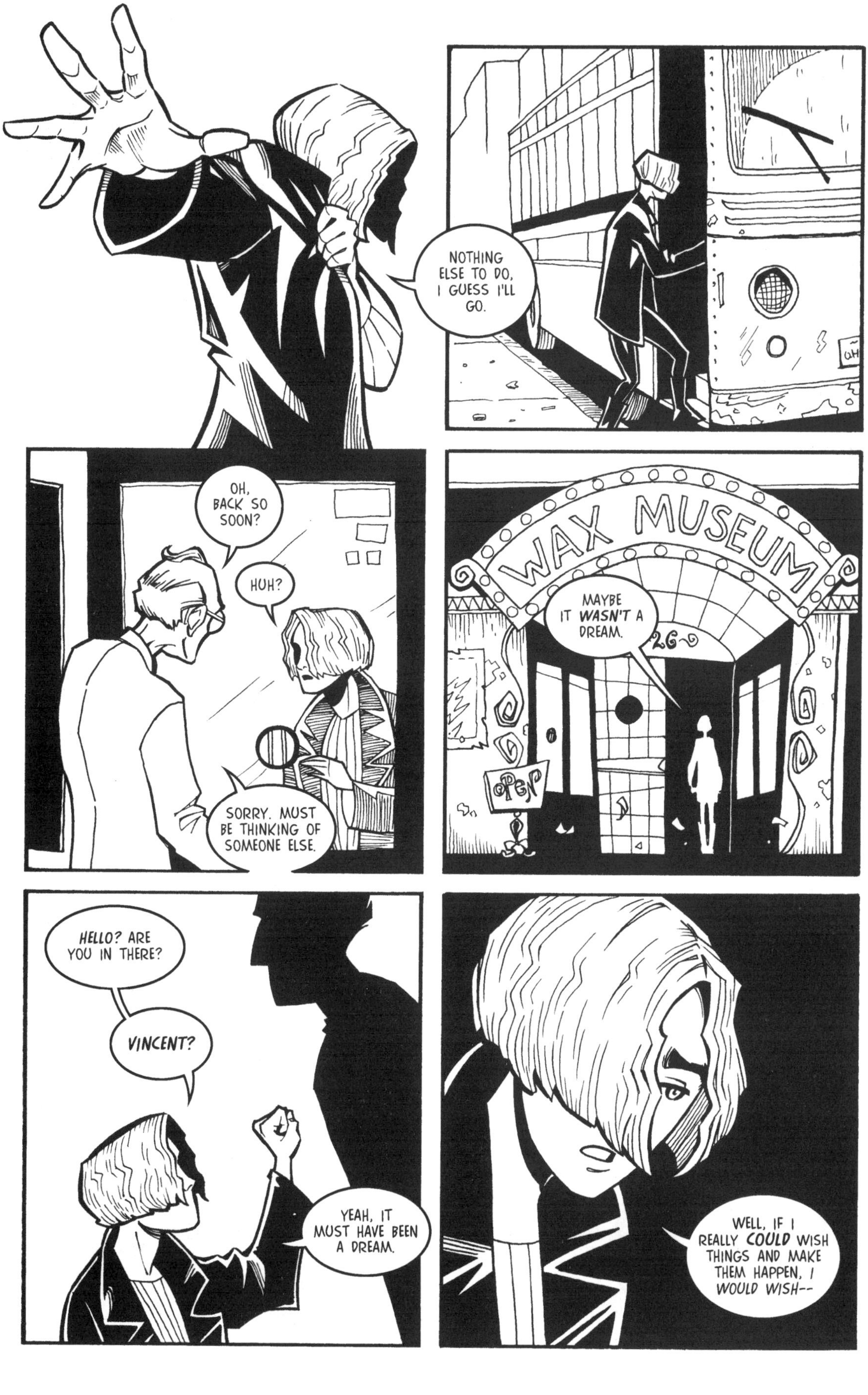

NOTHING ELSE TO DO, I GUESS I'LL GO.
OH, BACK SO SOON?
HUH?
SORRY. MUST BE THINKING OF SOMEONE ELSE.
WAX MUSEUM
MAYBE IT WASN'T A DREAM.
OPEN
HELLO? ARE YOU IN THERE?
VINCENT?
YEAH, IT MUST HAVE BEEN A DREAM.
WELL, IF I REALLY COULD WISH THINGS AND MAKE THEM HAPPEN, I WOULD WISH--

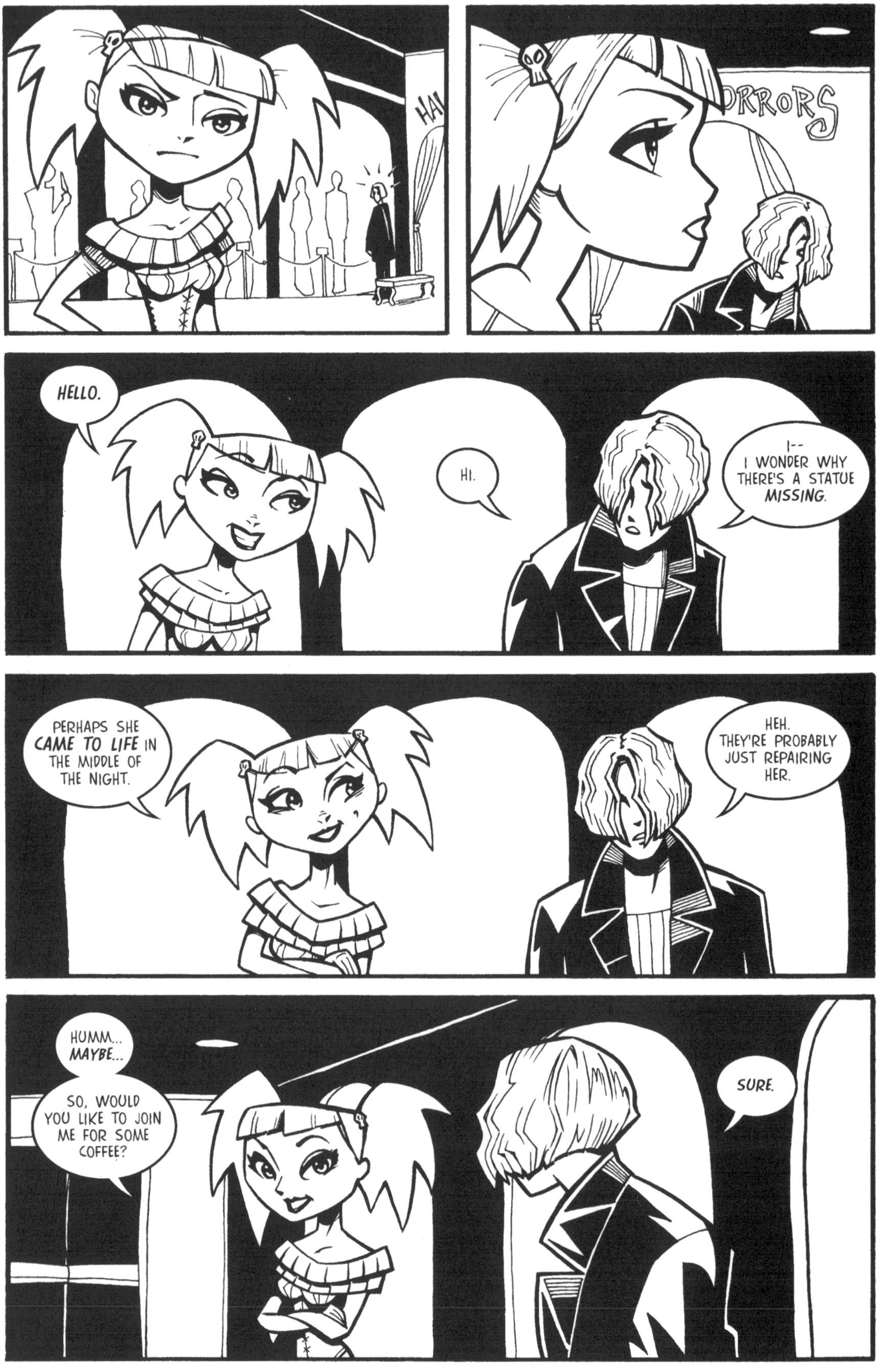

HA
ORRORS
HELLO.
HI.
I-- I WONDER WHY THERE'S A STATUE MISSING.
PERHAPS SHE CAME TO LIFE IN THE MIDDLE OF THE NIGHT.
HEH. THEY'RE PROBABLY JUST REPAIRING HER.
HUMM... MAYBE...
SO, WOULD YOU LIKE TO JOIN ME FOR SOME COFFEE?
SURE.

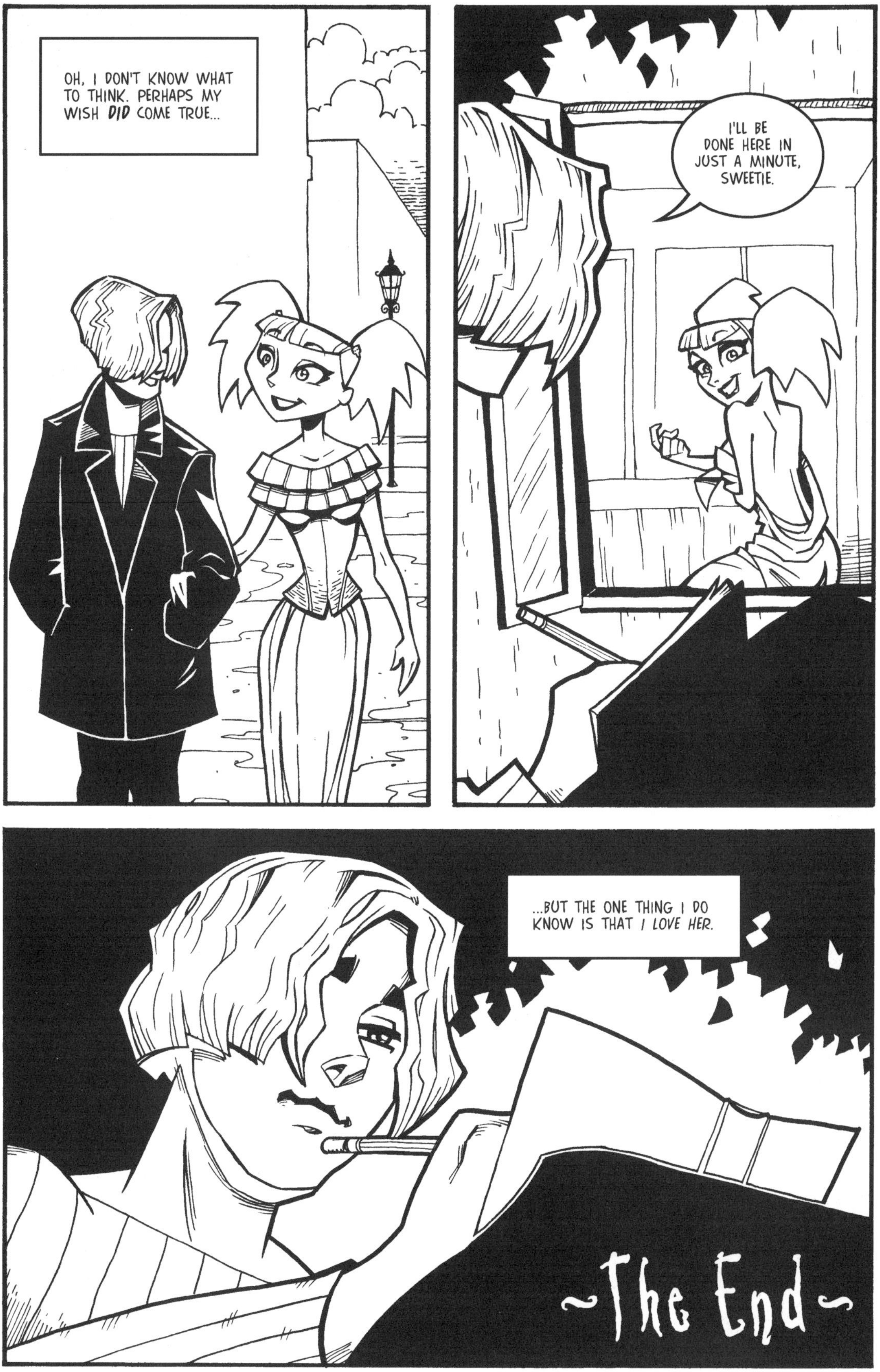
OH, I DON'T KNOW WHAT TO THINK. PERHAPS MY WISH DID COME TRUE...
I'LL BE DONE HERE IN JUST A MINUTE, SWEETIE.
...BUT THE ONE THING I DO KNOW IS THAT I LOVE HER.
~The End~

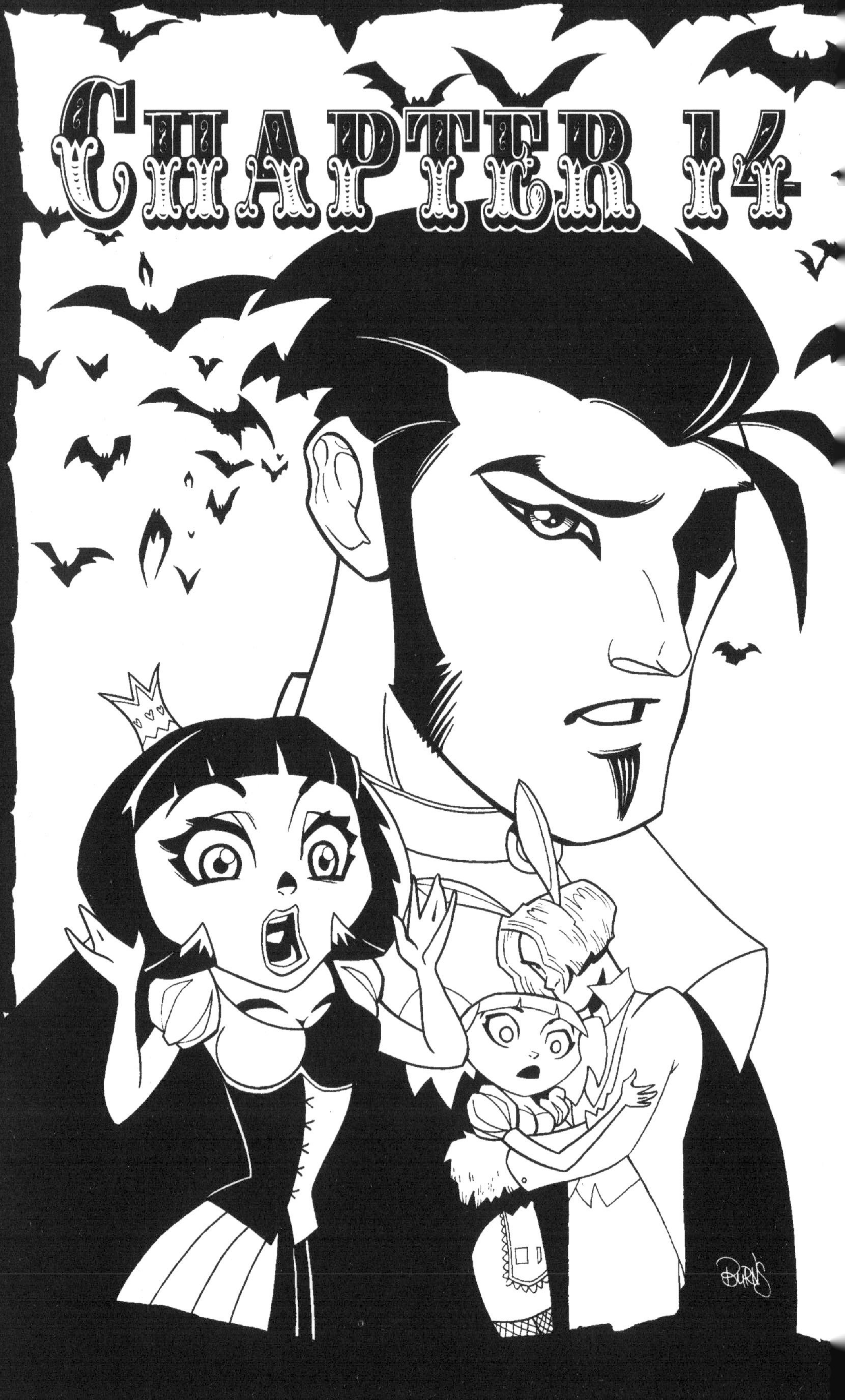
CHAPTER 14

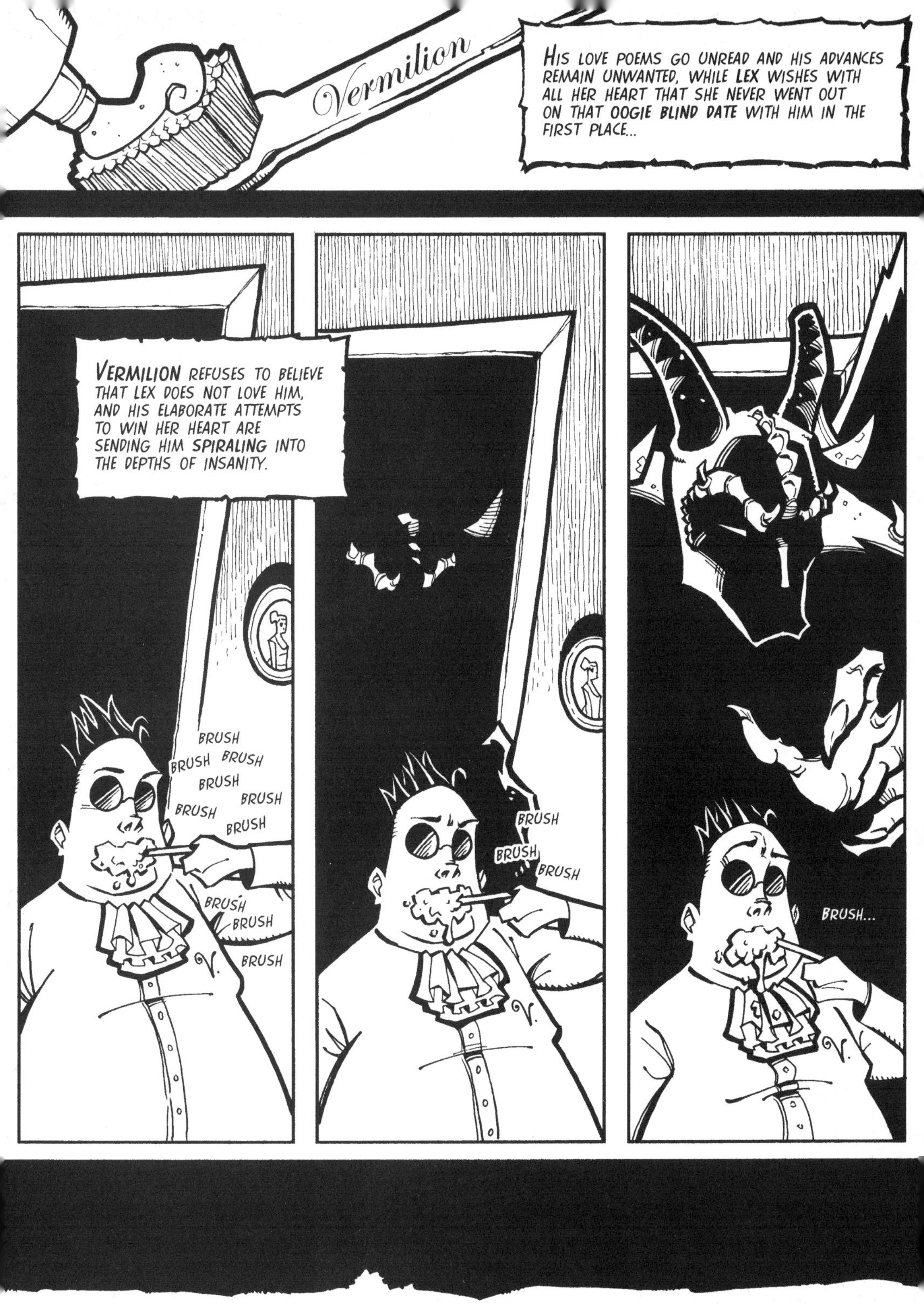
Vermilion
HIS LOVE POEMS GO UNREAD AND HIS ADVANCES REMAIN UNWANTED, WHILE LEX WISHES WITH ALL HER HEART THAT SHE NEVER WENT OUT ON THAT OOGIE BLIND DATE WITH HIM IN THE FIRST PLACE...
VERMILION REFUSES TO BELIEVE THAT LEX DOES NOT LOVE HIM, AND HIS ELABORATE ATTEMPTS TO WIN HER HEART ARE SENDING HIM SPIRALING INTO THE DEPTHS OF INSANITY.
BRUSH BRUSH BRUSH BRUSH BRUSH BRUSH BRUSH
BRUSH BRUSH BRUSH
V.
BRUSH BRUSH BRUSH
V.
BRUSH...
V.

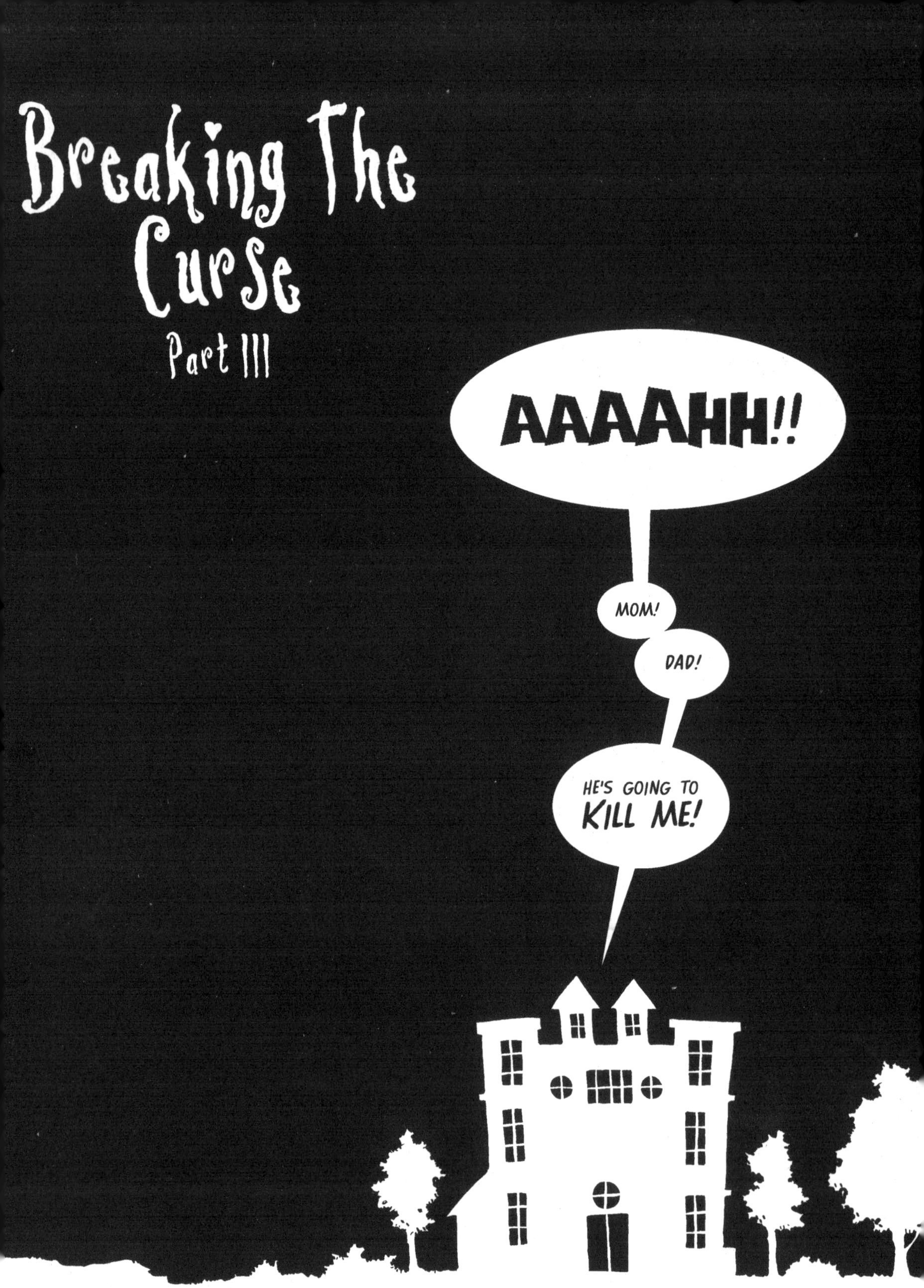
Breaking The Curse
Part III
AAAAHH!!
MOM!
DAD!
HE'S GOING TO KILL ME!

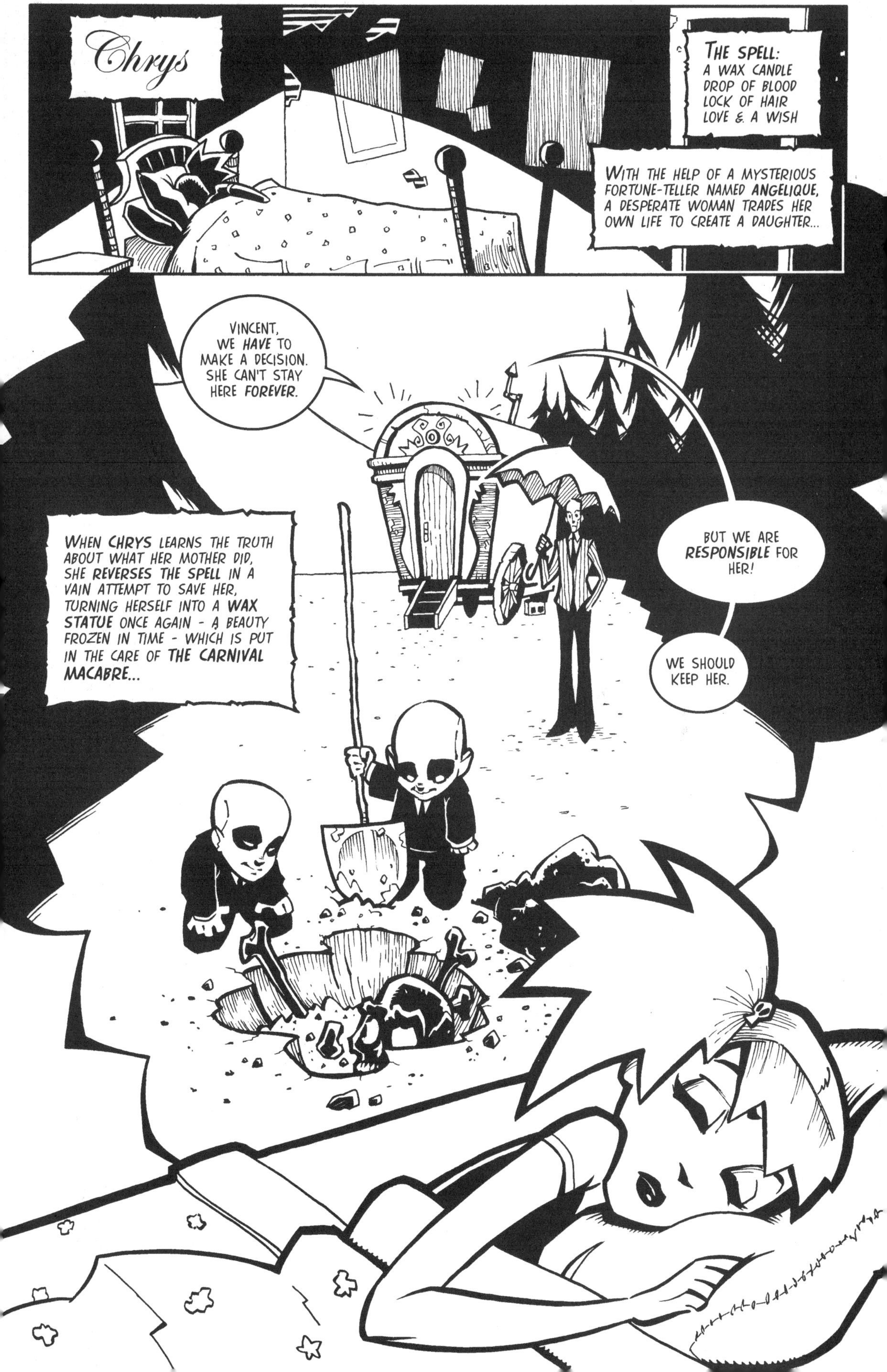
Chrys
THE SPELL:
A WAX CANDLE
DROP OF BLOOD
LOCK OF HAIR
LOVE & A WISH
WITH THE HELP OF A MYSTERIOUS FORTUNE-TELLER NAMED ANGELIQUE, A DESPERATE WOMAN TRADES HER OWN LIFE TO CREATE A DAUGHTER...
VINCENT, WE HAVE TO MAKE A DECISION. SHE CAN'T STAY HERE FOREVER.
BUT WE ARE RESPONSIBLE FOR HER!
WE SHOULD KEEP HER.
WHEN CHRYS LEARNS THE TRUTH ABOUT WHAT HER MOTHER DID, SHE REVERSES THE SPELL IN A VAIN ATTEMPT TO SAVE HER, TURNING HERSELF INTO A WAX STATUE ONCE AGAIN - A BEAUTY FROZEN IN TIME - WHICH IS PUT IN THE CARE OF THE CARNIVAL MACABRE...

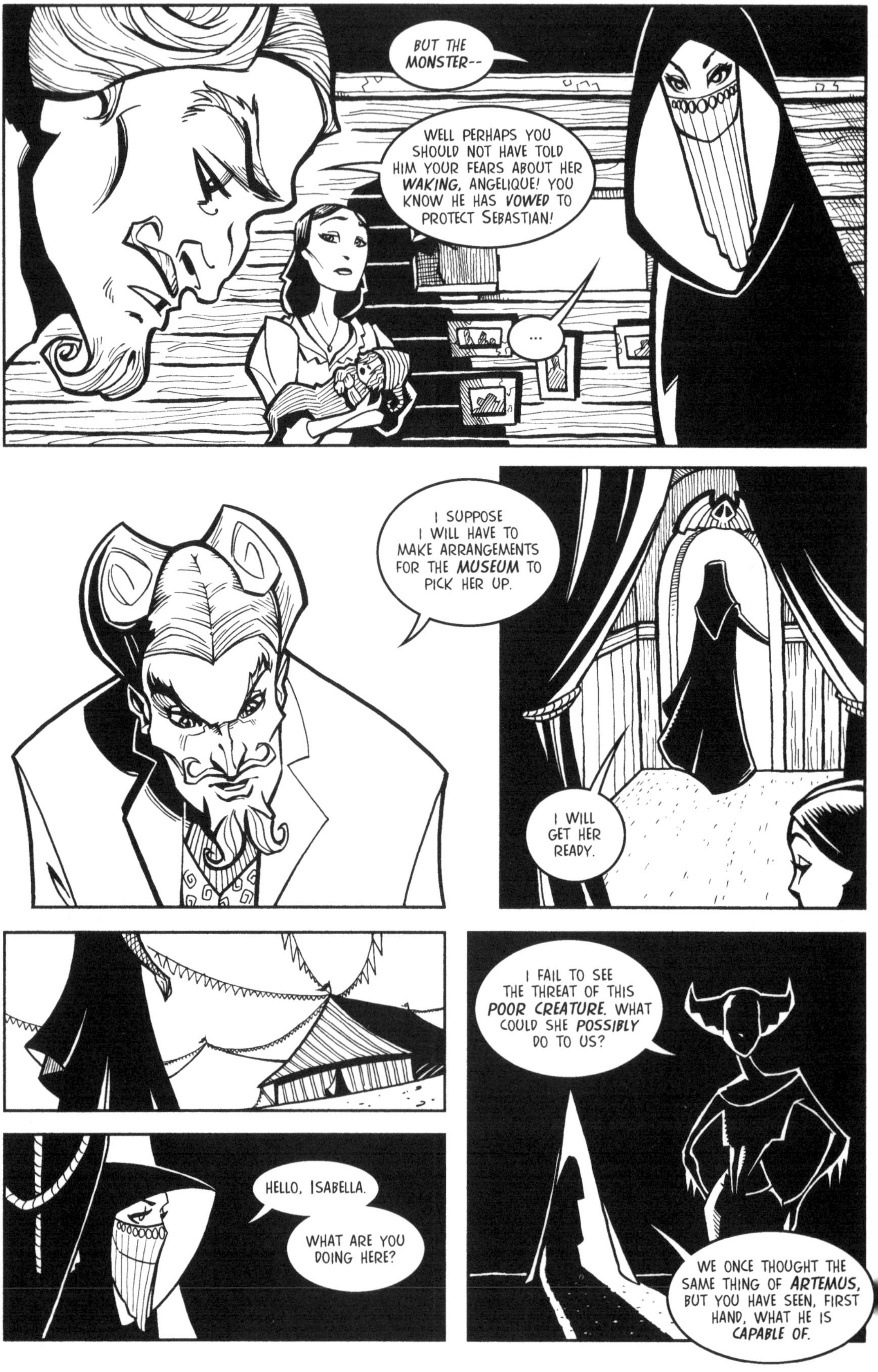
BUT THE MONSTER--
WELL PERHAPS YOU SHOULD NOT HAVE TOLD HIM YOUR FEARS ABOUT HER WAKING, ANGELIQUE! YOU KNOW HE HAS VOWED TO PROTECT SEBASTIAN!
...
I SUPPOSE I WILL HAVE TO MAKE ARRANGEMENTS FOR THE MUSEUM TO PICK HER UP.
I WILL GET HER READY.
HELLO, ISABELLA.
WHAT ARE YOU DOING HERE?
I FAIL TO SEE THE THREAT OF THIS POOR CREATURE. WHAT COULD SHE POSSIBLY DO TO US?
WE ONCE THOUGHT THE SAME THING OF ARTEMUS, BUT YOU HAVE SEEN, FIRST HAND, WHAT HE IS CAPABLE OF.

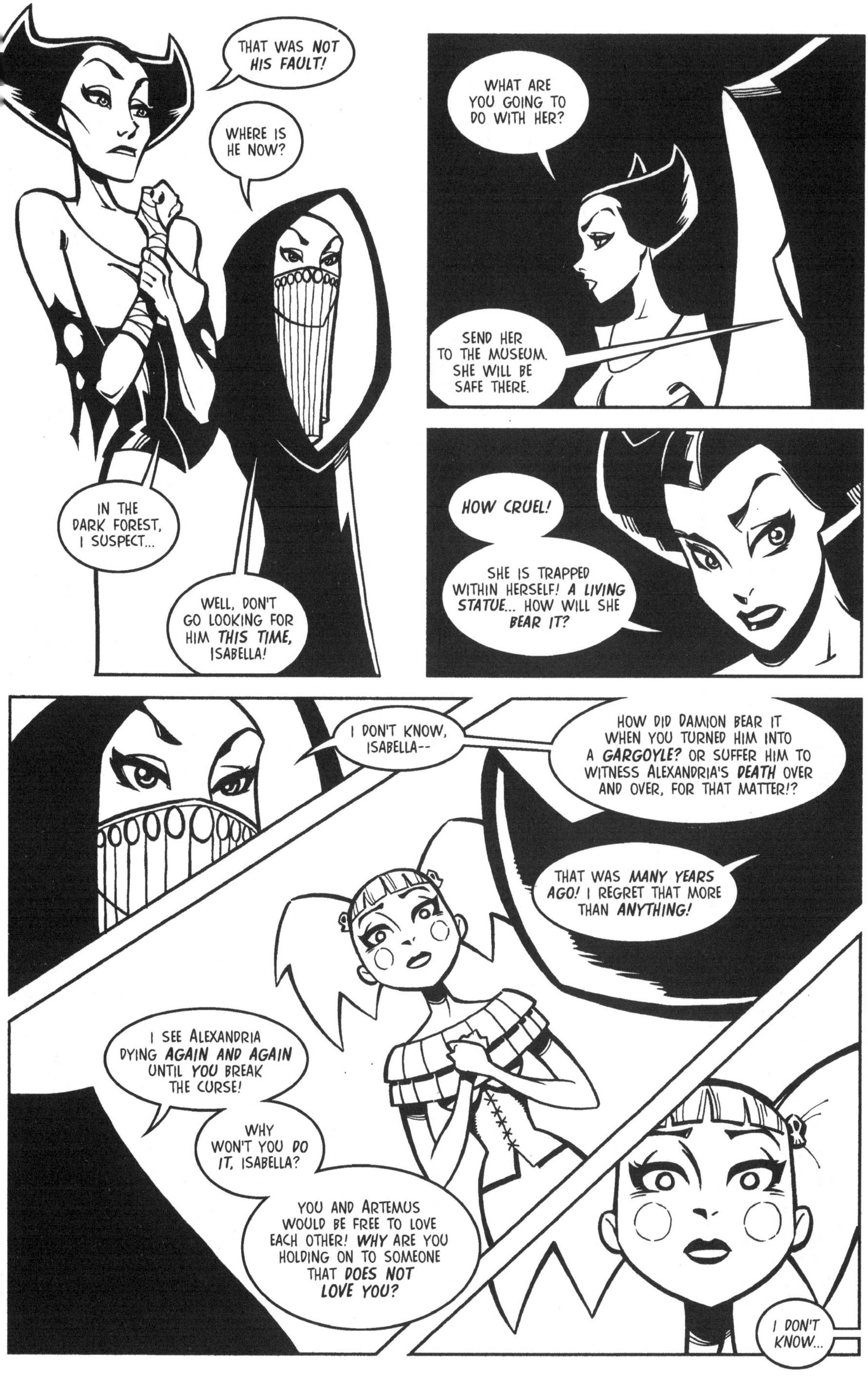
THAT WAS NOT HIS FAULT!
WHERE IS HE NOW?
IN THE DARK FOREST, I SUSPECT...
WELL, DON'T GO LOOKING FOR HIM THIS TIME, ISABELLA!
WHAT ARE YOU GOING TO DO WITH HER?
SEND HER TO THE MUSEUM. SHE WILL BE SAFE THERE.
HOW CRUEL!
SHE IS TRAPPED WITHIN HERSELF! A LIVING STATUE... HOW WILL SHE BEAR IT?
I DON'T KNOW, ISABELLA--
HOW DID DAMION BEAR IT WHEN YOU TURNED HIM INTO A GARGOYLE? OR SUFFER HIM TO WITNESS ALEXANDRIA'S DEATH OVER AND OVER, FOR THAT MATTER!?
THAT WAS MANY YEARS AGO! I REGRET THAT MORE THAN ANYTHING!
I SEE ALEXANDRIA DYING AGAIN AND AGAIN UNTIL YOU BREAK THE CURSE!
WHY WON'T YOU DO IT, ISABELLA?
YOU AND ARTEMUS WOULD BE FREE TO LOVE EACH OTHER! WHY ARE YOU HOLDING ON TO SOMEONE THAT DOES NOT LOVE YOU?
I DON'T KNOW...

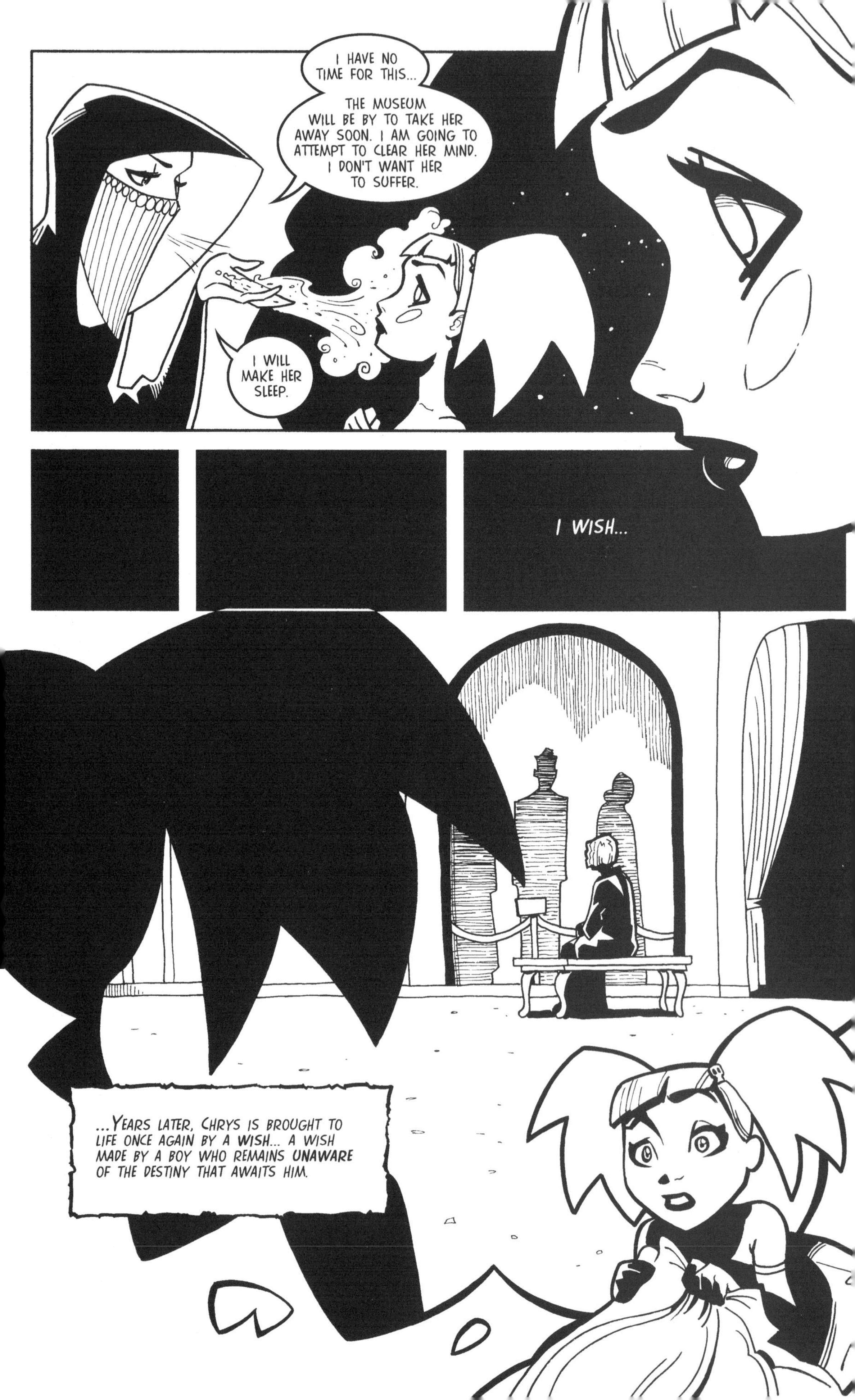
I HAVE NO TIME FOR THIS...
THE MUSEUM WILL BE BY TO TAKE HER AWAY SOON. I AM GOING TO ATTEMPT TO CLEAR HER MIND. I DON'T WANT HER TO SUFFER.
I WILL MAKE HER SLEEP.
I WISH...
...YEARS LATER, CHRYS IS BROUGHT TO LIFE ONCE AGAIN BY A WISH... A WISH MADE BY A BOY WHO REMAINS UNAWARE OF THE DESTINY THAT AWAITS HIM.

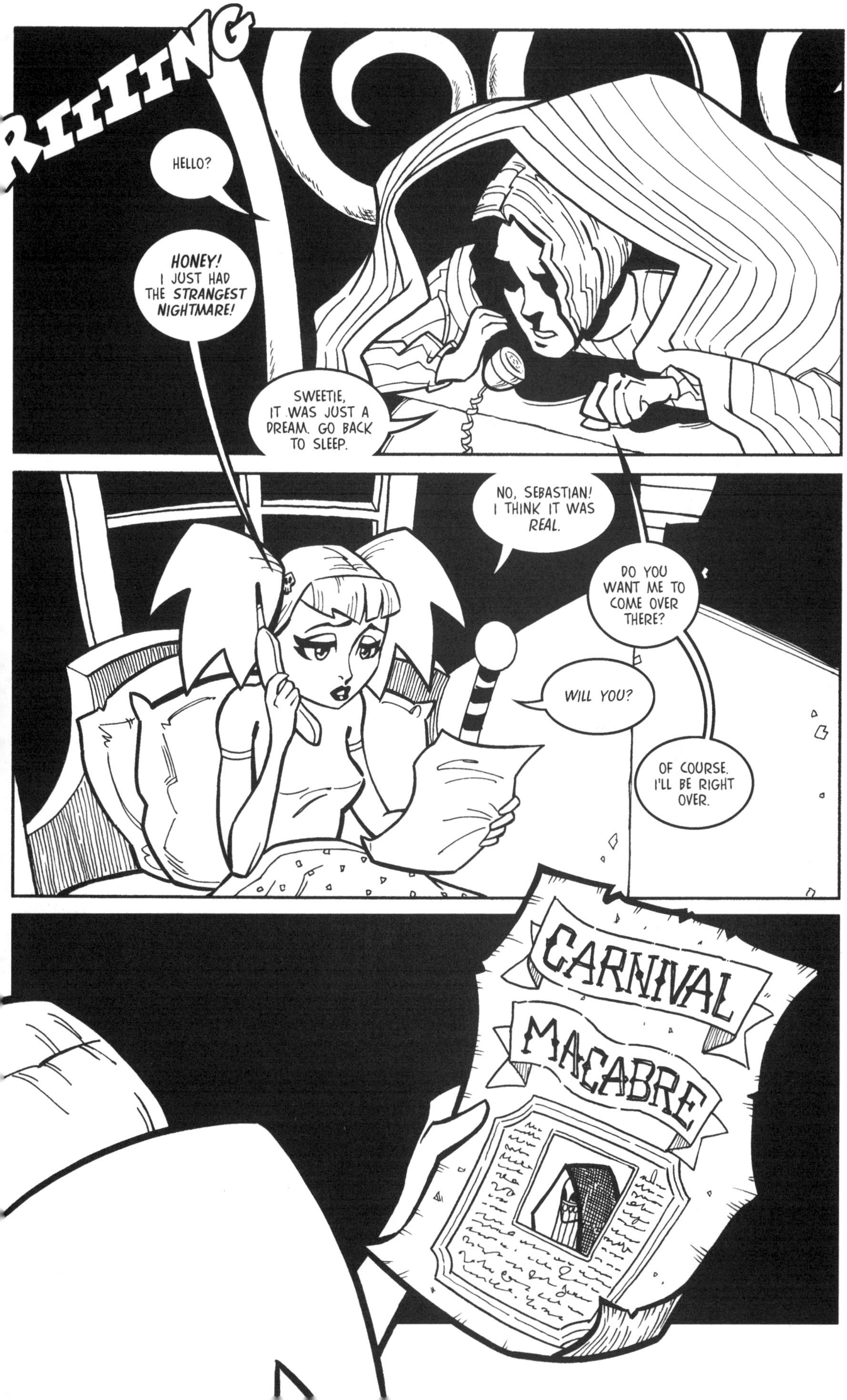
RIIIING
HELLO?
HONEY! I JUST HAD THE STRANGEST NIGHTMARE!
SWEETIE, IT WAS JUST A DREAM. GO BACK TO SLEEP.
NO, SEBASTIAN! I THINK IT WAS REAL.
DO YOU WANT ME TO COME OVER THERE?
WILL YOU?
OF COURSE. I'LL BE RIGHT OVER.
CARNIVAL
MACABRE

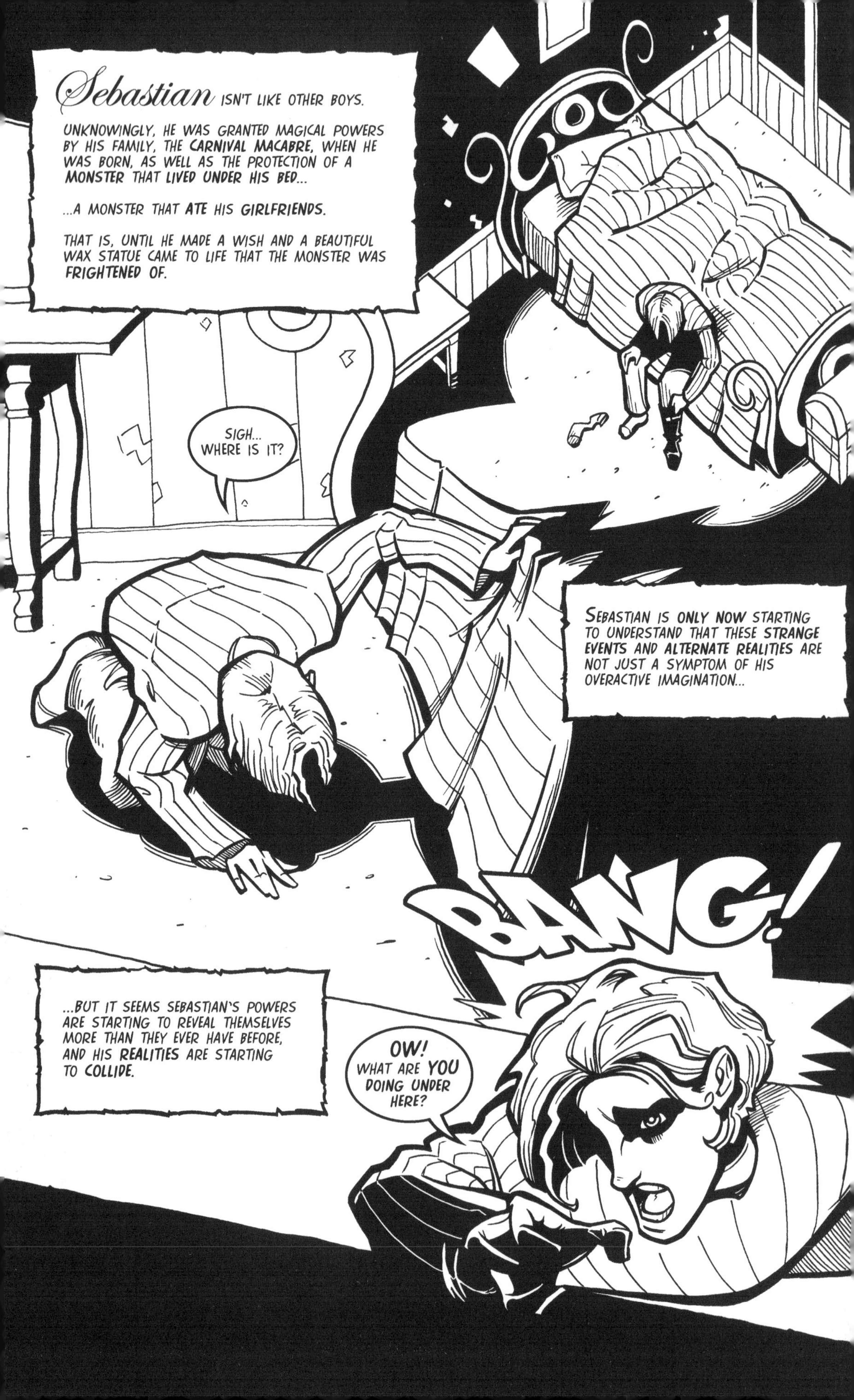
Sebastian ISN'T LIKE OTHER BOYS.
UNKNOWINGLY, HE WAS GRANTED MAGICAL POWERS BY HIS FAMILY, THE CARNIVAL MACABRE, WHEN HE WAS BORN, AS WELL AS THE PROTECTION OF A MONSTER THAT LIVED UNDER HIS BED...
...A MONSTER THAT ATE HIS GIRLFRIENDS.
THAT IS, UNTIL HE MADE A WISH AND A BEAUTIFUL WAX STATUE CAME TO LIFE THAT THE MONSTER WAS FRIGHTENED OF.
SIGH... WHERE IS IT?
SEBASTIAN IS ONLY NOW STARTING TO UNDERSTAND THAT THESE STRANGE EVENTS AND ALTERNATE REALITIES ARE NOT JUST A SYMPTOM OF HIS OVERACTIVE IMAGINATION...
BANG!
...BUT IT SEEMS SEBASTIAN'S POWERS ARE STARTING TO REVEAL THEMSELVES MORE THAN THEY EVER HAVE BEFORE, AND HIS REALITIES ARE STARTING TO COLLIDE.
OW! WHAT ARE YOU DOING UNDER HERE?

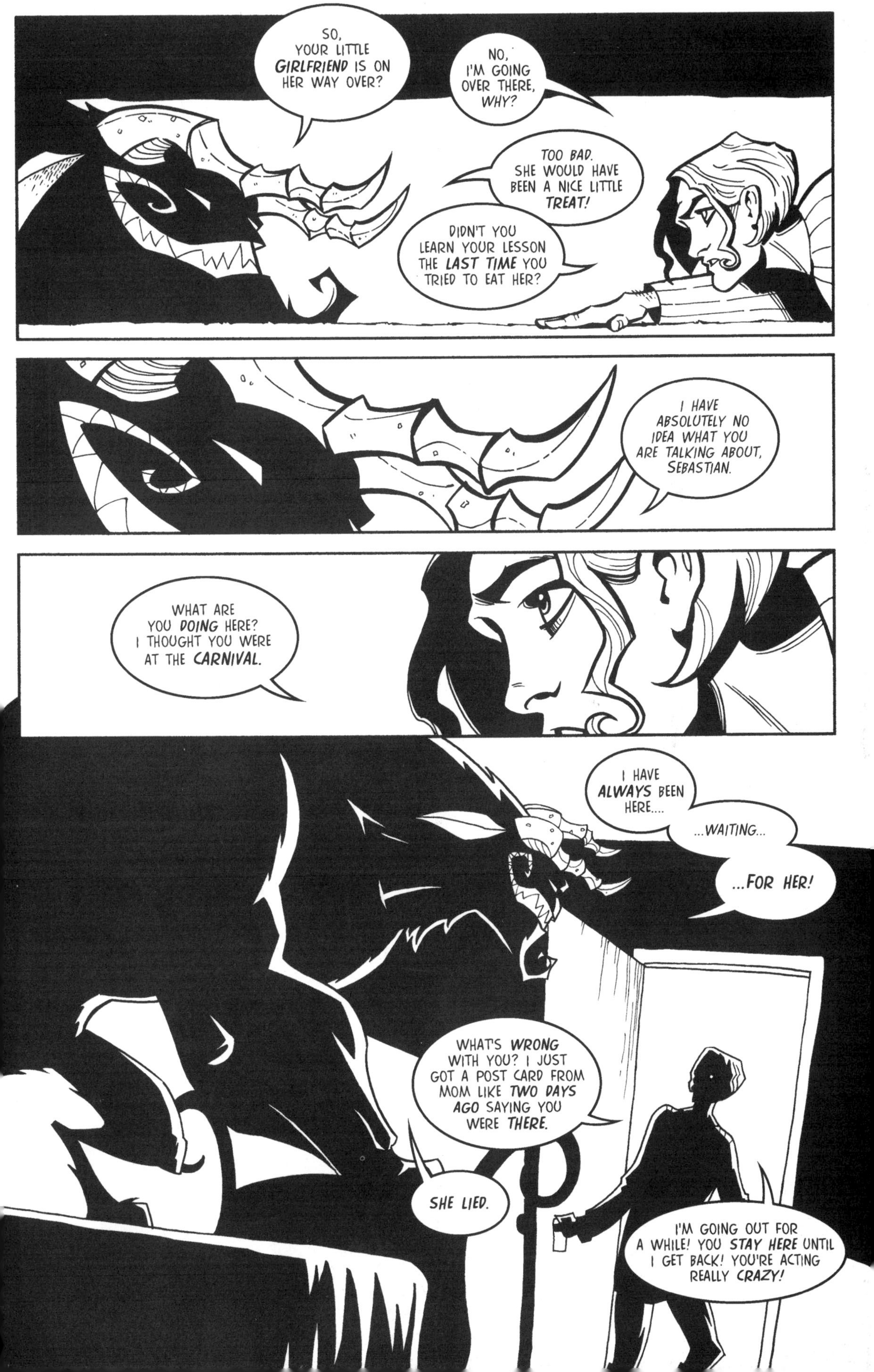
SO, YOUR LITTLE GIRLFRIEND IS ON HER WAY OVER?
NO, I'M GOING OVER THERE, WHY?
TOO BAD. SHE WOULD HAVE BEEN A NICE LITTLE TREAT!
DIDN'T YOU LEARN YOUR LESSON THE LAST TIME YOU TRIED TO EAT HER?
I HAVE ABSOLUTELY NO IDEA WHAT YOU ARE TALKING ABOUT, SEBASTIAN.
WHAT ARE YOU DOING HERE? I THOUGHT YOU WERE AT THE CARNIVAL.
I HAVE ALWAYS BEEN HERE....
...WAITING...
...FOR HER!
WHAT'S WRONG WITH YOU? I JUST GOT A POST CARD FROM MOM LIKE TWO DAYS AGO SAYING YOU WERE THERE.
SHE LIED.
I'M GOING OUT FOR A WHILE! YOU STAY HERE UNTIL I GET BACK! YOU'RE ACTING REALLY CRAZY!

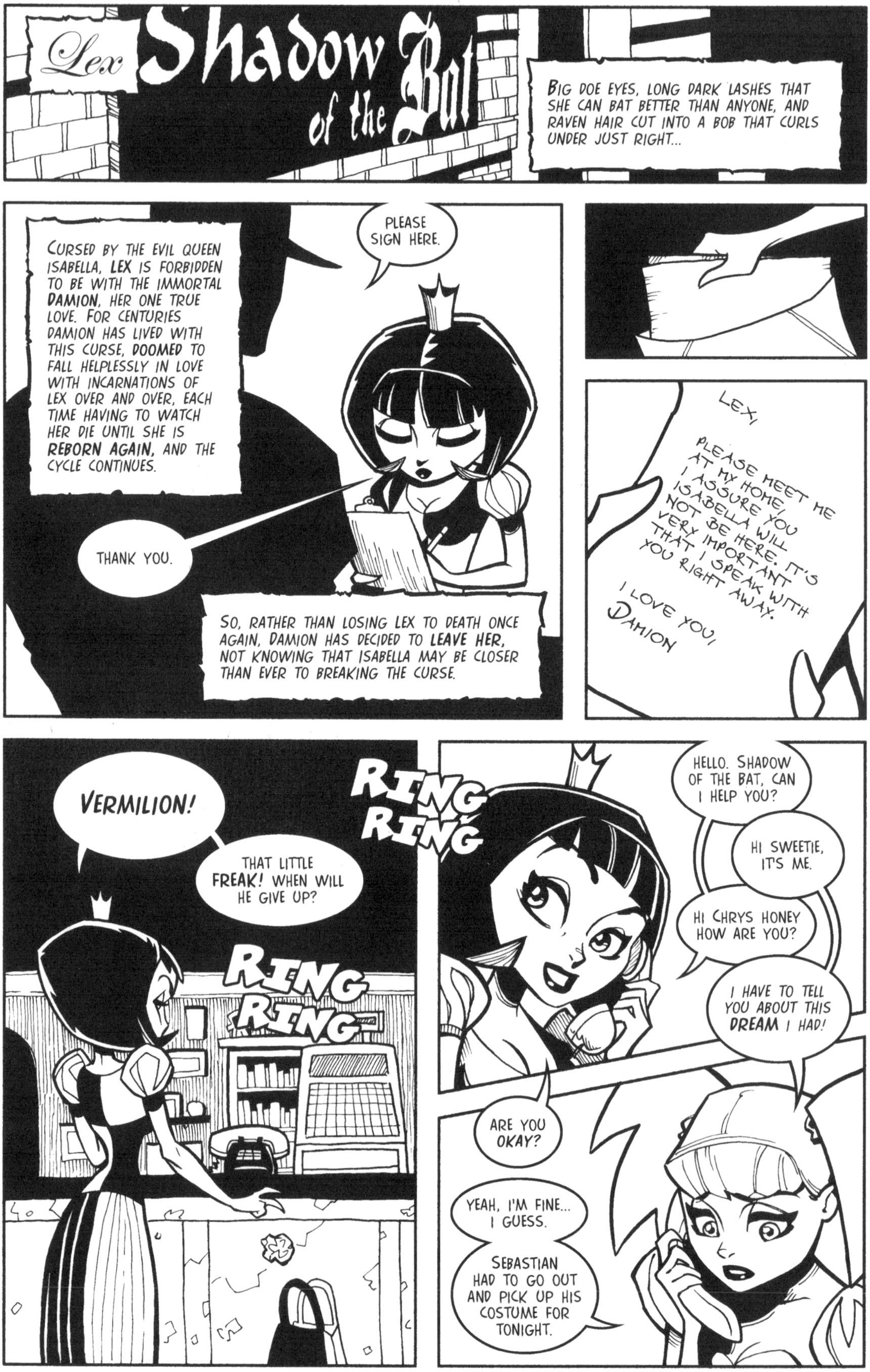
Lex
Shadow of the Bat
Big doe eyes, long dark lashes that she can bat better than anyone, and raven hair cut into a bob that curls under just right...
Cursed by the evil queen Isabella, Lex is forbidden to be with the immortal Damion, her one true love. For centuries Damion has lived with this curse, doomed to fall helplessly in love with incarnations of Lex over and over, each time having to watch her die until she is reborn again, and the cycle continues.
Please sign here.
Thank you.
So, rather than losing Lex to death once again, Damion has decided to leave her, not knowing that Isabella may be closer than ever to breaking the curse.
Lex, Please meet me at my home, I assure you Isabella will not be here. It's very important that I speak with you right away. I love you, Damion
Vermilion!
That little freak! When will he give up?
Ring Ring
Ring Ring
Hello. Shadow of the Bat, can I help you?
Hi sweetie, it's me.
Hi Chrys honey how are you?
I have to tell you about this dream I had!
Are you okay?
Yeah, I'm fine... I guess.
Sebastian had to go out and pick up his costume for tonight.

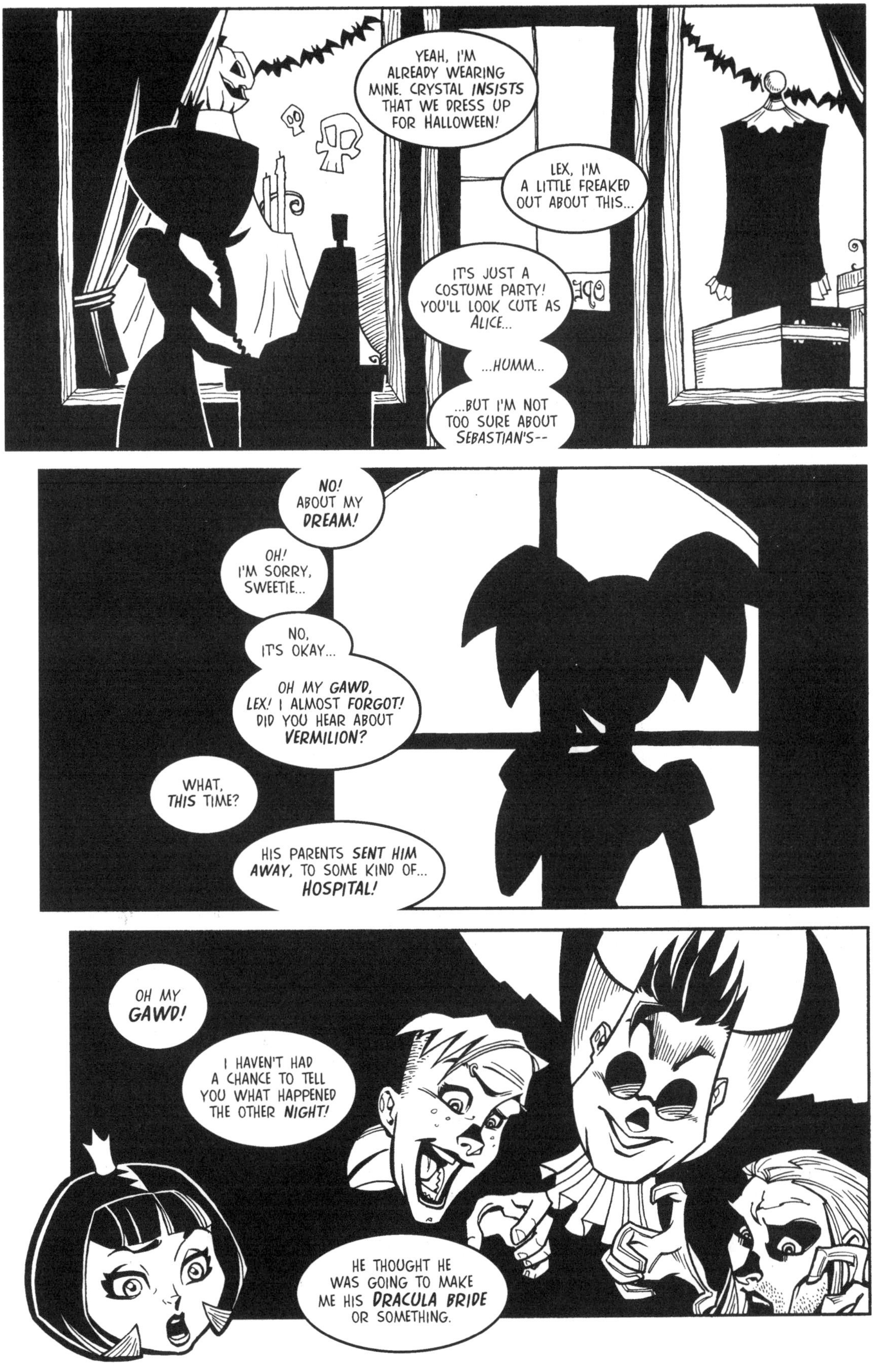
YEAH, I'M ALREADY WEARING MINE. CRYSTAL INSISTS THAT WE DRESS UP FOR HALLOWEEN!
LEX, I'M A LITTLE FREAKED OUT ABOUT THIS...
IT'S JUST A COSTUME PARTY! YOU'LL LOOK CUTE AS ALICE...
...HUMM...
...BUT I'M NOT TOO SURE ABOUT SEBASTIAN'S--
NO! ABOUT MY DREAM!
OH! I'M SORRY, SWEETIE...
NO, IT'S OKAY...
OH MY GAWD, LEX! I ALMOST FORGOT! DID YOU HEAR ABOUT VERMILION?
WHAT, THIS TIME?
HIS PARENTS SENT HIM AWAY, TO SOME KIND OF... HOSPITAL!
OH MY GAWD!
I HAVEN'T HAD A CHANCE TO TELL YOU WHAT HAPPENED THE OTHER NIGHT!
HE THOUGHT HE WAS GOING TO MAKE ME HIS DRACULA BRIDE OR SOMETHING.

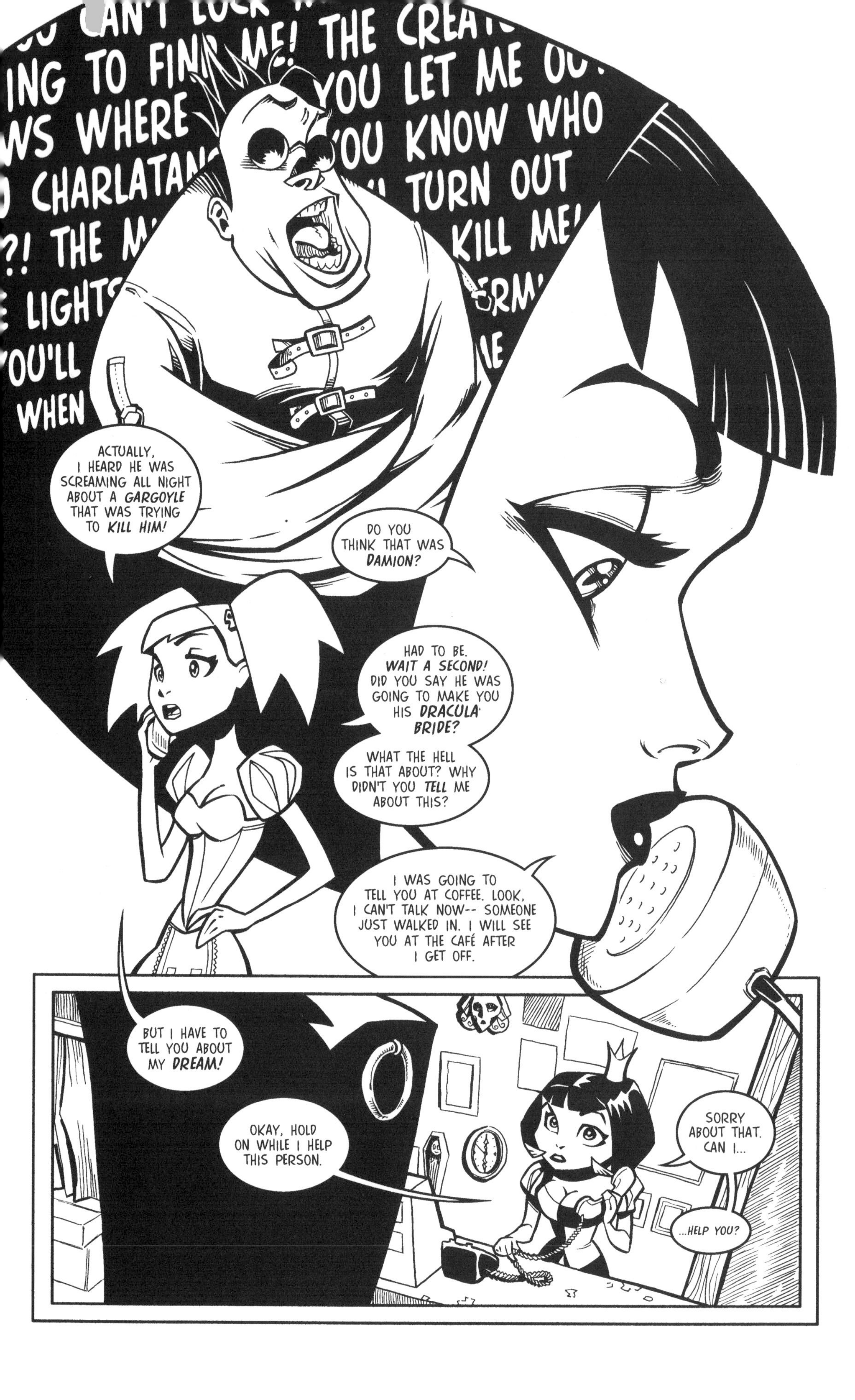
ACTUALLY, I HEARD HE WAS SCREAMING ALL NIGHT ABOUT A GARGOYLE THAT WAS TRYING TO KILL HIM!
DO YOU THINK THAT WAS DAMION?
HAD TO BE. WAIT A SECOND! DID YOU SAY HE WAS GOING TO MAKE YOU HIS DRACULA BRIDE?
WHAT THE HELL IS THAT ABOUT? WHY DIDN'T YOU TELL ME ABOUT THIS?
I WAS GOING TO TELL YOU AT COFFEE. LOOK, I CAN'T TALK NOW-- SOMEONE JUST WALKED IN. I WILL SEE YOU AT THE CAFÉ AFTER I GET OFF.
BUT I HAVE TO TELL YOU ABOUT MY DREAM!
OKAY, HOLD ON WHILE I HELP THIS PERSON.
SORRY ABOUT THAT. CAN I...
...HELP YOU?

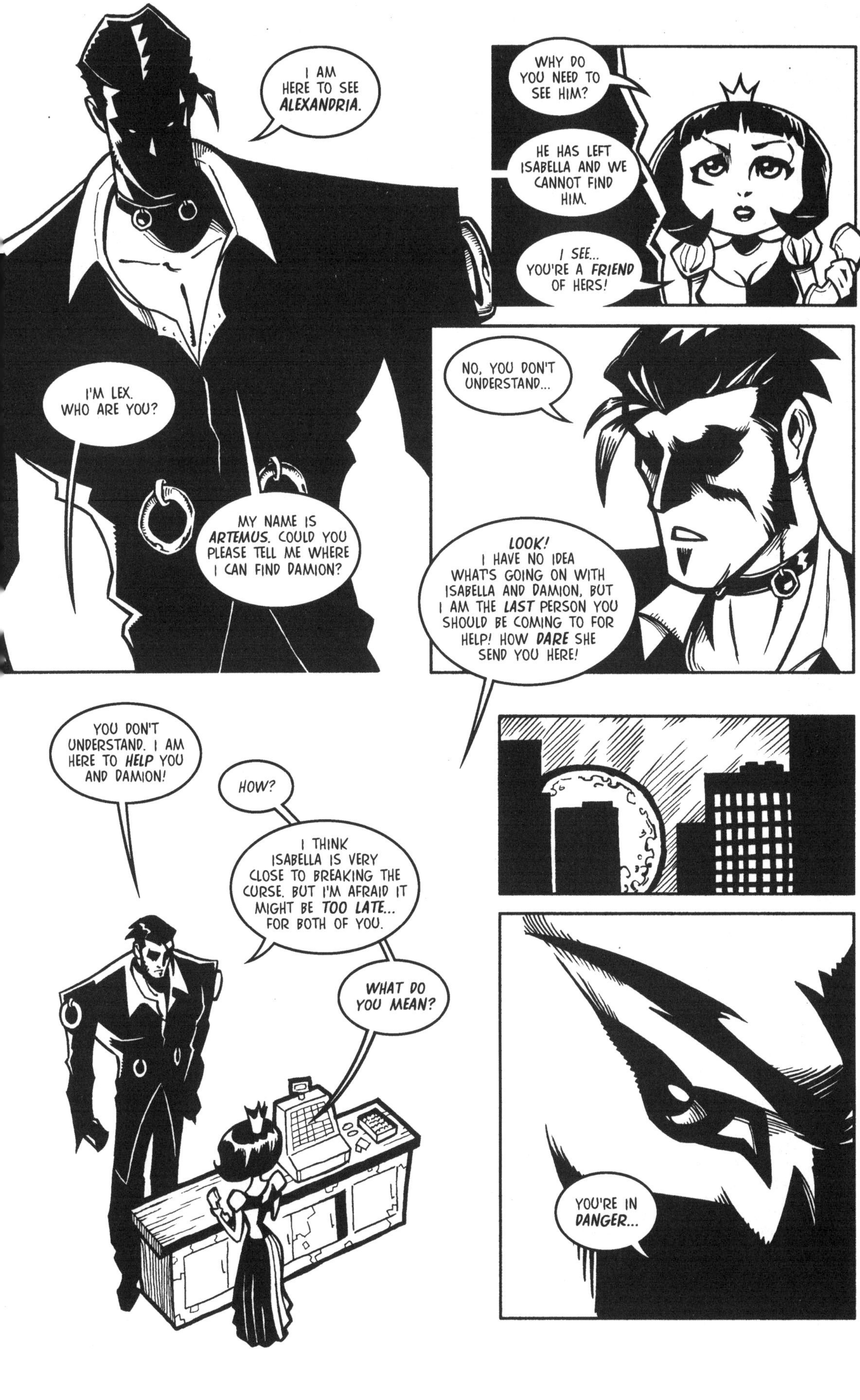
I AM HERE TO SEE ALEXANDRIA.
WHY DO YOU NEED TO SEE HIM?
HE HAS LEFT ISABELLA AND WE CANNOT FIND HIM.
I SEE... YOU'RE A FRIEND OF HERS!
I'M LEX. WHO ARE YOU?
MY NAME IS ARTEMUS. COULD YOU PLEASE TELL ME WHERE I CAN FIND DAMION?
NO, YOU DON'T UNDERSTAND...
LOOK! I HAVE NO IDEA WHAT'S GOING ON WITH ISABELLA AND DAMION, BUT I AM THE LAST PERSON YOU SHOULD BE COMING TO FOR HELP! HOW DARE SHE SEND YOU HERE!
YOU DON'T UNDERSTAND. I AM HERE TO HELP YOU AND DAMION!
HOW?
I THINK ISABELLA IS VERY CLOSE TO BREAKING THE CURSE. BUT I'M AFRAID IT MIGHT BE TOO LATE... FOR BOTH OF YOU.
WHAT DO YOU MEAN?
YOU'RE IN DANGER...

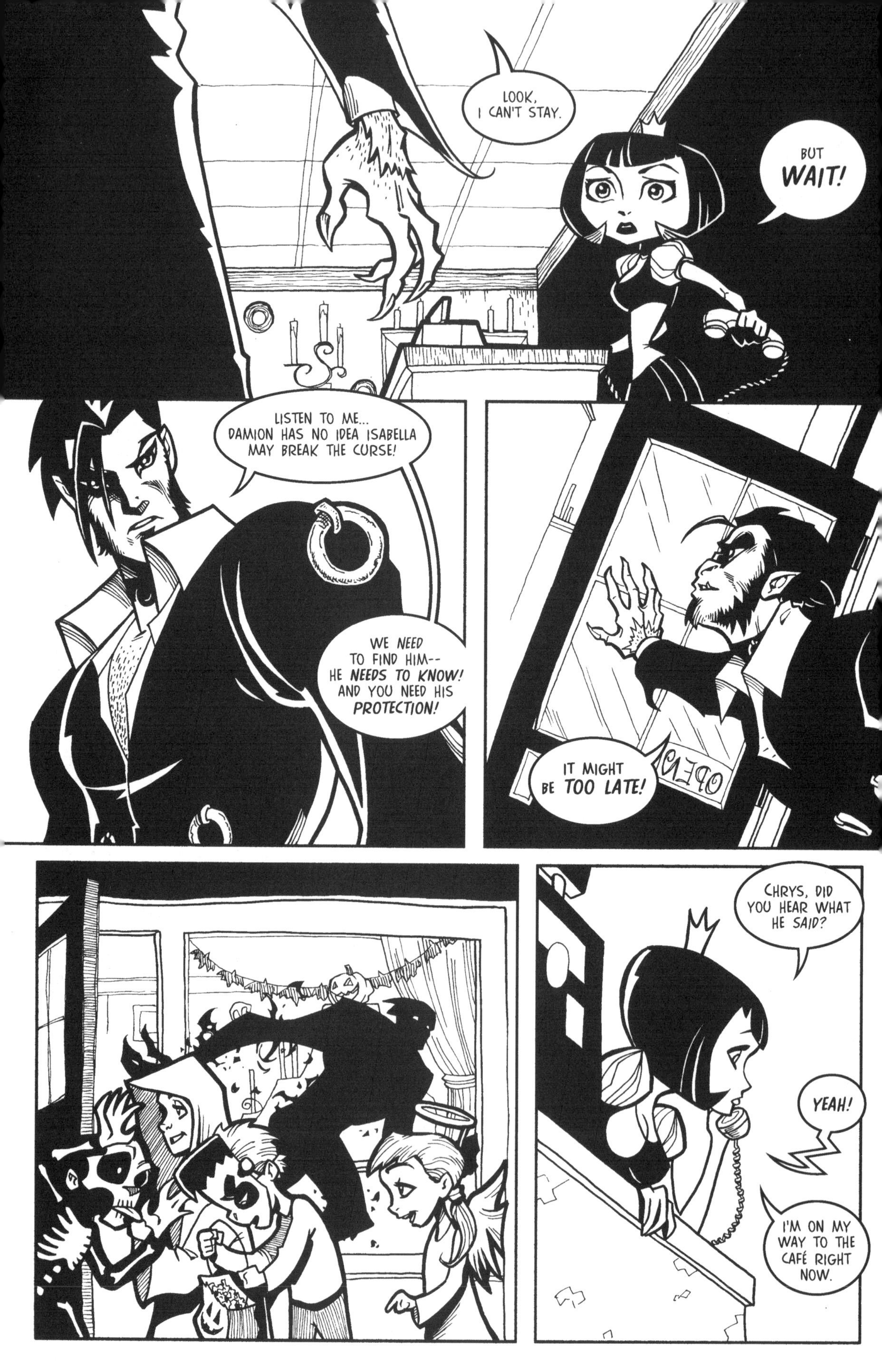
LOOK, I CAN'T STAY.
BUT WAIT!
LISTEN TO ME... DAMION HAS NO IDEA ISABELLA MAY BREAK THE CURSE!
WE NEED TO FIND HIM-- HE NEEDS TO KNOW! AND YOU NEED HIS PROTECTION!
IT MIGHT BE TOO LATE!
OPEN
CHRYS, DID YOU HEAR WHAT HE SAID?
YEAH!
I'M ON MY WAY TO THE CAFÉ RIGHT NOW.

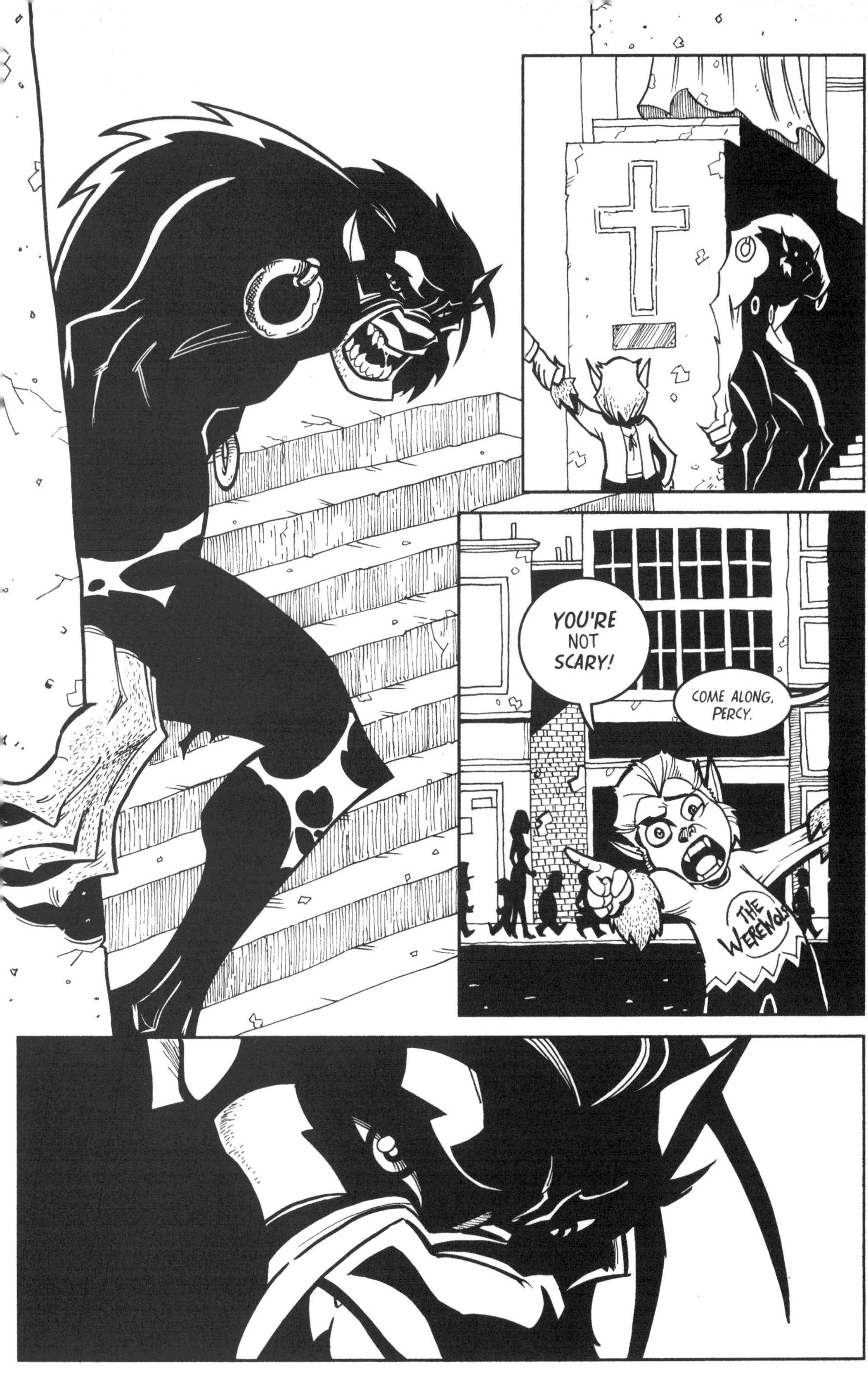
YOU'RE NOT SCARY!
COME ALONG, PERCY.
THE WEREWOLF

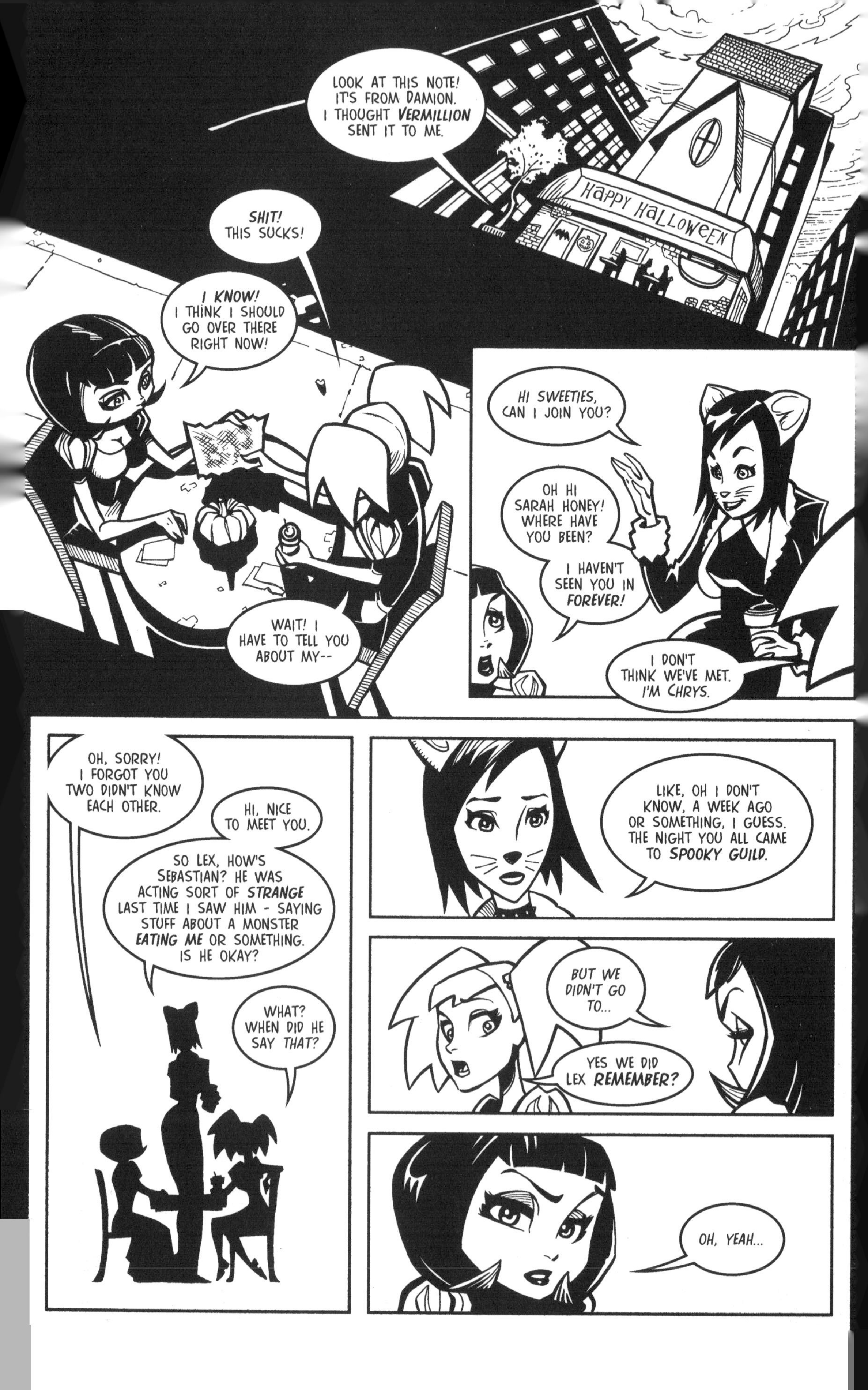
LOOK AT THIS NOTE! IT'S FROM DAMION. I THOUGHT VERMILLION SENT IT TO ME.
HAPPY HALLOWEEN
SHIT! THIS SUCKS!
I KNOW! I THINK I SHOULD GO OVER THERE RIGHT NOW!
WAIT! I HAVE TO TELL YOU ABOUT MY--
HI SWEETIES, CAN I JOIN YOU?
OH HI SARAH HONEY! WHERE HAVE YOU BEEN?
I HAVEN'T SEEN YOU IN FOREVER!
I DON'T THINK WE'VE MET. I'M CHRYS.
OH, SORRY! I FORGOT YOU TWO DIDN'T KNOW EACH OTHER.
HI, NICE TO MEET YOU.
SO LEX, HOW'S SEBASTIAN? HE WAS ACTING SORT OF STRANGE LAST TIME I SAW HIM - SAYING STUFF ABOUT A MONSTER EATING ME OR SOMETHING. IS HE OKAY?
WHAT? WHEN DID HE SAY THAT?
LIKE, OH I DON'T KNOW, A WEEK AGO OR SOMETHING, I GUESS. THE NIGHT YOU ALL CAME TO SPOOKY GUILD.
BUT WE DIDN'T GO TO...
YES WE DID LEX REMEMBER?
OH, YEAH...

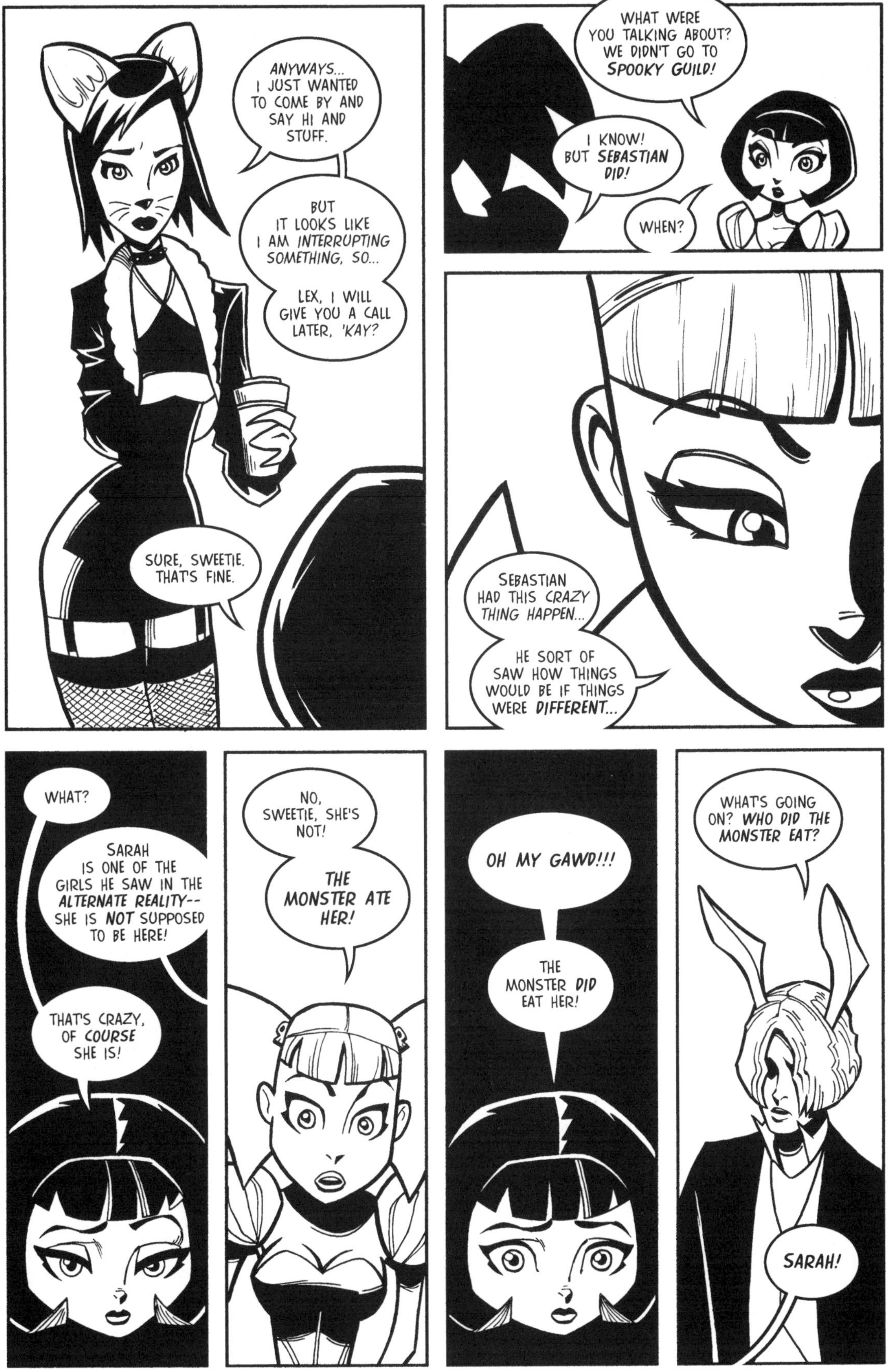
ANYWAYS... I JUST WANTED TO COME BY AND SAY HI AND STUFF.
BUT IT LOOKS LIKE I AM INTERRUPTING SOMETHING, SO...
LEX, I WILL GIVE YOU A CALL LATER, 'KAY?
SURE, SWEETIE. THAT'S FINE.
WHAT WERE YOU TALKING ABOUT? WE DIDN'T GO TO SPOOKY GUILD!
I KNOW! BUT SEBASTIAN DID!
WHEN?
SEBASTIAN HAD THIS CRAZY THING HAPPEN...
HE SORT OF SAW HOW THINGS WOULD BE IF THINGS WERE DIFFERENT...
WHAT?
SARAH IS ONE OF THE GIRLS HE SAW IN THE ALTERNATE REALITY-- SHE IS NOT SUPPOSED TO BE HERE!
THAT'S CRAZY, OF COURSE SHE IS!
NO, SWEETIE, SHE'S NOT!
THE MONSTER ATE HER!
OH MY GAWD!!!
THE MONSTER DID EAT HER!
WHAT'S GOING ON? WHO DID THE MONSTER EAT?
SARAH!

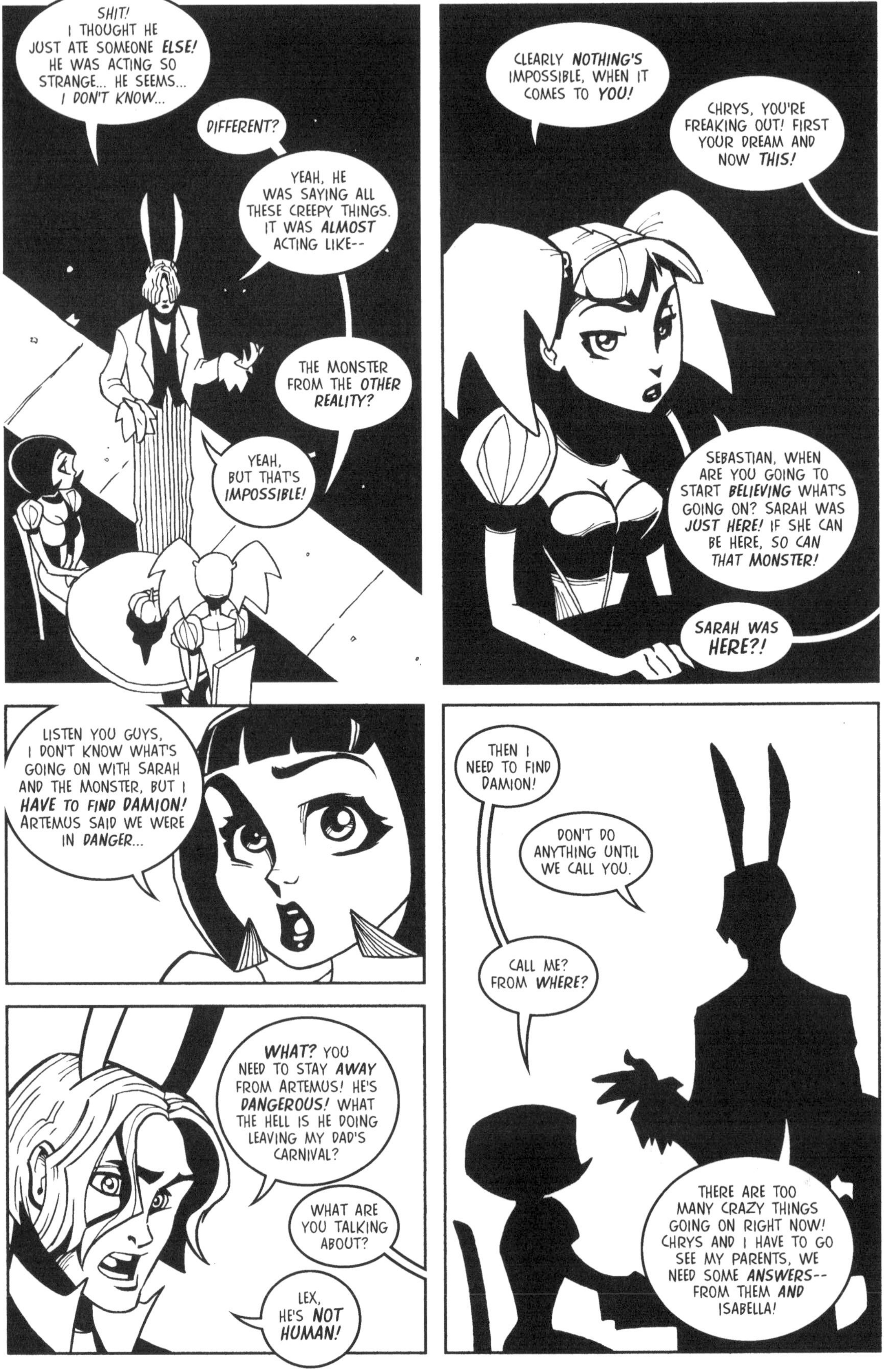
SHIT! I THOUGHT HE JUST ATE SOMEONE ELSE! HE WAS ACTING SO STRANGE... HE SEEMS... I DON'T KNOW...
DIFFERENT?
YEAH, HE WAS SAYING ALL THESE CREEPY THINGS. IT WAS ALMOST ACTING LIKE--
THE MONSTER FROM THE OTHER REALITY?
YEAH, BUT THAT'S IMPOSSIBLE!
CLEARLY NOTHING'S IMPOSSIBLE, WHEN IT COMES TO YOU!
CHRYS, YOU'RE FREAKING OUT! FIRST YOUR DREAM AND NOW THIS!
SEBASTIAN, WHEN ARE YOU GOING TO START BELIEVING WHAT'S GOING ON? SARAH WAS JUST HERE! IF SHE CAN BE HERE, SO CAN THAT MONSTER!
SARAH WAS HERE?!
LISTEN YOU GUYS, I DON'T KNOW WHAT'S GOING ON WITH SARAH AND THE MONSTER, BUT I HAVE TO FIND DAMION! ARTEMUS SAID WE WERE IN DANGER...
WHAT? YOU NEED TO STAY AWAY FROM ARTEMUS! HE'S DANGEROUS! WHAT THE HELL IS HE DOING LEAVING MY DAD'S CARNIVAL?
WHAT ARE YOU TALKING ABOUT?
LEX, HE'S NOT HUMAN!
THEN I NEED TO FIND DAMION!
DON'T DO ANYTHING UNTIL WE CALL YOU.
CALL ME? FROM WHERE?
THERE ARE TOO MANY CRAZY THINGS GOING ON RIGHT NOW! CHRYS AND I HAVE TO GO SEE MY PARENTS, WE NEED SOME ANSWERS-- FROM THEM AND ISABELLA!

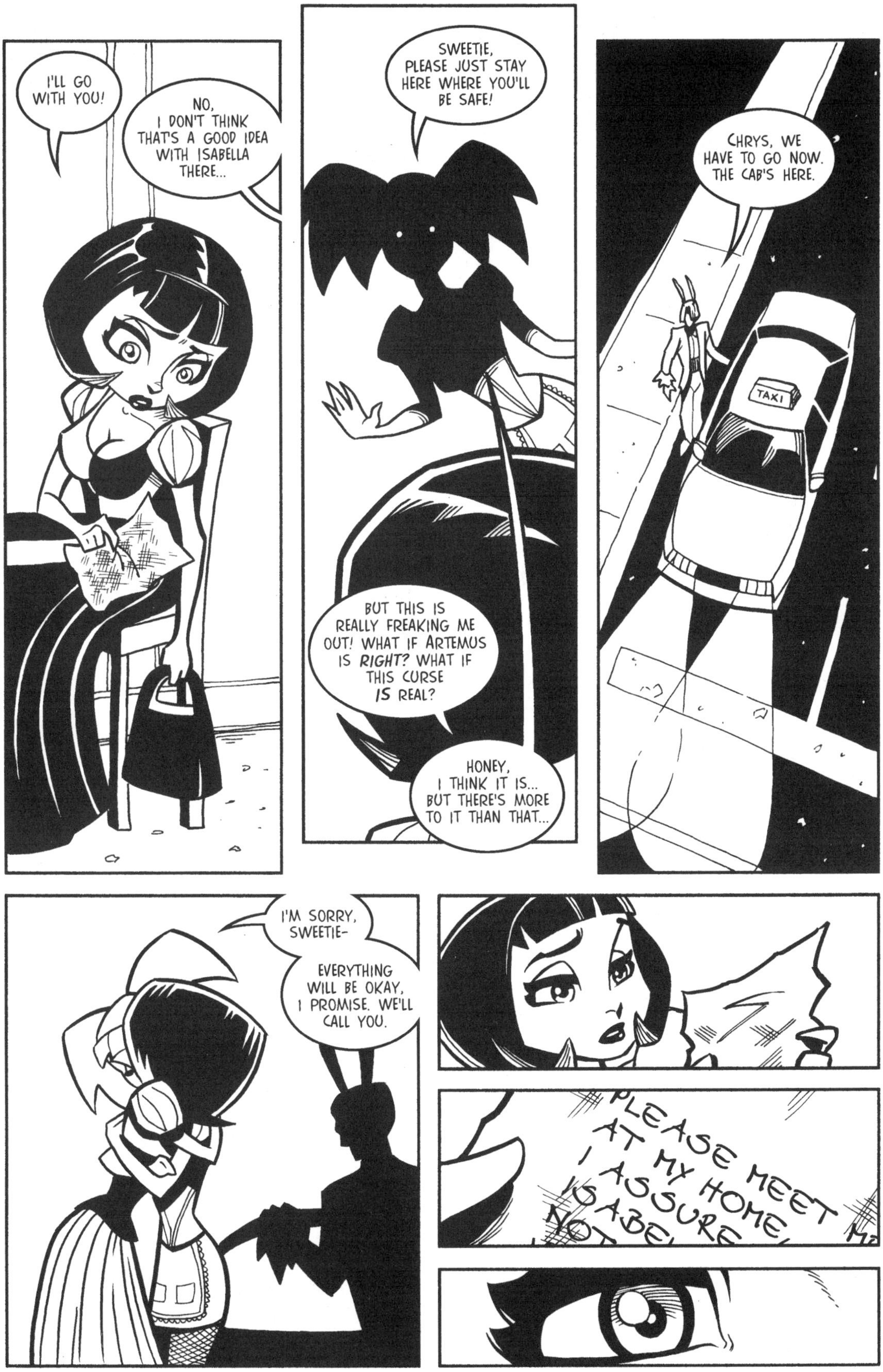

I'LL GO WITH YOU!
NO, I DON'T THINK THAT'S A GOOD IDEA WITH ISABELLA THERE...
SWEETIE, PLEASE JUST STAY HERE WHERE YOU'LL BE SAFE!
BUT THIS IS REALLY FREAKING ME OUT! WHAT IF ARTEMUS IS RIGHT? WHAT IF THIS CURSE IS REAL?
HONEY, I THINK IT IS... BUT THERE'S MORE TO IT THAN THAT...
CHRYS, WE HAVE TO GO NOW. THE CAB'S HERE.
TAXI
I'M SORRY, SWEETIE-
EVERYTHING WILL BE OKAY, I PROMISE. WE'LL CALL YOU.
PLEASE MEET
AT MY HOME
I ASSURE

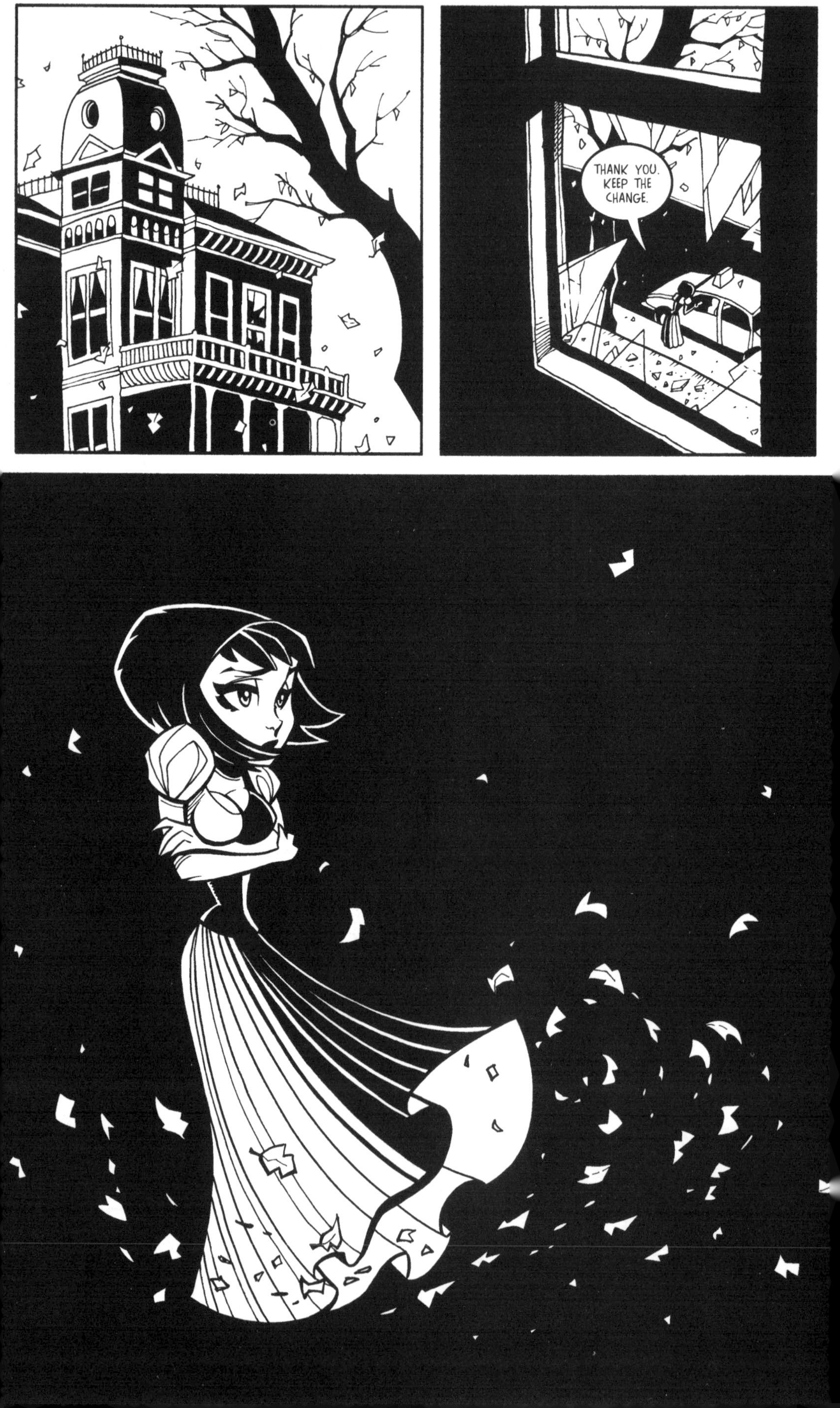
THANK YOU. KEEP THE CHANGE.

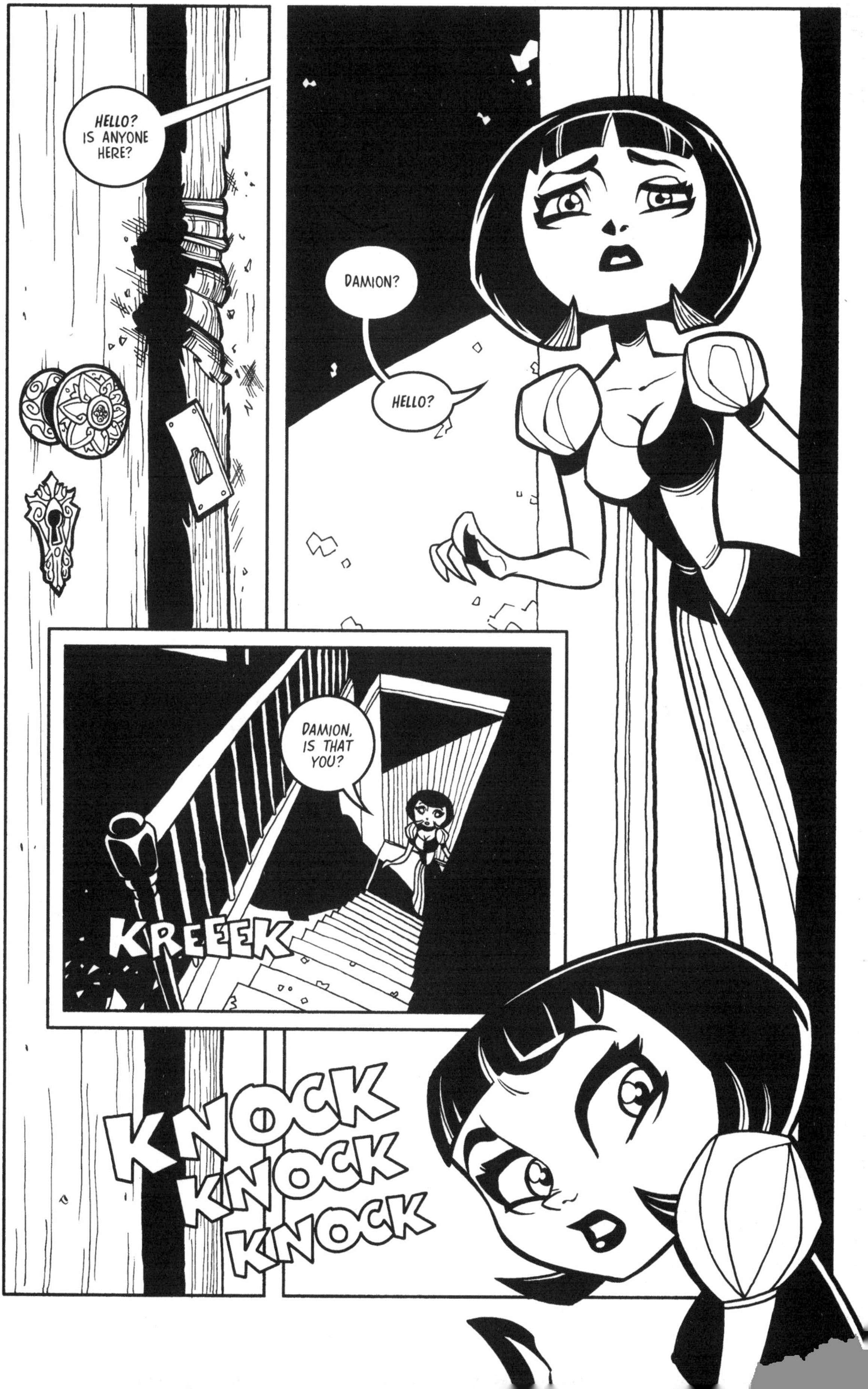
HELLO? IS ANYONE HERE?
DAMION?
HELLO?
DAMION, IS THAT YOU?
KREEEK
KNOCK KNOCK KNOCK

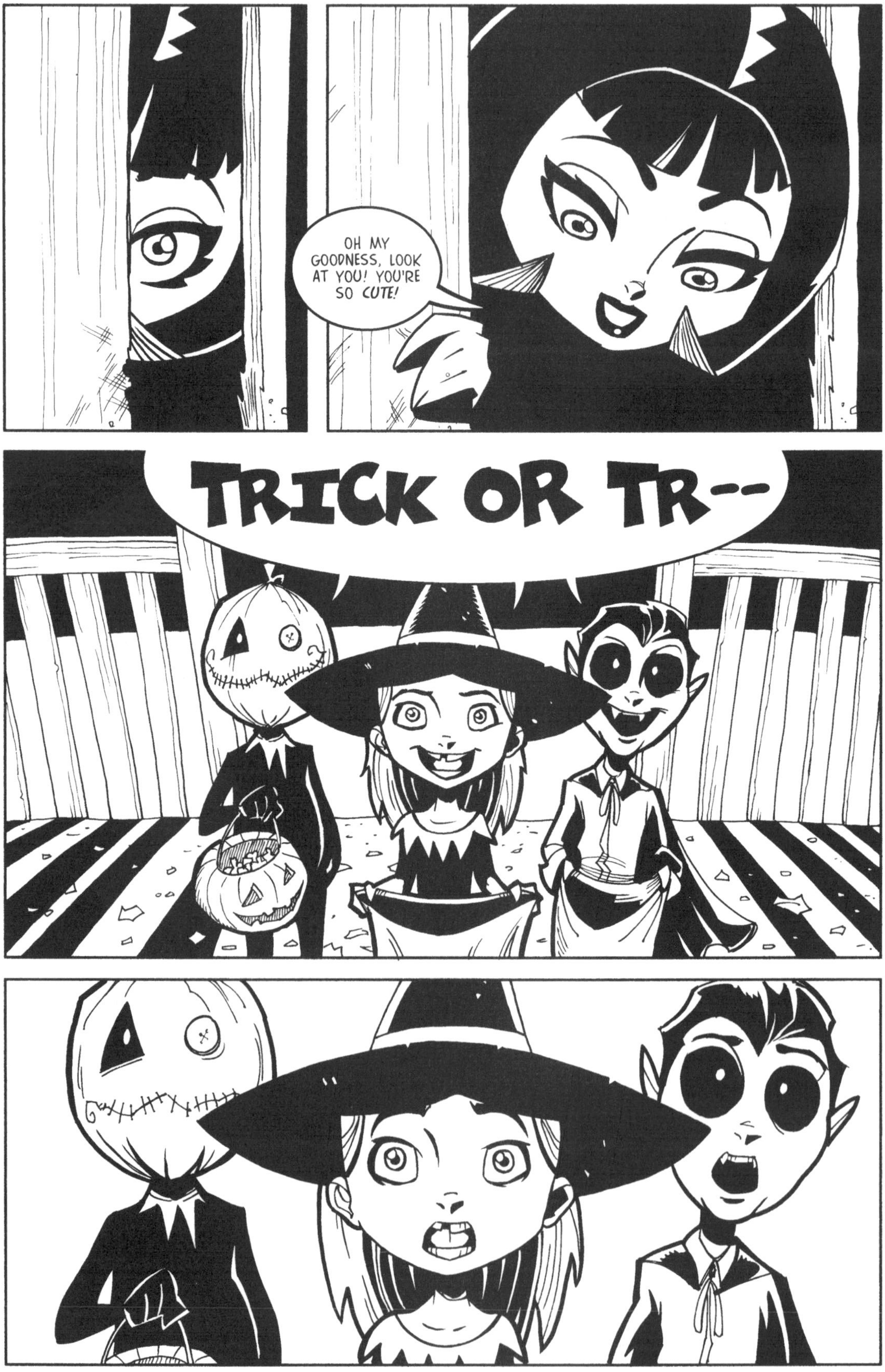
OH MY GOODNESS, LOOK AT YOU! YOU'RE SO *CUTE!*
TRICK OR TR--

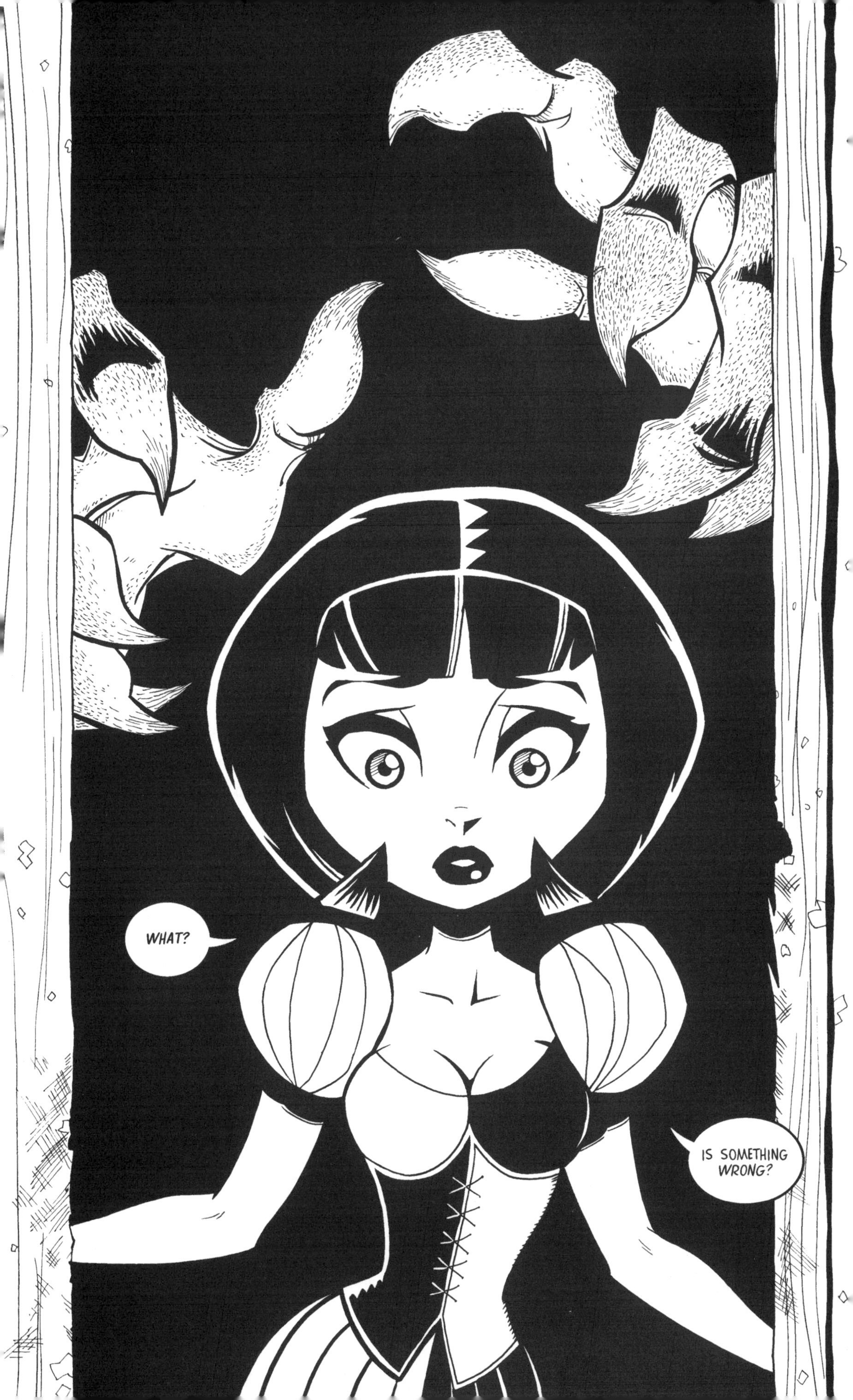
WHAT?
IS SOMETHING WRONG?

CHAPTER 15

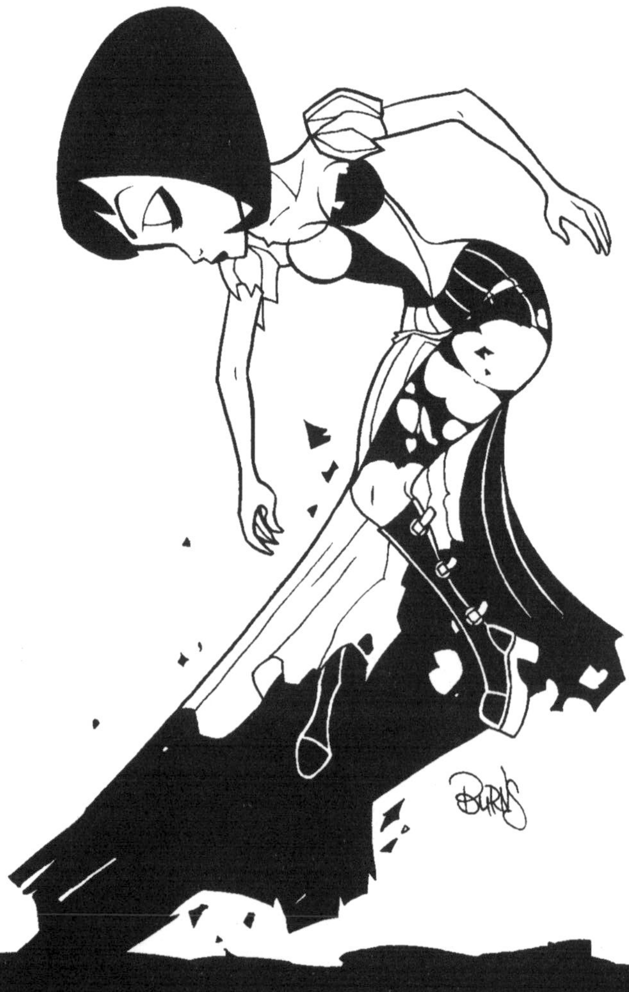
BURNS

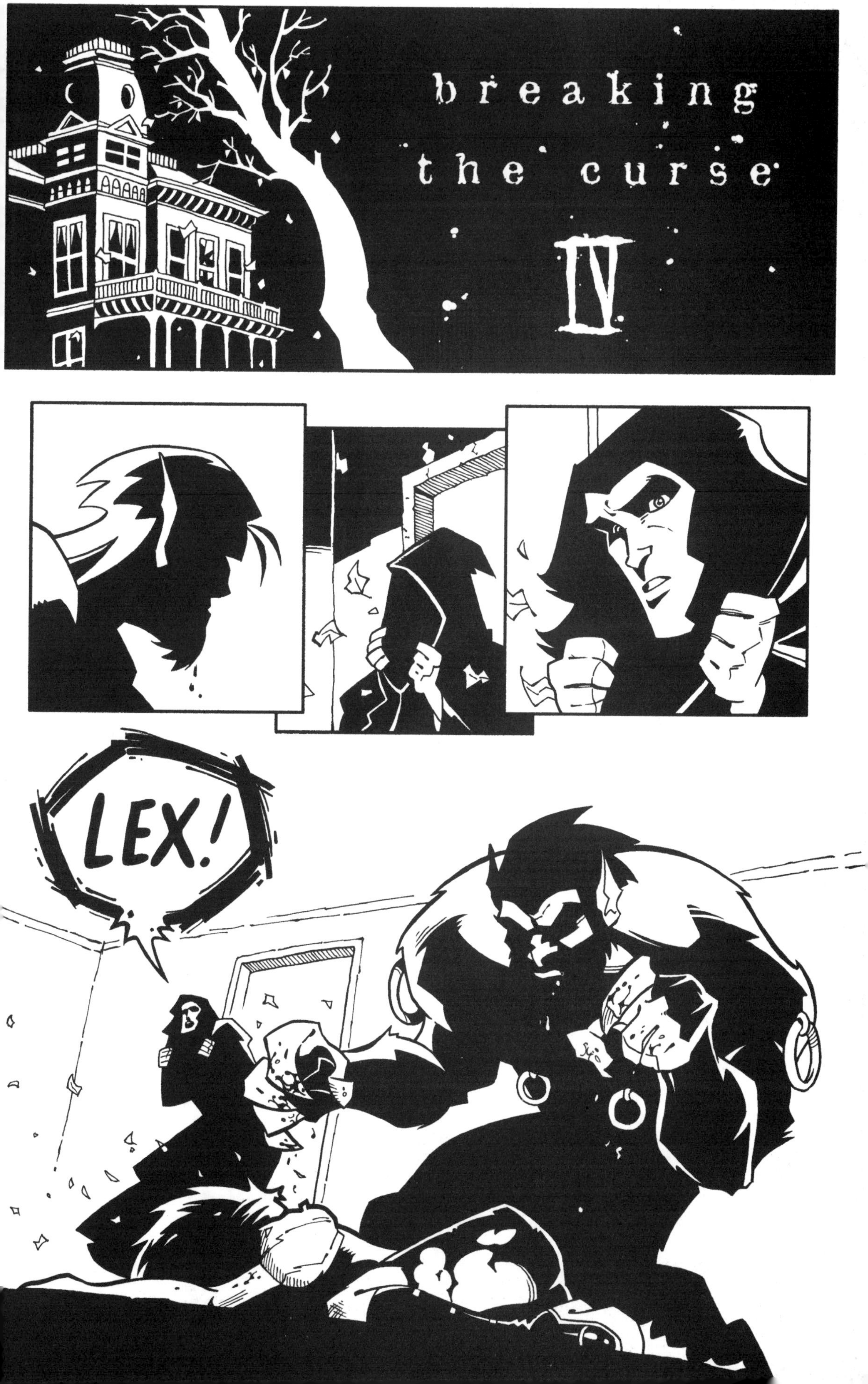
breaking the curse
IV
LEX!

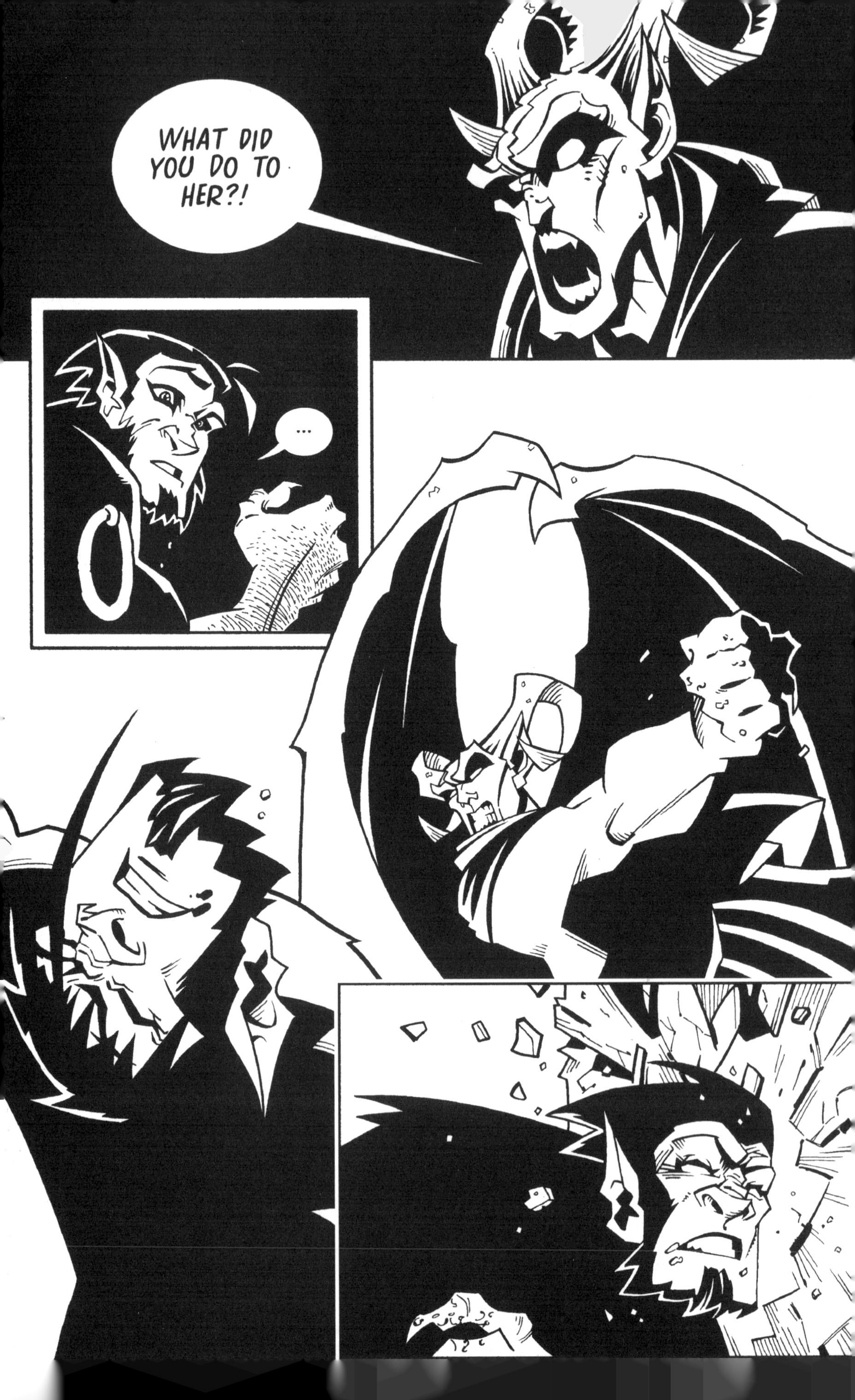
WHAT DID YOU DO TO HER?!
...

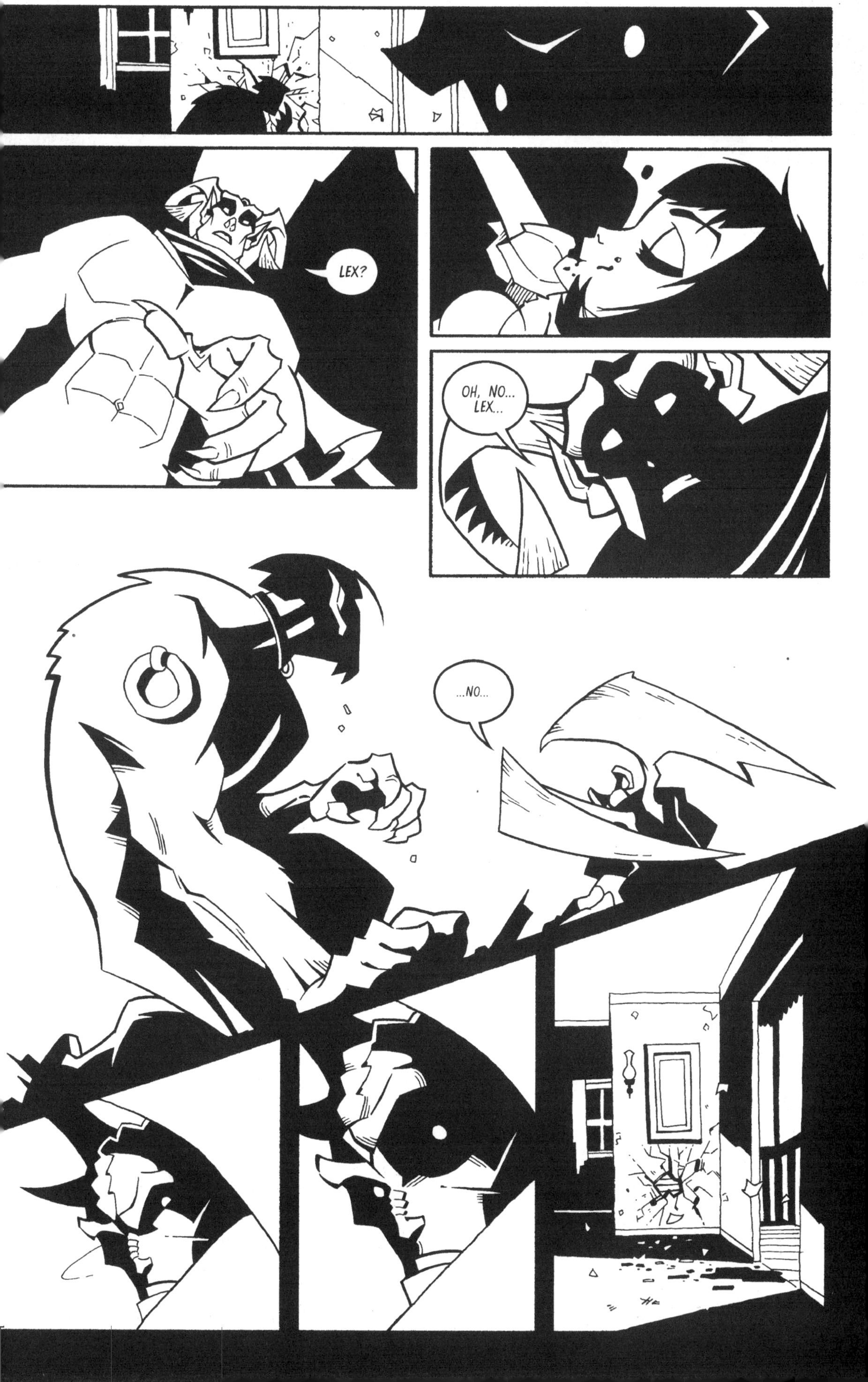
LEX?
OH, NO... LEX...
...NO...

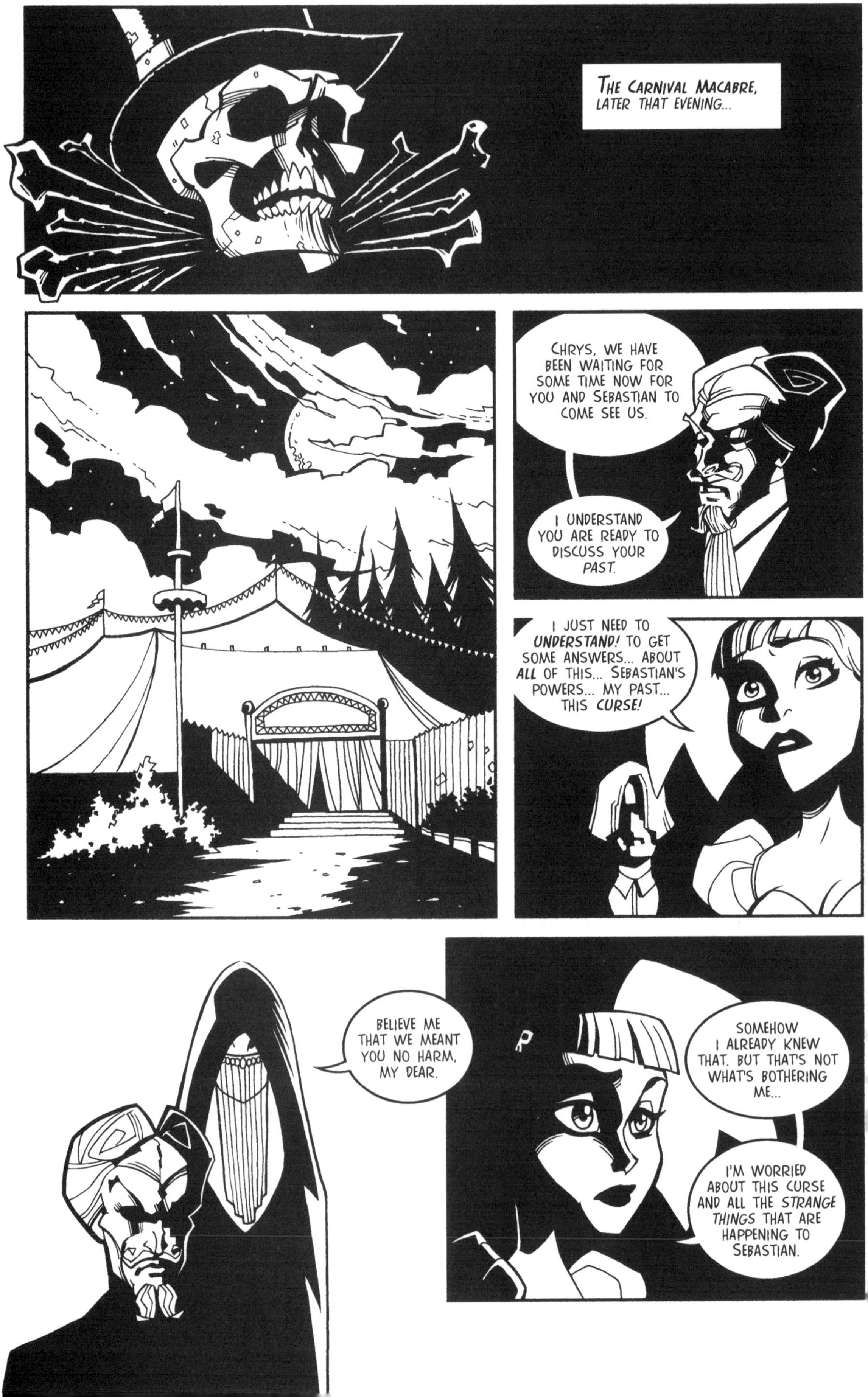
THE CARNIVAL MACABRE, LATER THAT EVENING...
CHRYS, WE HAVE BEEN WAITING FOR SOME TIME NOW FOR YOU AND SEBASTIAN TO COME SEE US.
I UNDERSTAND YOU ARE READY TO DISCUSS YOUR *PAST*.
I JUST NEED TO *UNDERSTAND!* TO GET SOME ANSWERS... ABOUT *ALL* OF THIS... SEBASTIAN'S POWERS... MY PAST... THIS *CURSE!*
BELIEVE ME THAT WE MEANT YOU NO HARM, MY DEAR.
SOMEHOW I ALREADY KNEW THAT. BUT THAT'S NOT WHAT'S BOTHERING ME...
I'M WORRIED ABOUT THIS CURSE AND ALL THE *STRANGE THINGS* THAT ARE HAPPENING TO SEBASTIAN.

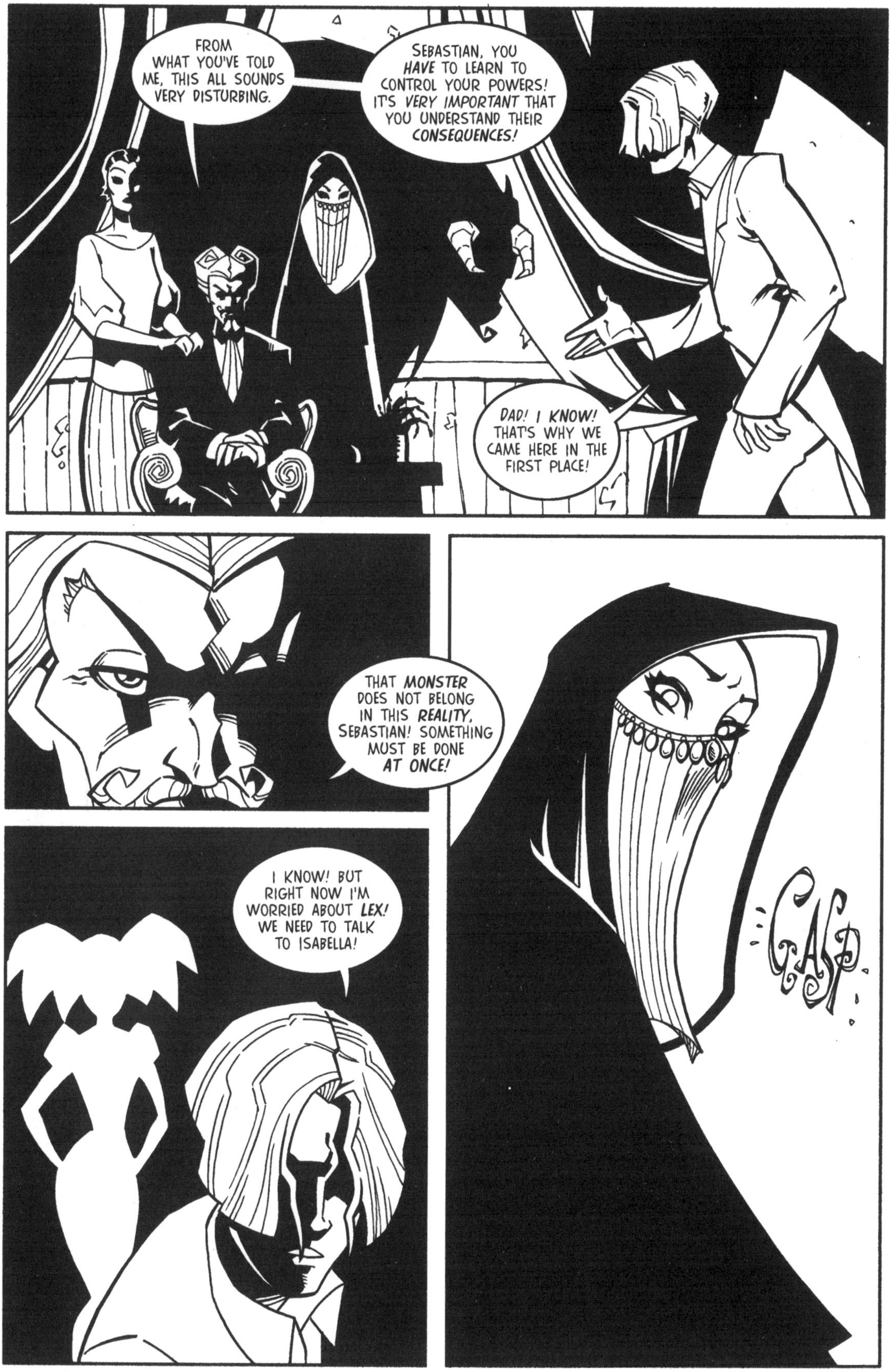
FROM WHAT YOU'VE TOLD ME, THIS ALL SOUNDS VERY DISTURBING.
SEBASTIAN, YOU HAVE TO LEARN TO CONTROL YOUR POWERS! IT'S VERY IMPORTANT THAT YOU UNDERSTAND THEIR CONSEQUENCES!
DAD! I KNOW! THAT'S WHY WE CAME HERE IN THE FIRST PLACE!
THAT MONSTER DOES NOT BELONG IN THIS REALITY, SEBASTIAN! SOMETHING MUST BE DONE AT ONCE!
I KNOW! BUT RIGHT NOW I'M WORRIED ABOUT LEX! WE NEED TO TALK TO ISABELLA!
GASP

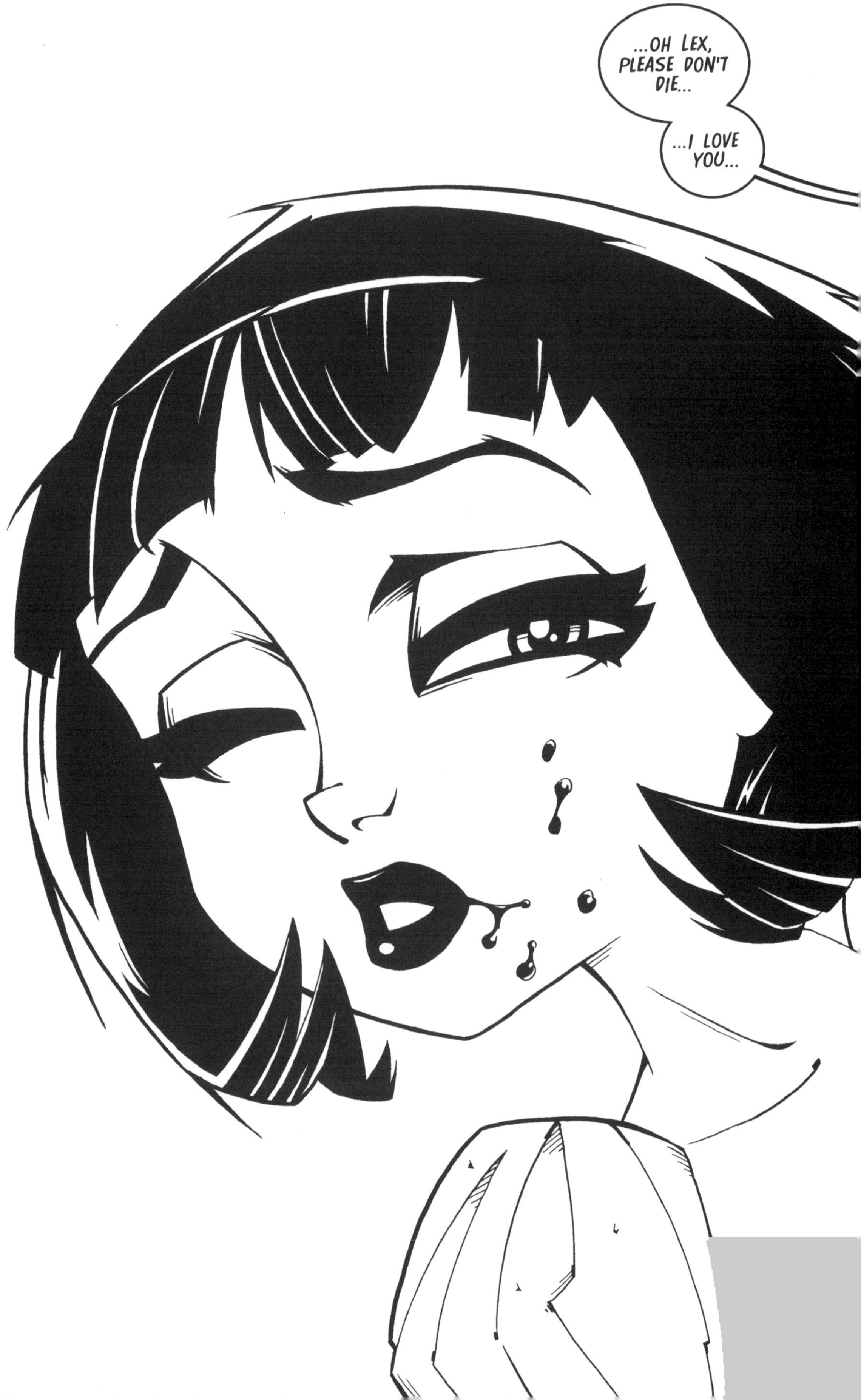
...OH LEX, PLEASE DON'T DIE...
...I LOVE YOU...

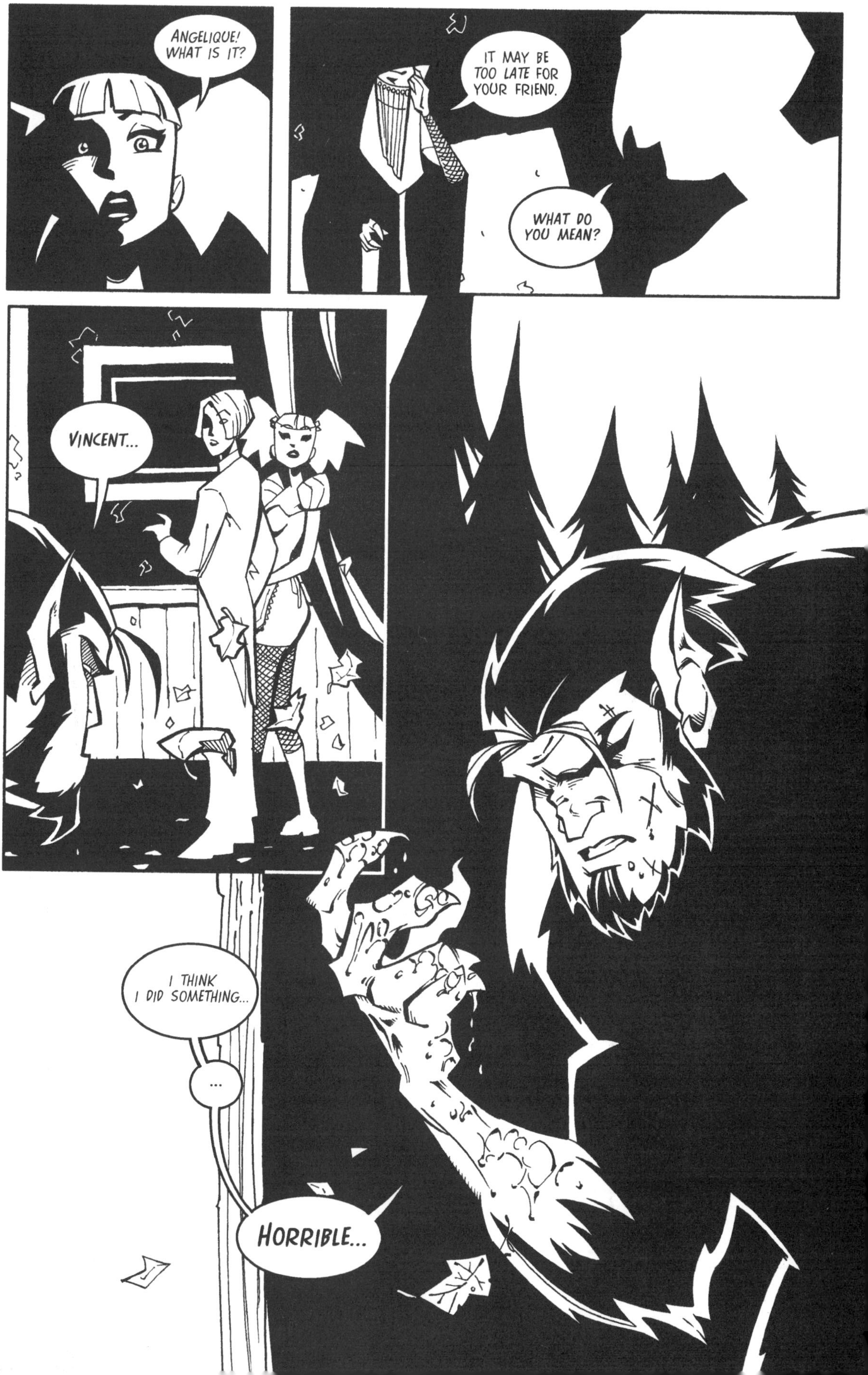
ANGELIQUE! WHAT IS IT?
IT MAY BE TOO LATE FOR YOUR FRIEND.
WHAT DO YOU MEAN?
VINCENT...
I THINK I DID SOMETHING...
...
HORRIBLE...

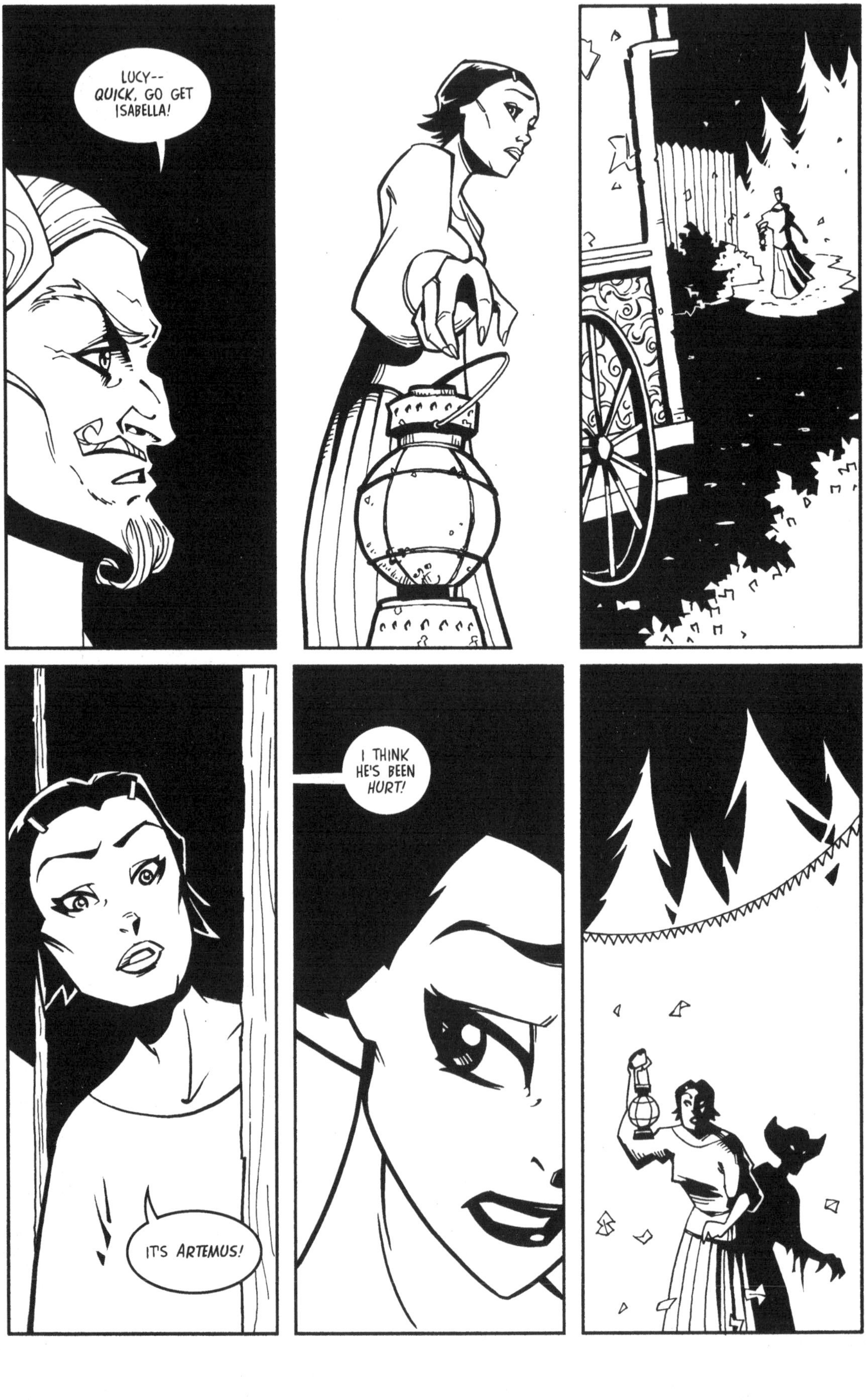
LUCY--
QUICK, GO GET
ISABELLA!
IT'S ARTEMUS!
I THINK
HE'S BEEN
HURT!

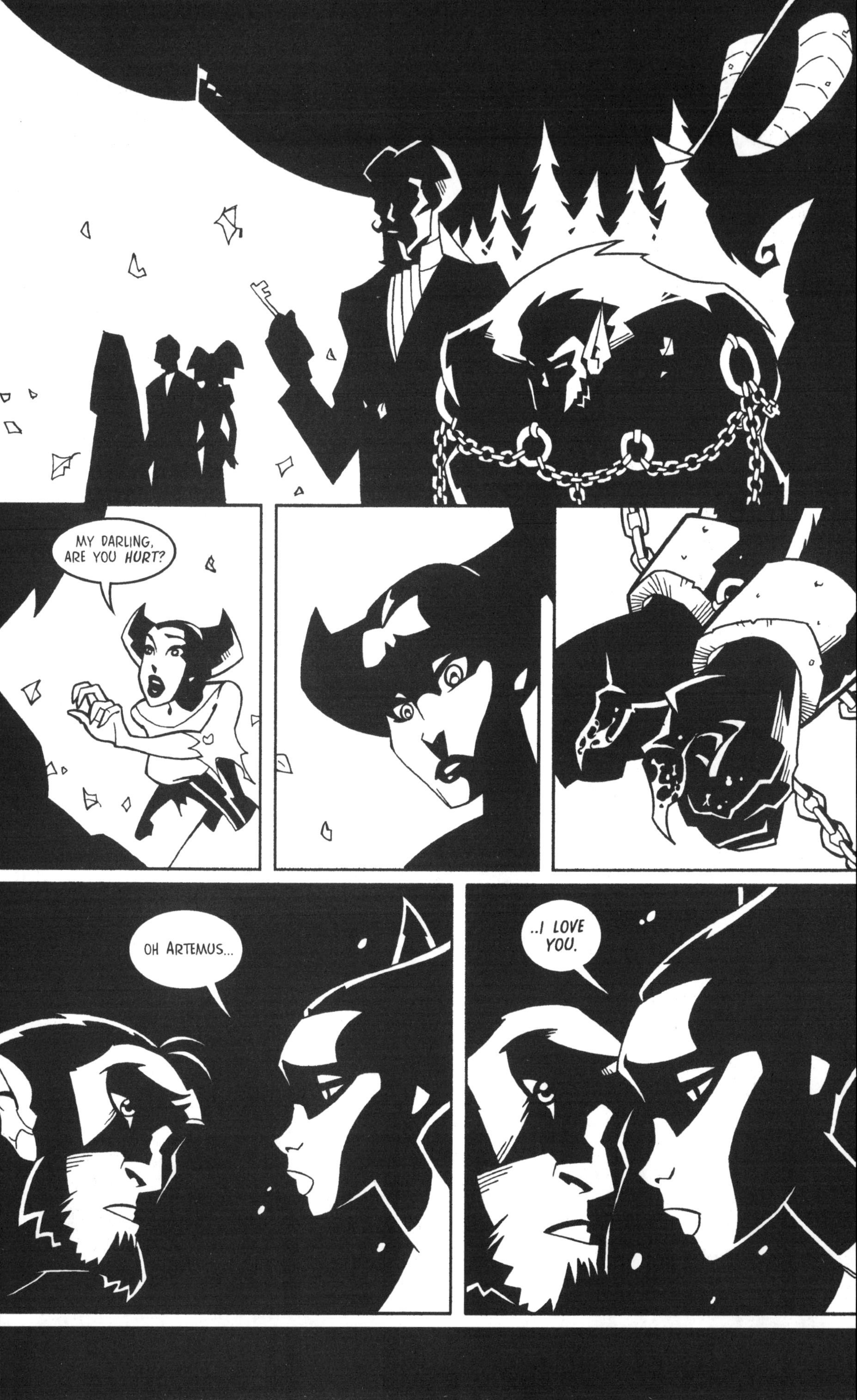
MY DARLING, ARE YOU HURT?
OH ARTEMUS...
..I LOVE YOU.

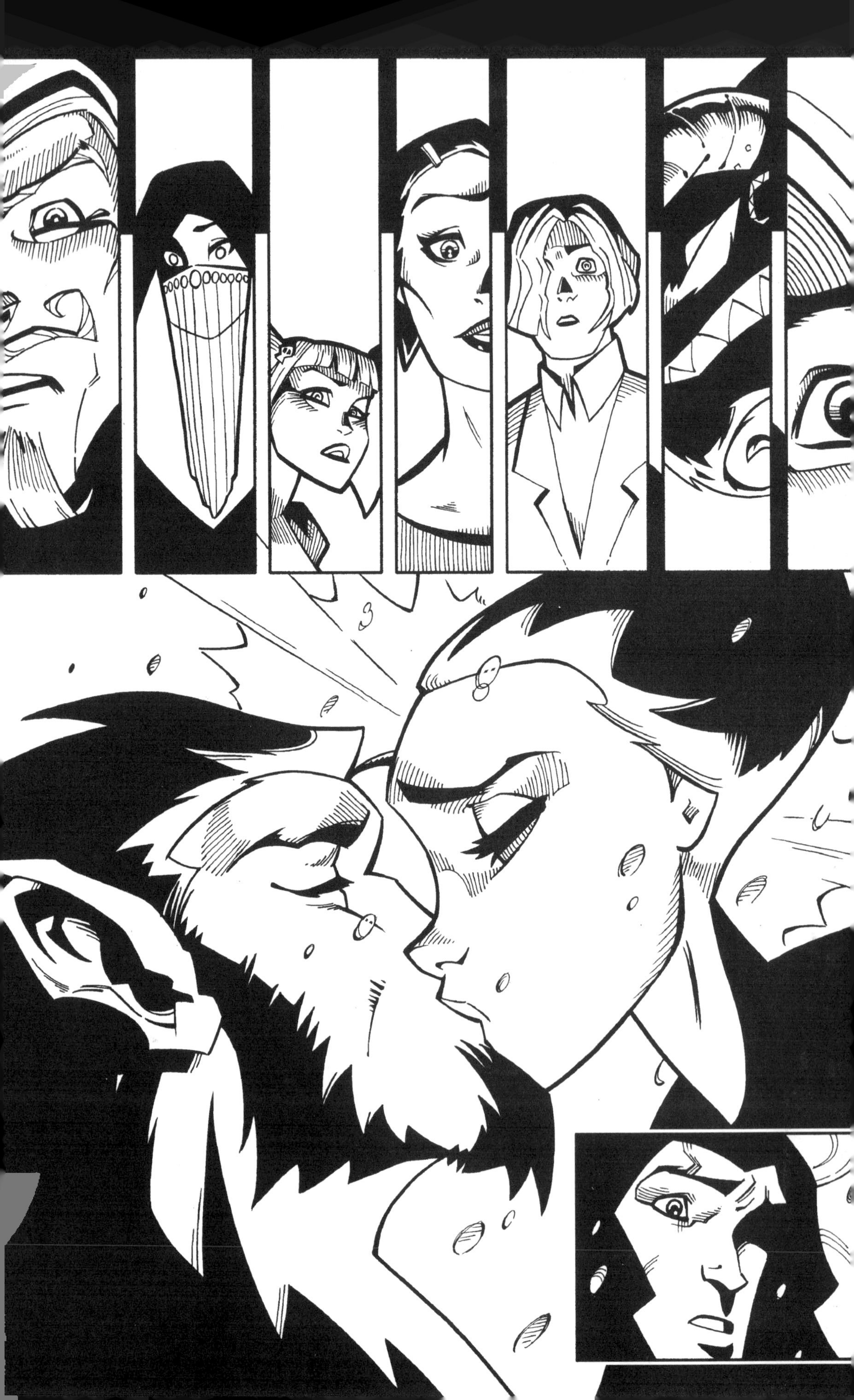

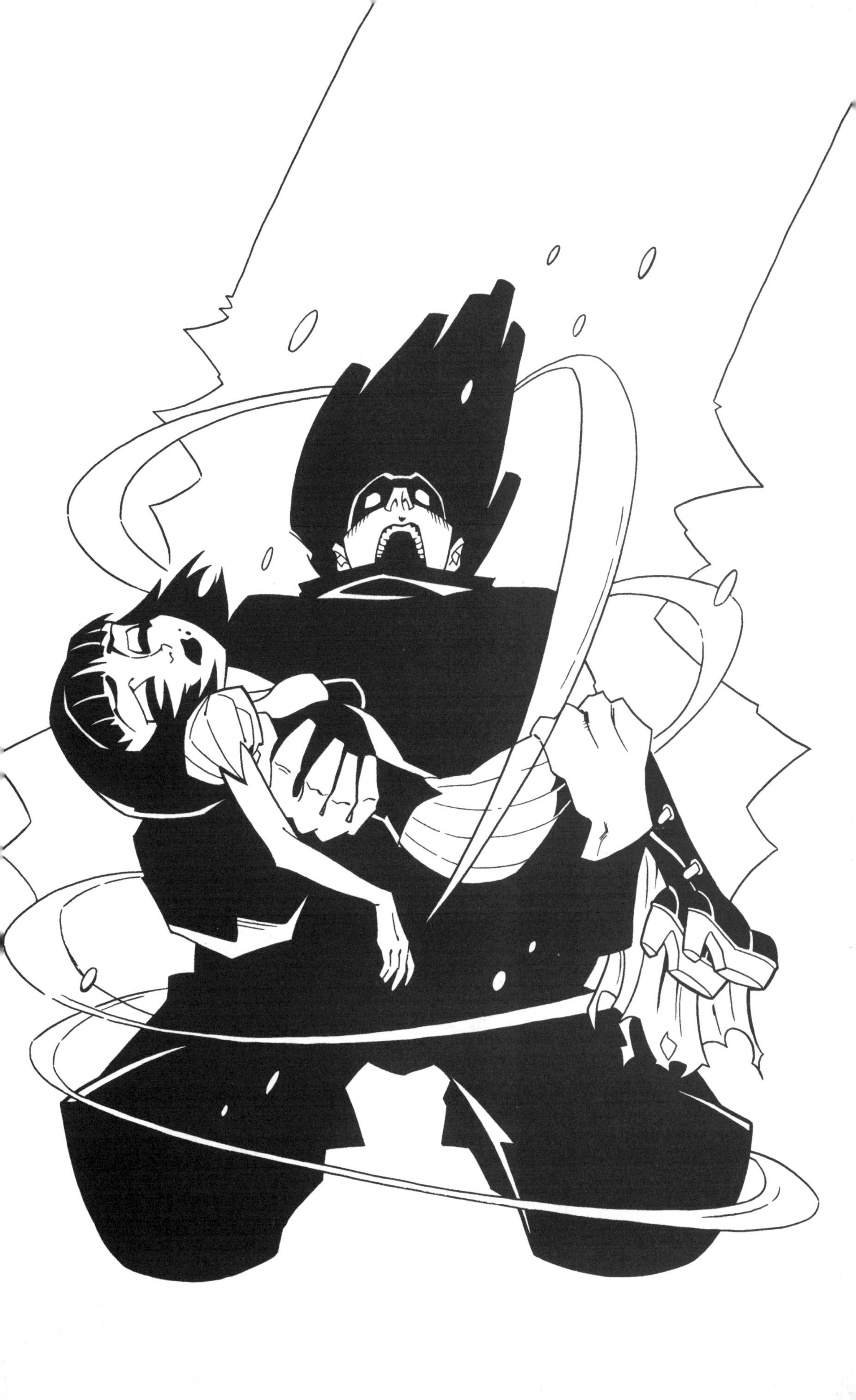

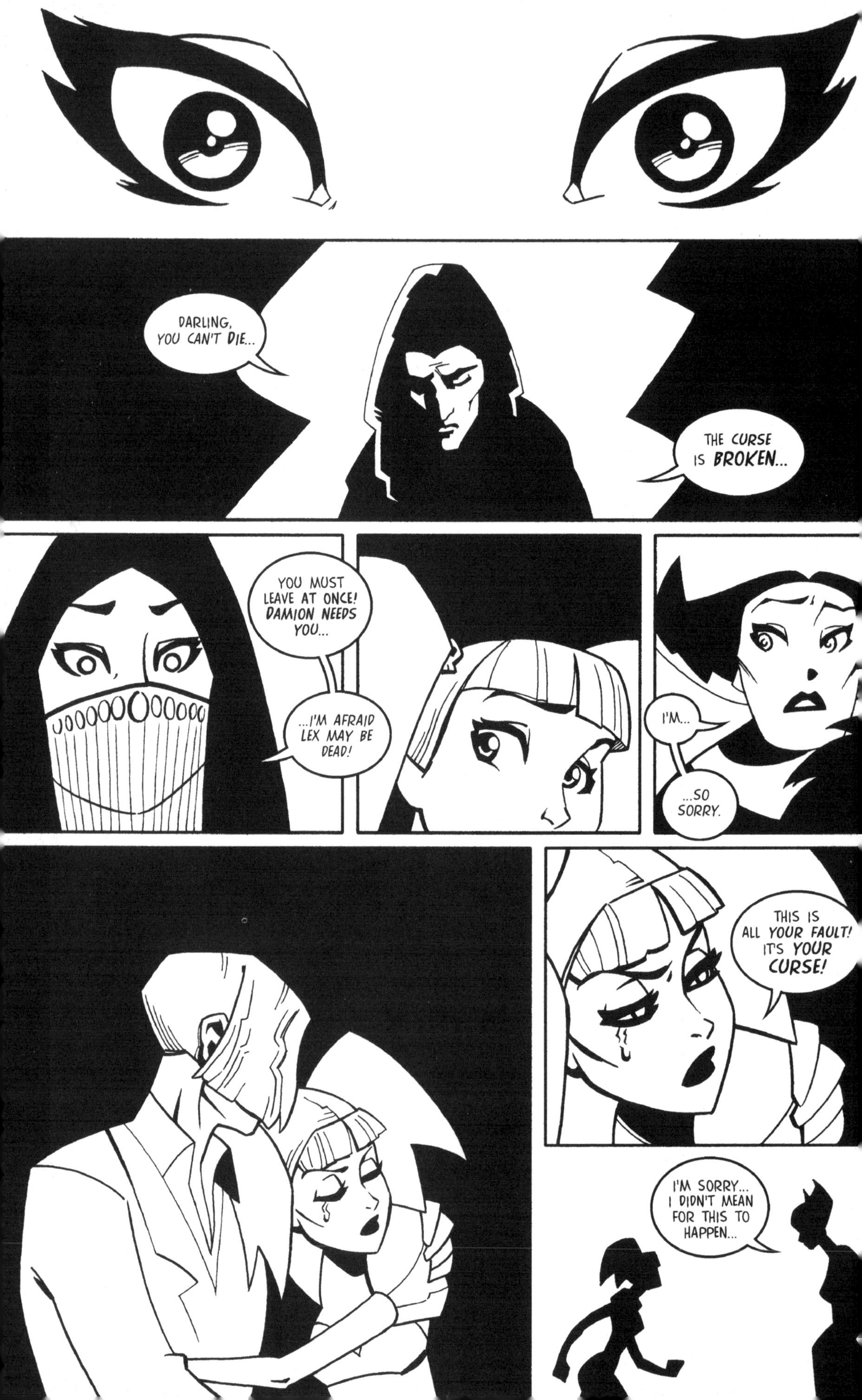
DARLING, YOU CAN'T DIE...
THE CURSE IS BROKEN...
YOU MUST LEAVE AT ONCE! DAMION NEEDS YOU...
...I'M AFRAID LEX MAY BE DEAD!
I'M...
...SO SORRY.
THIS IS ALL YOUR FAULT! IT'S YOUR CURSE!
I'M SORRY... I DIDN'T MEAN FOR THIS TO HAPPEN...

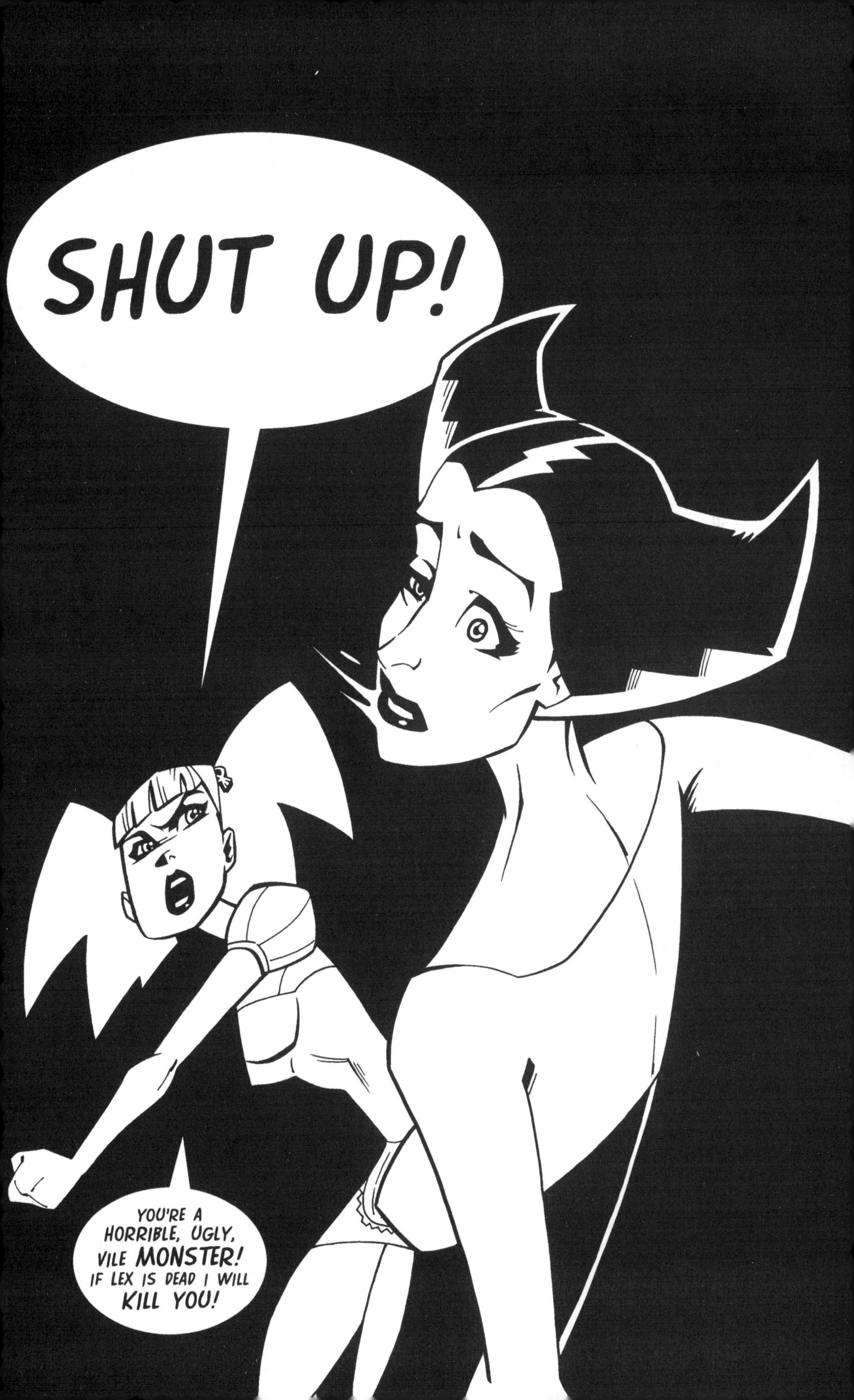
SHUT UP!
YOU'RE A HORRIBLE, UGLY, VILE MONSTER! IF LEX IS DEAD I WILL KILL YOU!

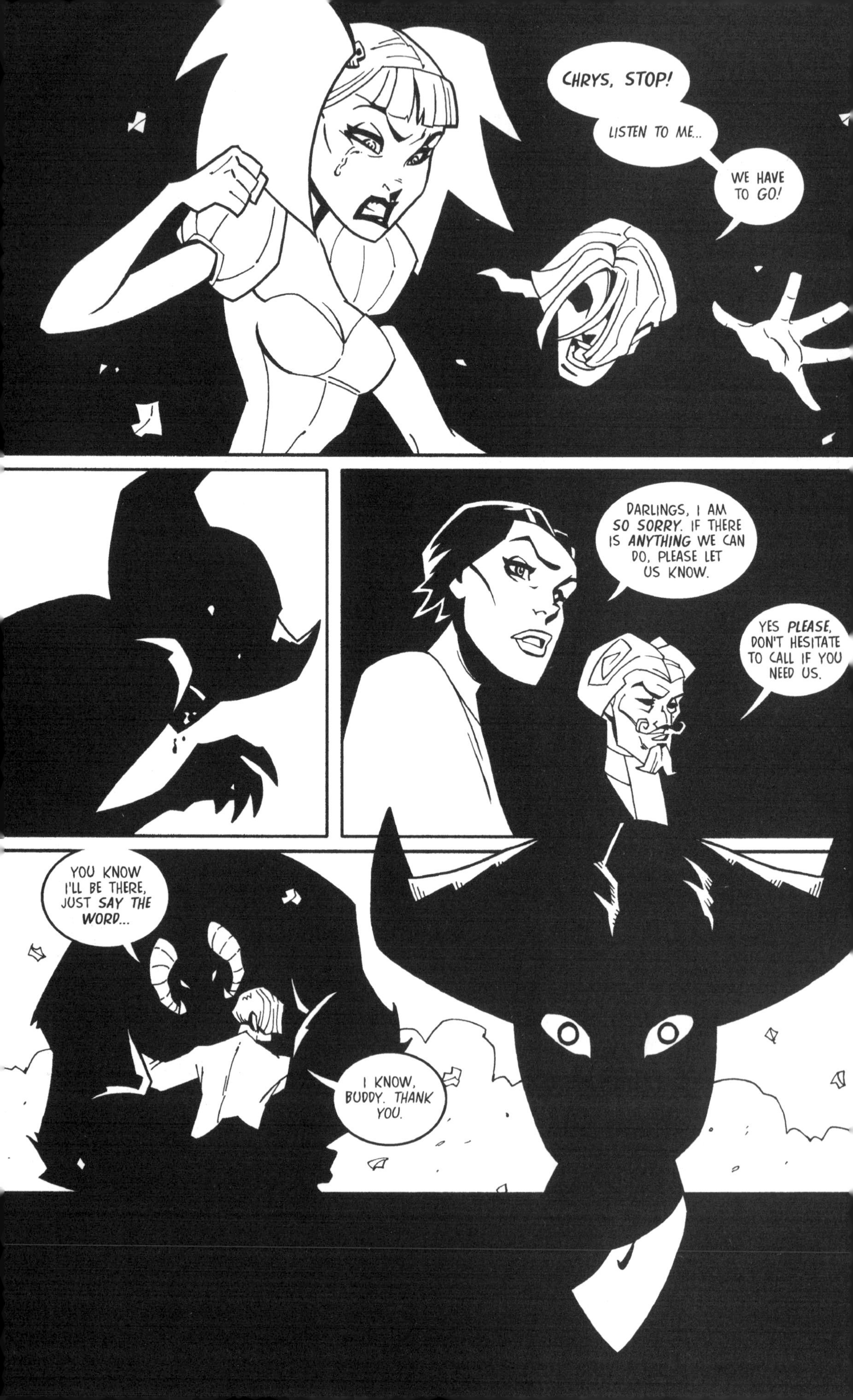
CHRYS, STOP!
LISTEN TO ME...
WE HAVE TO GO!
DARLINGS, I AM SO SORRY. IF THERE IS ANYTHING WE CAN DO, PLEASE LET US KNOW.
YES PLEASE, DON'T HESITATE TO CALL IF YOU NEED US.
YOU KNOW I'LL BE THERE, JUST SAY THE WORD...
I KNOW, BUDDY. THANK YOU.

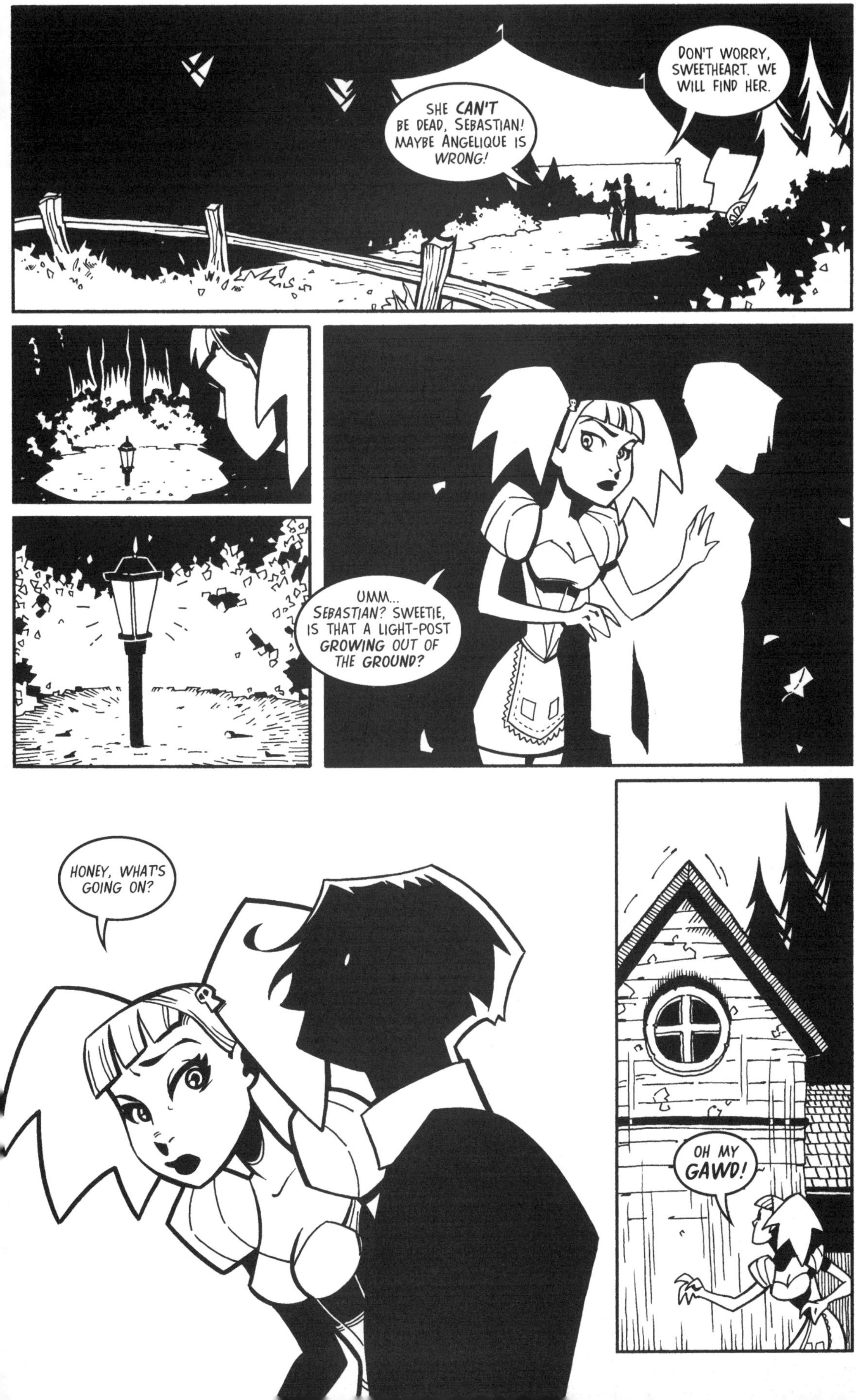
SHE CAN'T BE DEAD, SEBASTIAN! MAYBE ANGELIQUE IS WRONG!
DON'T WORRY, SWEETHEART. WE WILL FIND HER.
UMM... SEBASTIAN? SWEETIE, IS THAT A LIGHT-POST GROWING OUT OF THE GROUND?
HONEY, WHAT'S GOING ON?
OH MY GAWD!

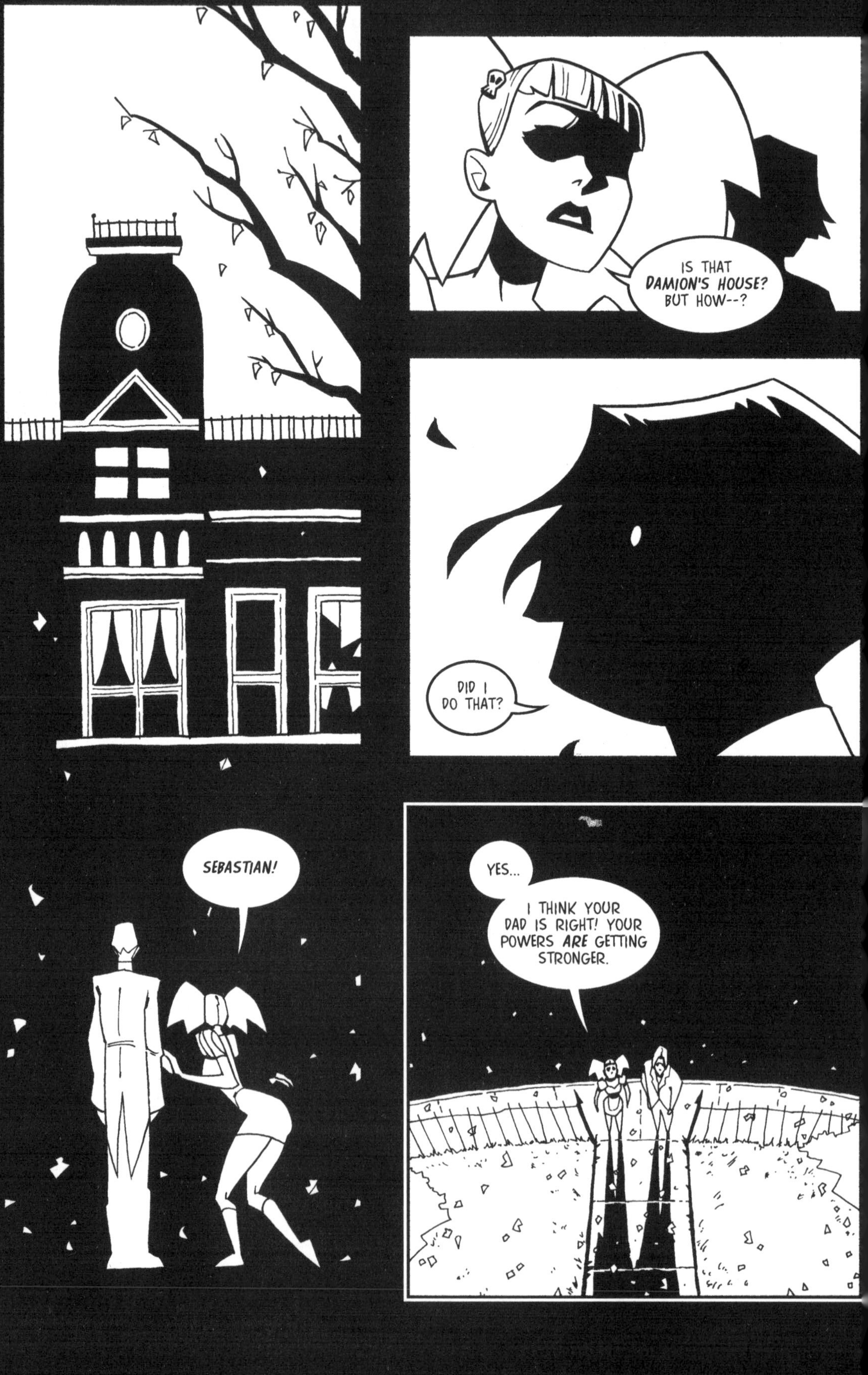
IS THAT DAMION'S HOUSE? BUT HOW--?
DID I DO THAT?
SEBASTIAN!
YES...
I THINK YOUR DAD IS RIGHT! YOUR POWERS ARE GETTING STRONGER.

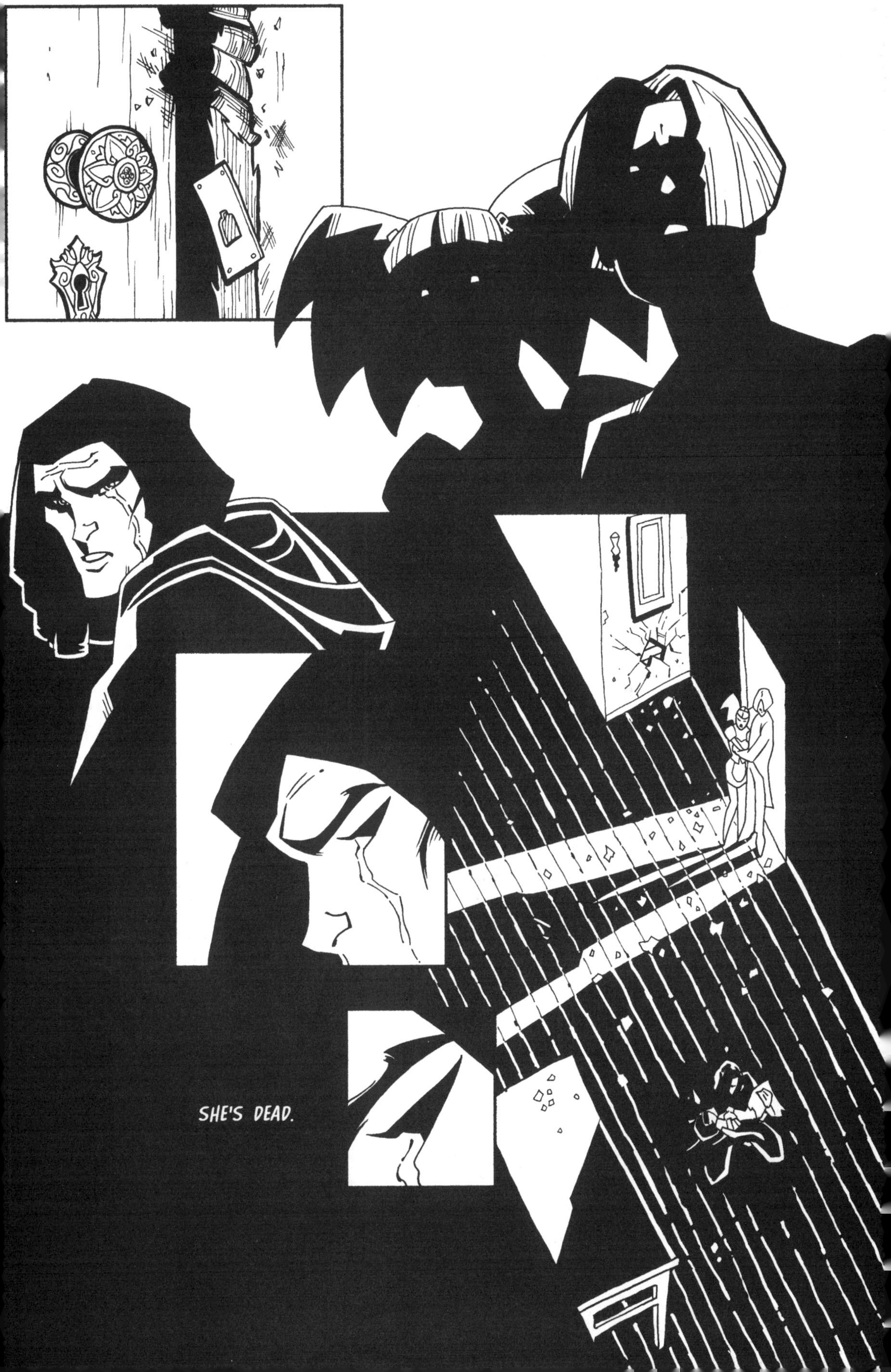
SHE'S DEAD.

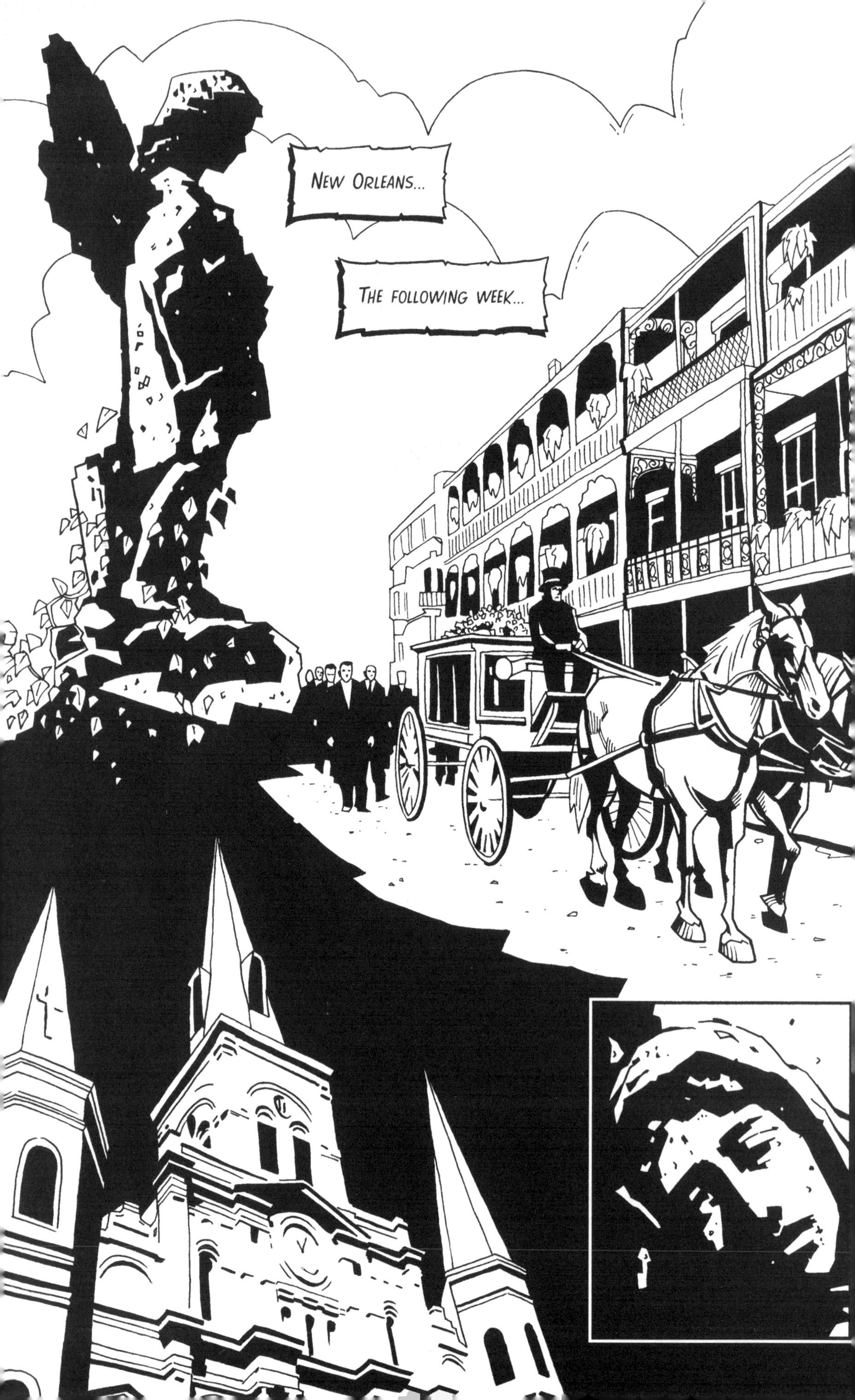
NEW ORLEANS...
THE FOLLOWING WEEK...

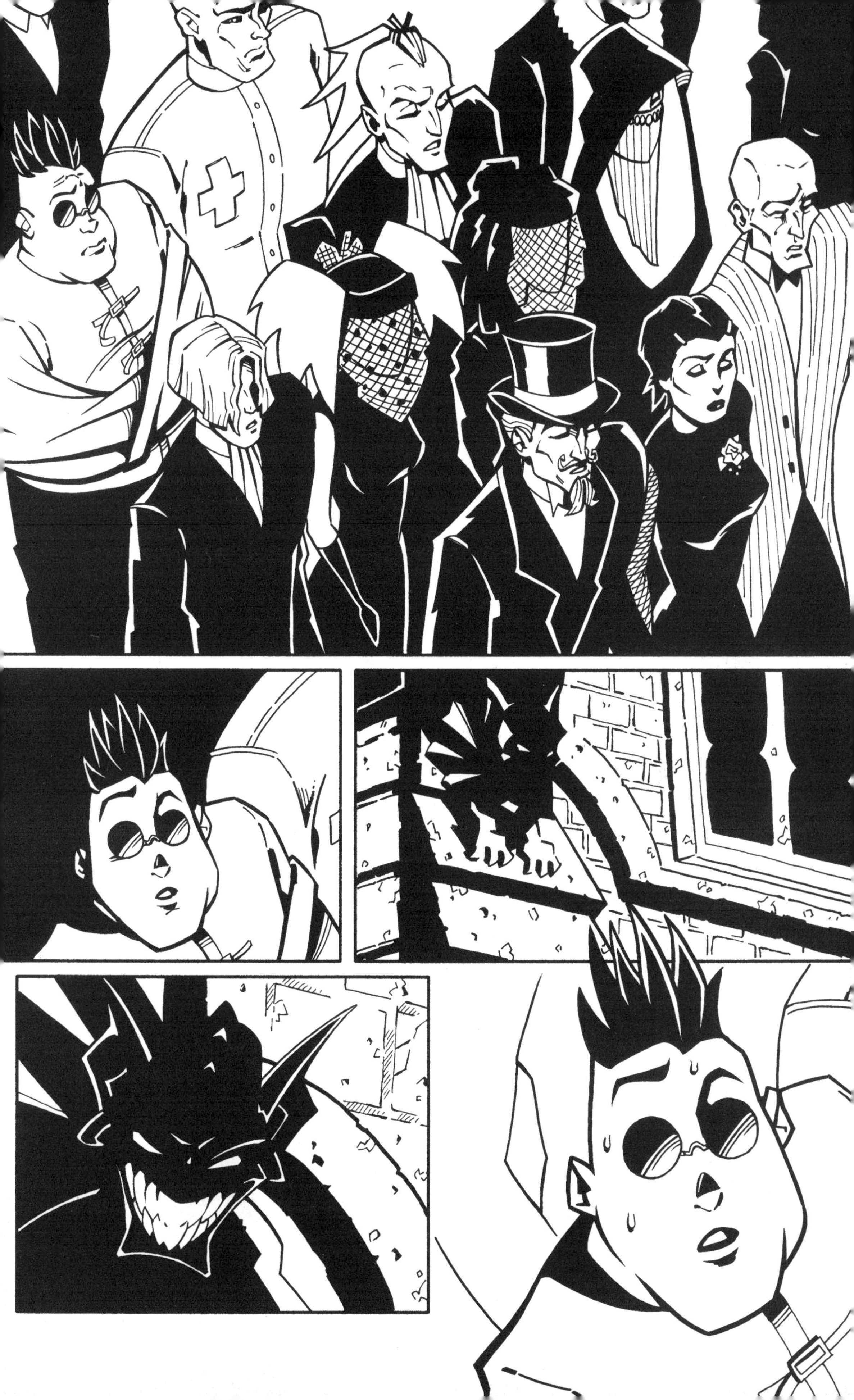

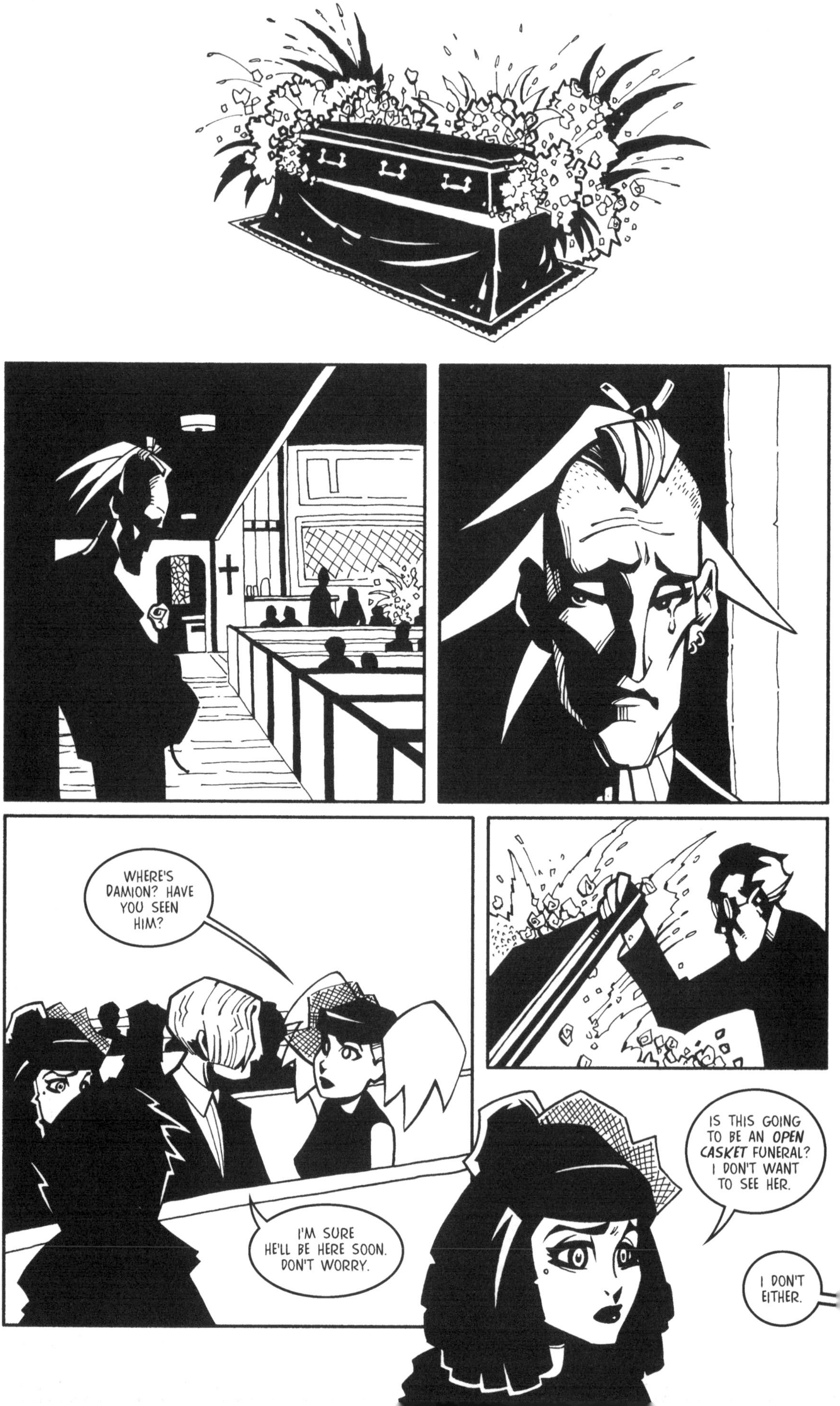
WHERE'S DAMION? HAVE YOU SEEN HIM?
I'M SURE HE'LL BE HERE SOON. DON'T WORRY.
IS THIS GOING TO BE AN *OPEN CASKET* FUNERAL? I DON'T WANT TO SEE HER.
I DON'T EITHER.

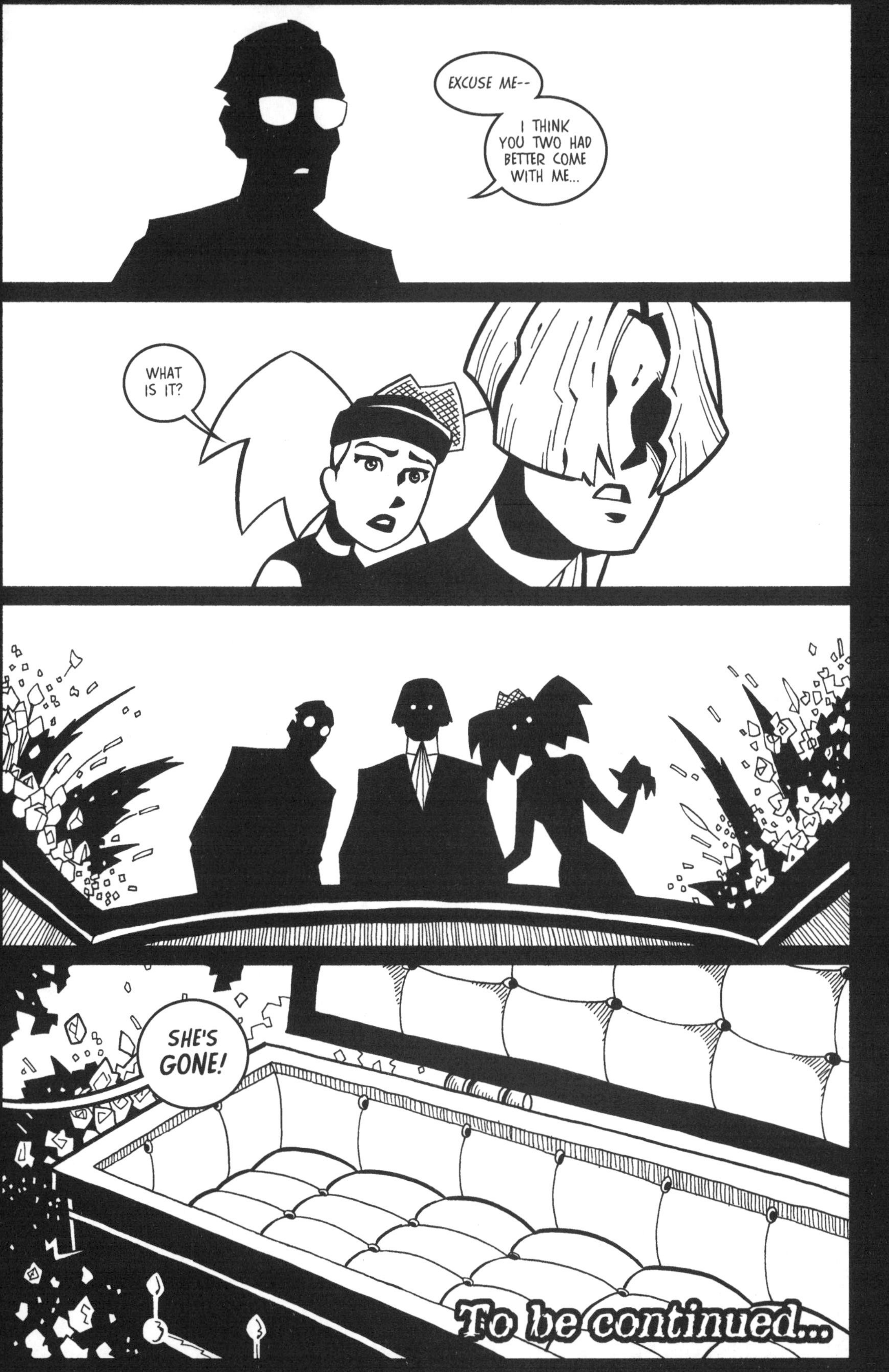
EXCUSE ME--
I THINK YOU TWO HAD BETTER COME WITH ME...
WHAT IS IT?
SHE'S GONE!
To be continued...

CHAPTER 16

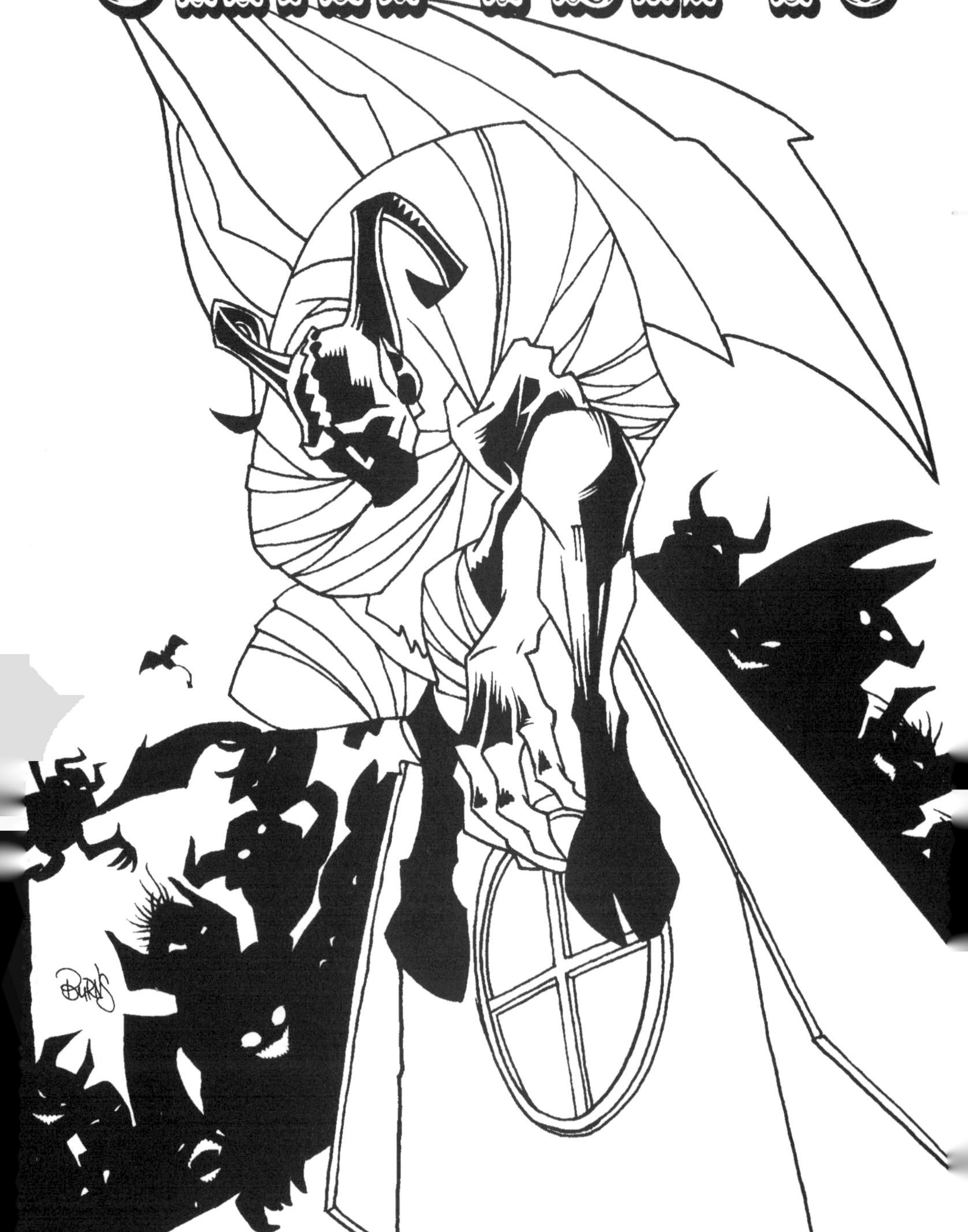

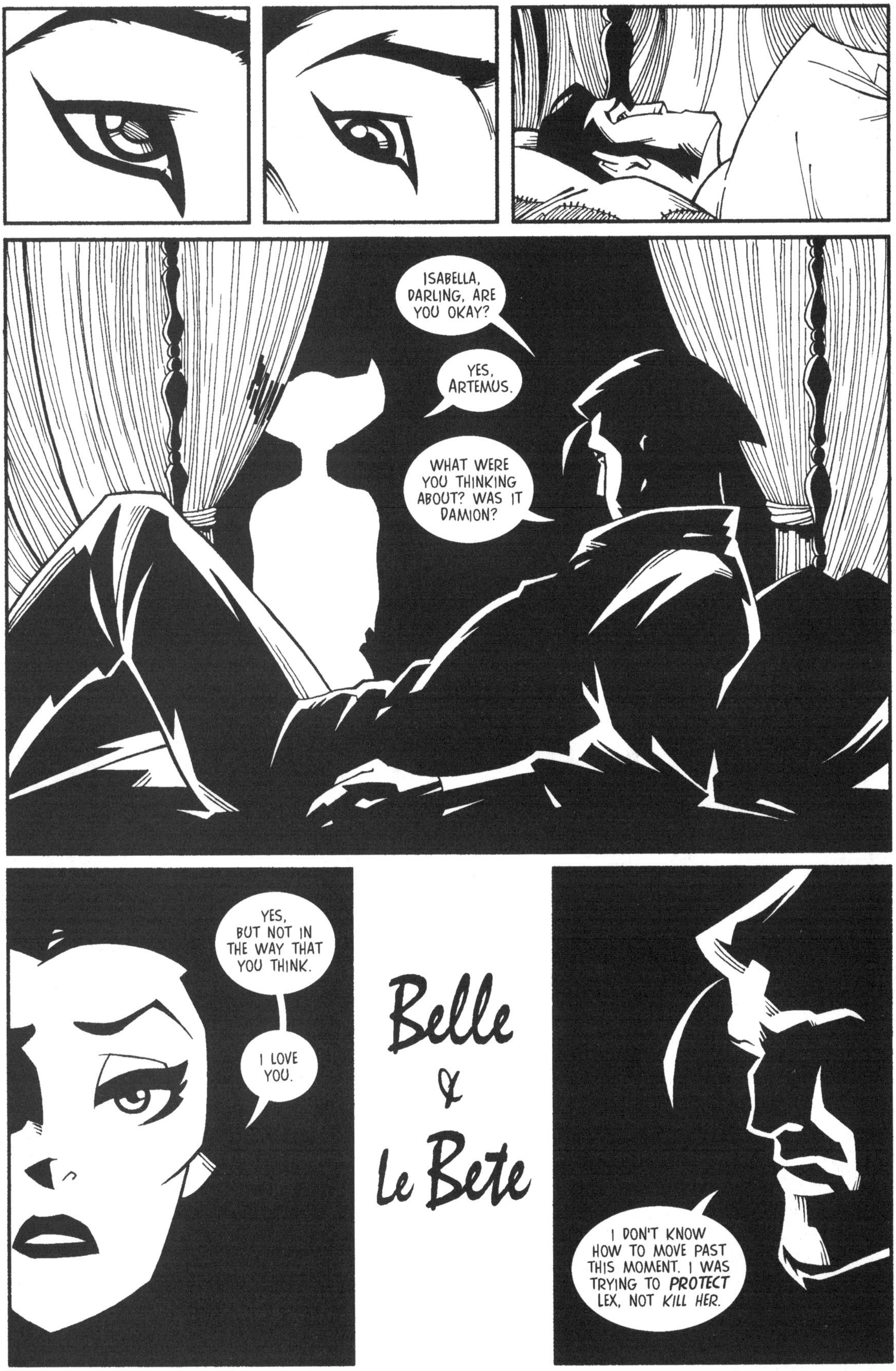
ISABELLA, DARLING, ARE YOU OKAY?
YES, ARTEMUS.
WHAT WERE YOU THINKING ABOUT? WAS IT DAMION?
YES, BUT NOT IN THE WAY THAT YOU THINK.
I LOVE YOU.
Belle & le Bete
I DON'T KNOW HOW TO MOVE PAST THIS MOMENT. I WAS TRYING TO PROTECT LEX, NOT KILL HER.

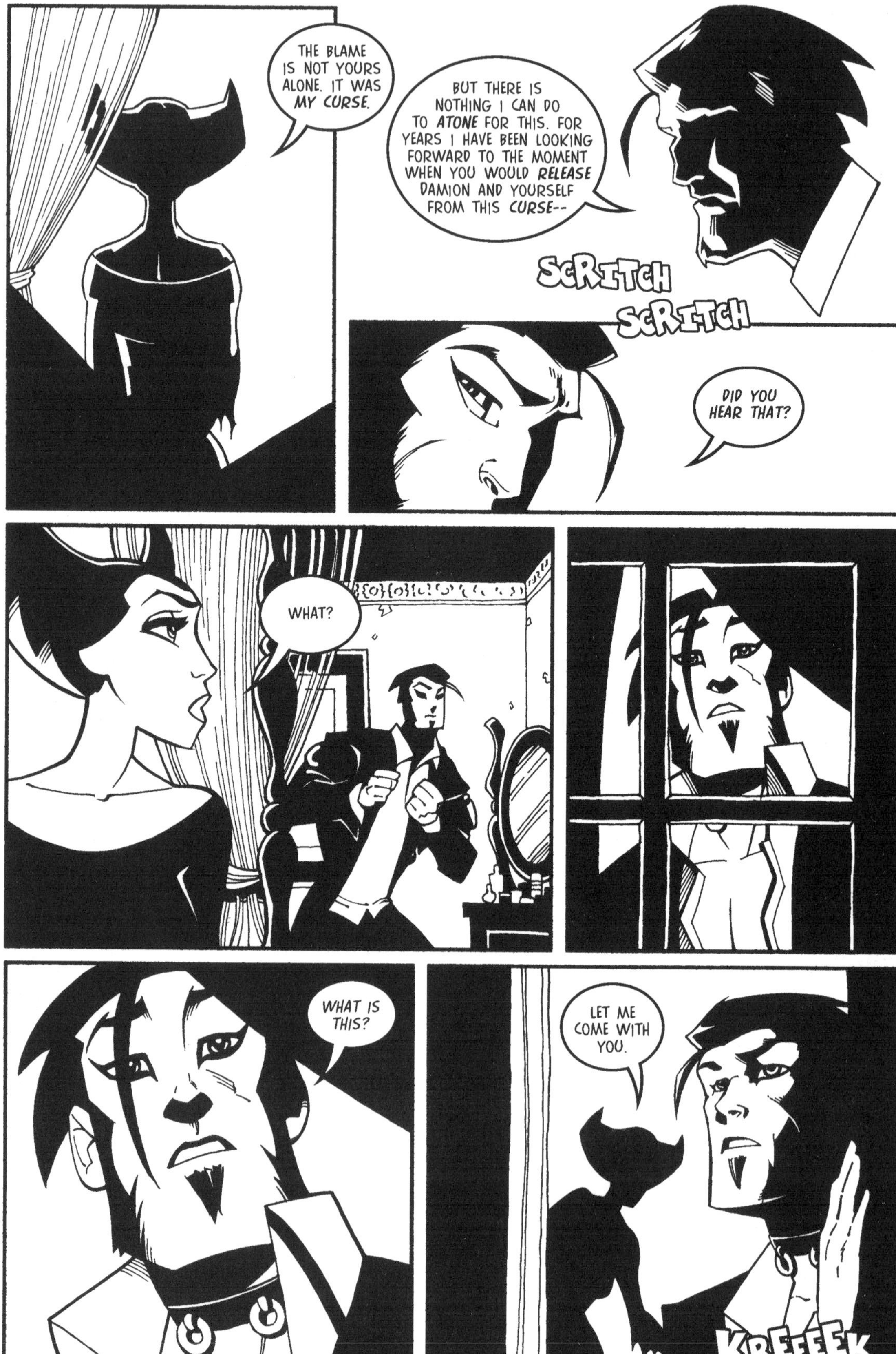
THE BLAME IS NOT YOURS ALONE. IT WAS MY CURSE.
BUT THERE IS NOTHING I CAN DO TO ATONE FOR THIS. FOR YEARS I HAVE BEEN LOOKING FORWARD TO THE MOMENT WHEN YOU WOULD RELEASE DAMION AND YOURSELF FROM THIS CURSE--
SCRITCH
SCRITCH
DID YOU HEAR THAT?
WHAT?
WHAT IS THIS?
LET ME COME WITH YOU.
KREEEEK

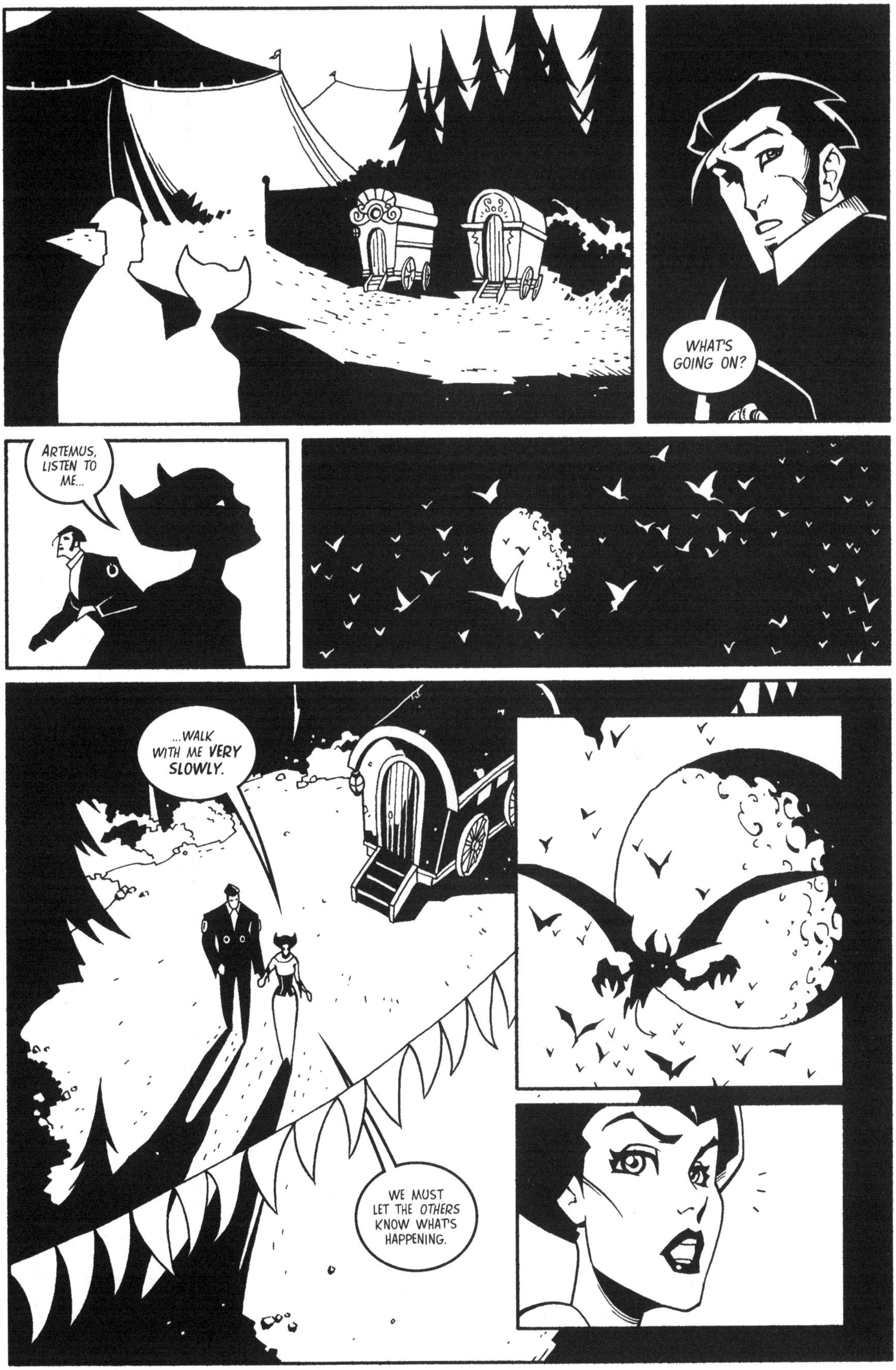
WHAT'S GOING ON?
ARTEMUS, LISTEN TO ME...
...WALK WITH ME VERY SLOWLY.
WE MUST LET THE OTHERS KNOW WHAT'S HAPPENING.

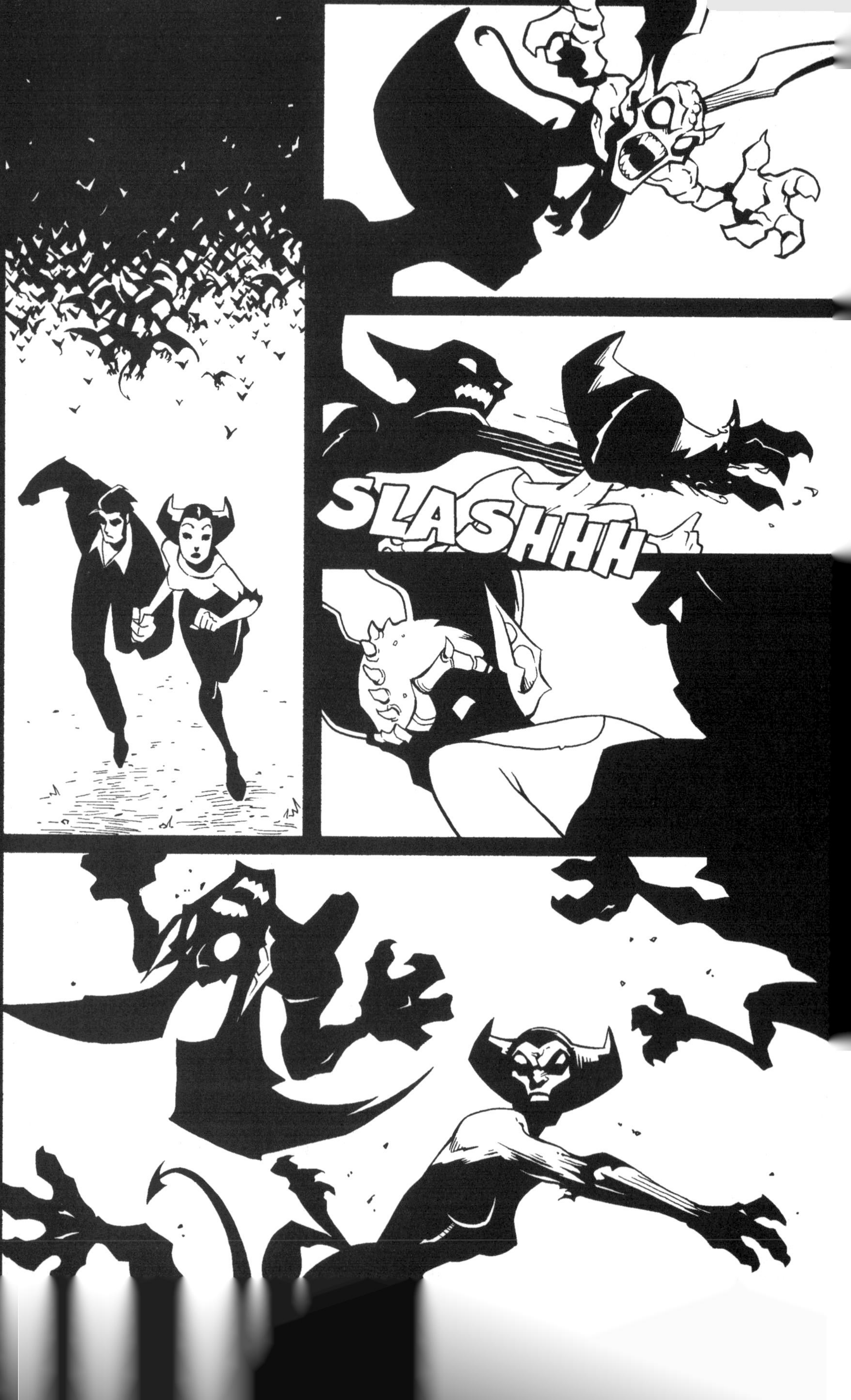
SLASHHH

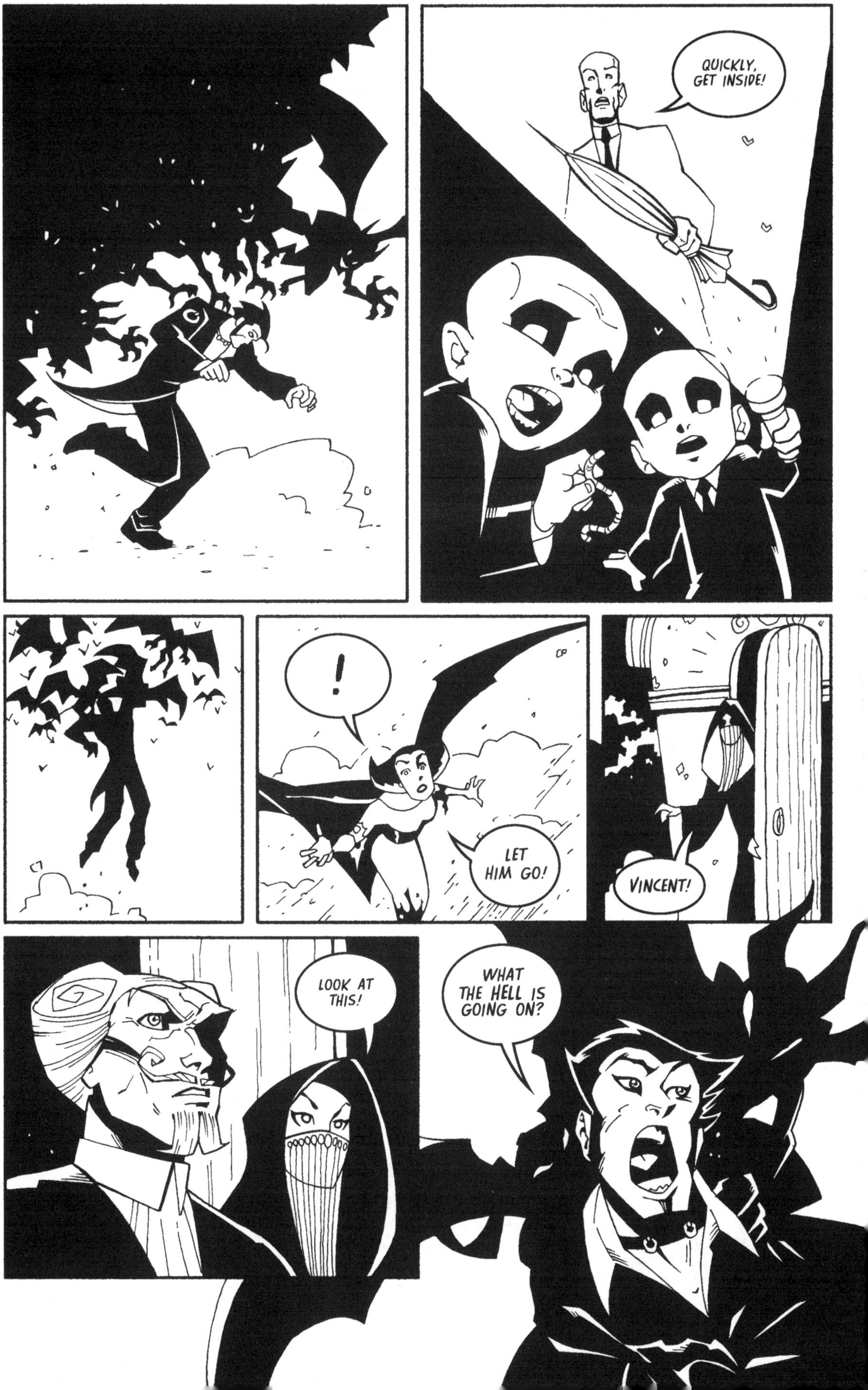
QUICKLY, GET INSIDE!
!
LET HIM GO!
VINCENT!
LOOK AT THIS!
WHAT THE HELL IS GOING ON?

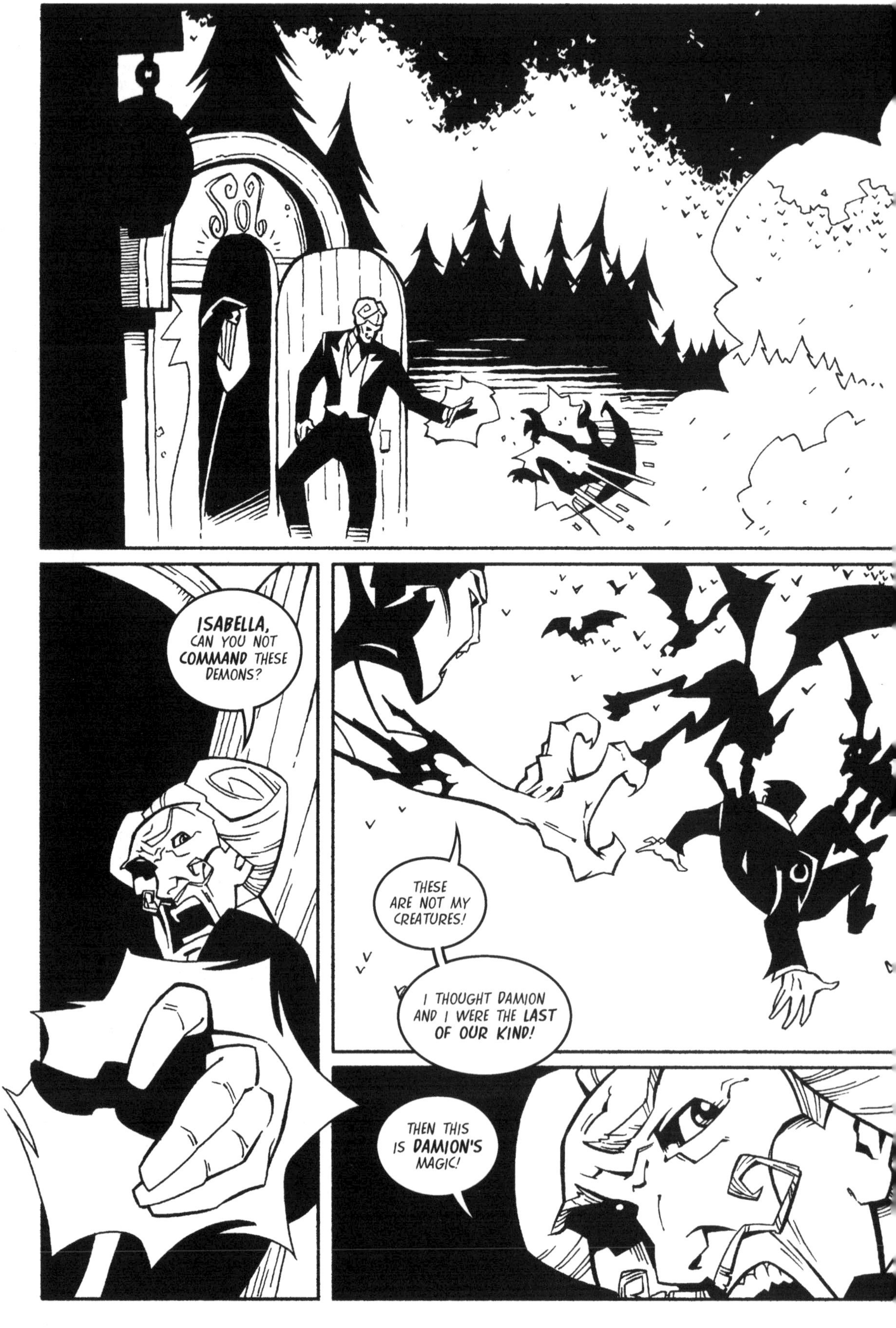
ISABELLA, CAN YOU NOT COMMAND THESE DEMONS?
THESE ARE NOT MY CREATURES!
I THOUGHT DAMION AND I WERE THE LAST OF OUR KIND!
THEN THIS IS DAMION'S MAGIC!

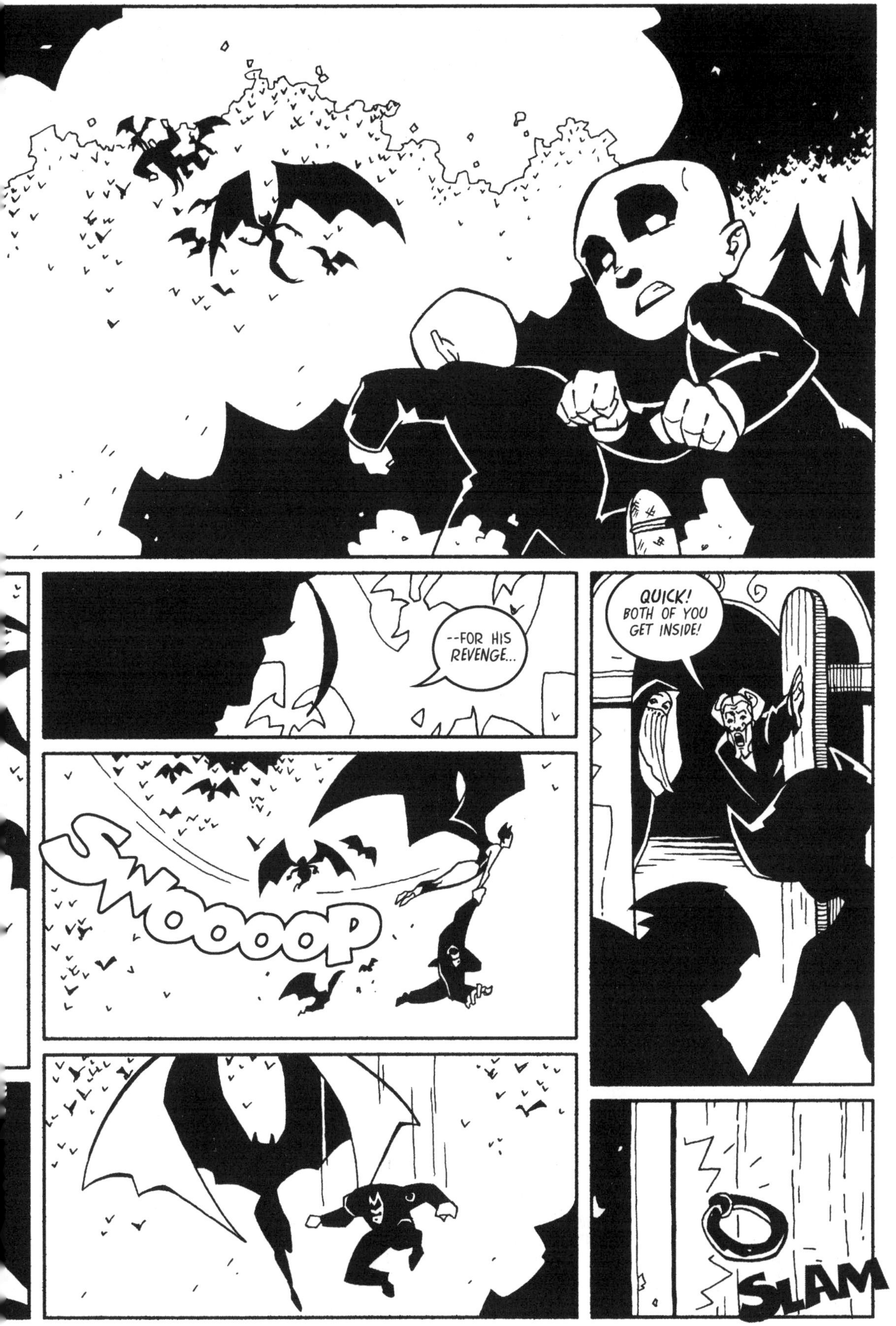
--FOR HIS REVENGE...
SWOOOOP
QUICK! BOTH OF YOU GET INSIDE!
SLAM

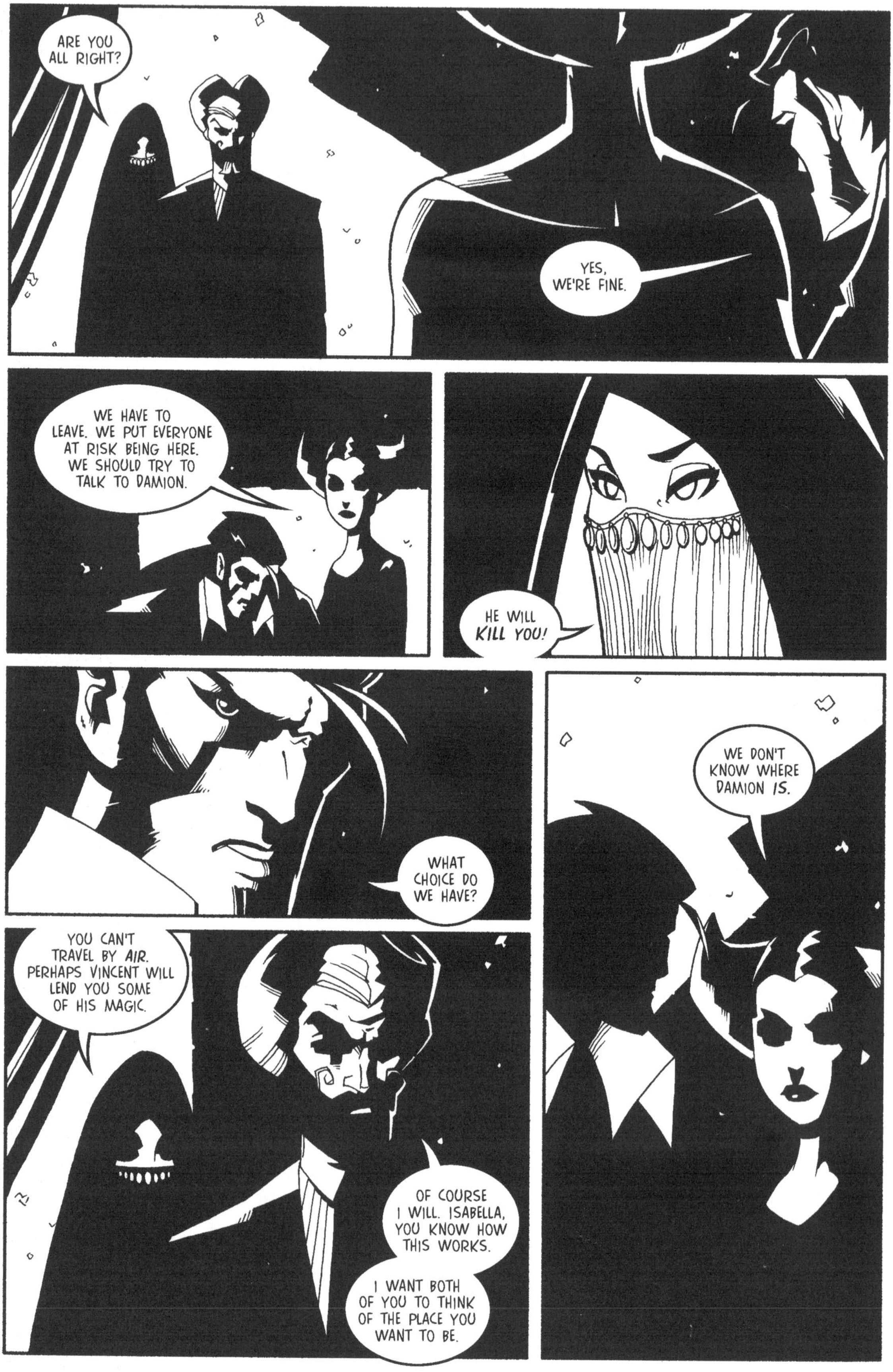

ARE YOU ALL RIGHT?
YES, WE'RE FINE.
WE HAVE TO LEAVE. WE PUT EVERYONE AT RISK BEING HERE. WE SHOULD TRY TO TALK TO DAMION.
HE WILL *KILL YOU!*
WHAT CHOICE DO WE HAVE?
WE DON'T KNOW WHERE DAMION *IS.*
YOU CAN'T TRAVEL BY *AIR.* PERHAPS VINCENT WILL LEND YOU SOME OF HIS MAGIC.
OF COURSE I WILL. ISABELLA, YOU KNOW HOW THIS WORKS.
I WANT BOTH OF YOU TO THINK OF THE PLACE YOU WANT TO BE.

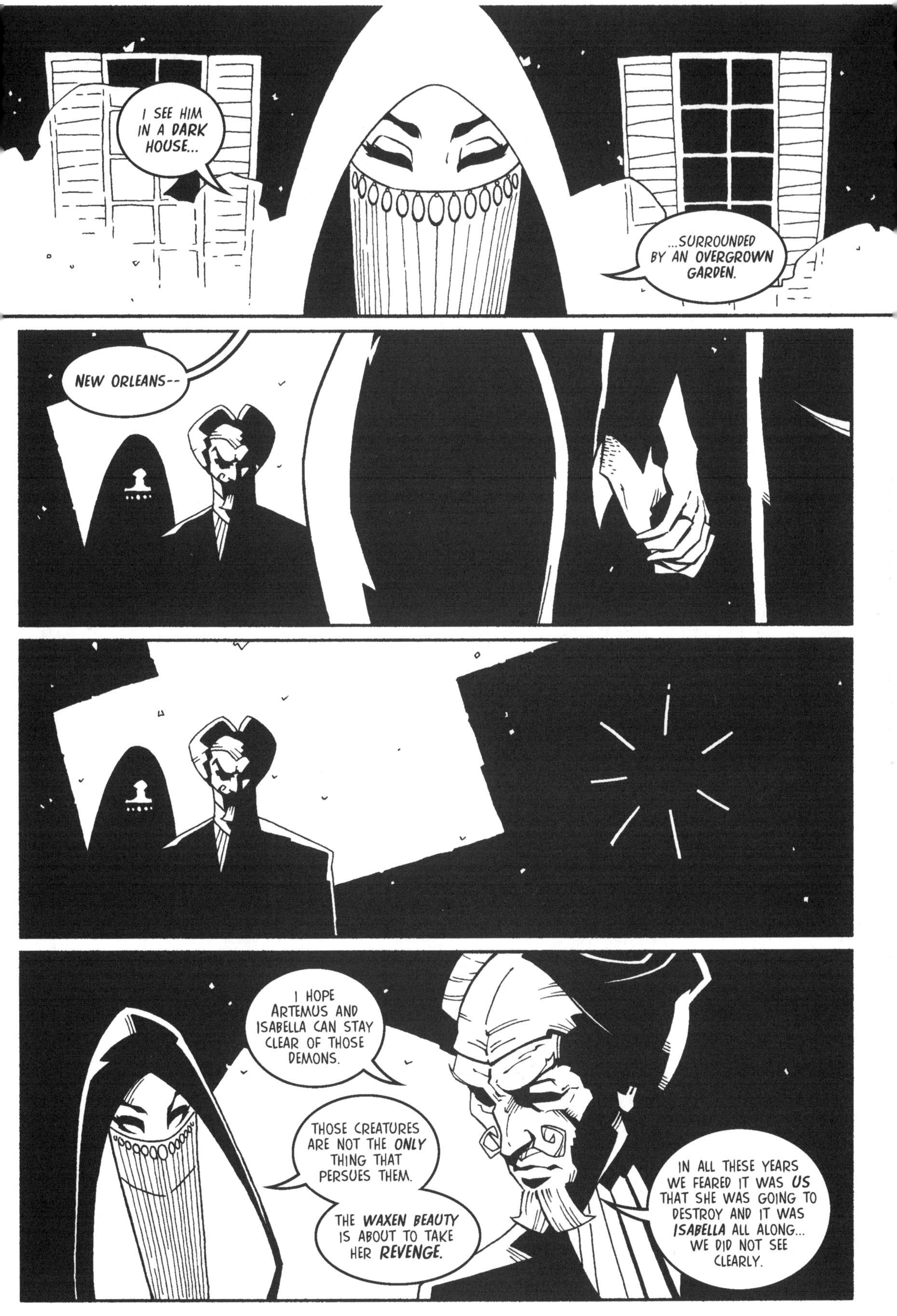
I SEE HIM IN A DARK HOUSE...
...SURROUNDED BY AN OVERGROWN GARDEN.
NEW ORLEANS--
I HOPE ARTEMUS AND ISABELLA CAN STAY CLEAR OF THOSE DEMONS.
THOSE CREATURES ARE NOT THE ONLY THING THAT PERSUES THEM.
THE WAXEN BEAUTY IS ABOUT TO TAKE HER REVENGE.
IN ALL THESE YEARS WE FEARED IT WAS US THAT SHE WAS GOING TO DESTROY AND IT WAS ISABELLA ALL ALONG... WE DID NOT SEE CLEARLY.

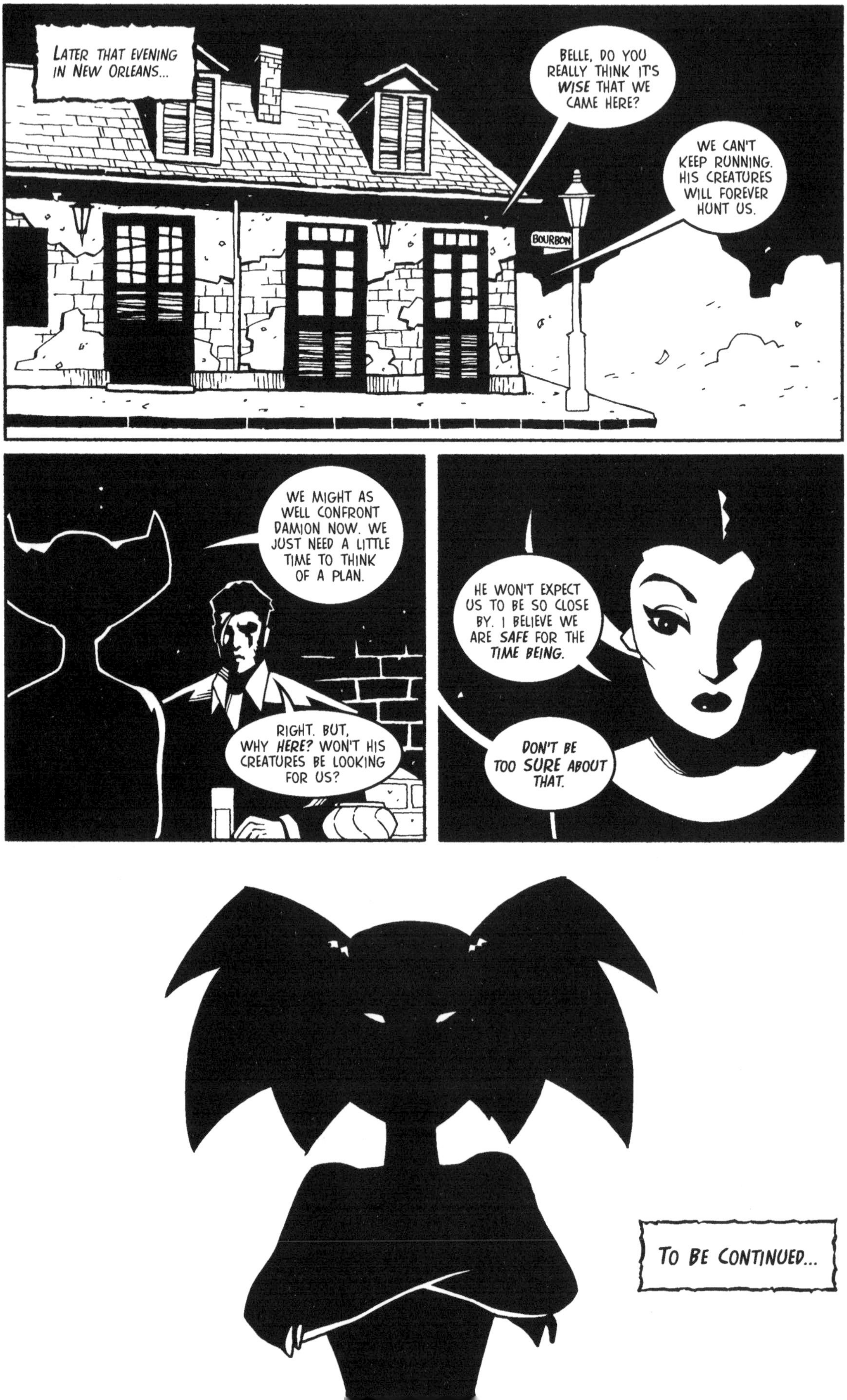
LATER THAT EVENING IN NEW ORLEANS...
BELLE, DO YOU REALLY THINK IT'S *WISE* THAT WE CAME HERE?
WE CAN'T KEEP RUNNING. HIS CREATURES WILL FOREVER HUNT US.
BOURBON
WE MIGHT AS WELL CONFRONT DAMION NOW. WE JUST NEED A LITTLE TIME TO THINK OF A PLAN.
RIGHT. BUT, WHY *HERE*? WON'T HIS CREATURES BE LOOKING FOR US?
HE WON'T EXPECT US TO BE SO CLOSE BY. I BELIEVE WE ARE *SAFE* FOR THE *TIME BEING*.
*DON'T BE TOO **SURE** ABOUT THAT.*
TO BE CONTINUED...

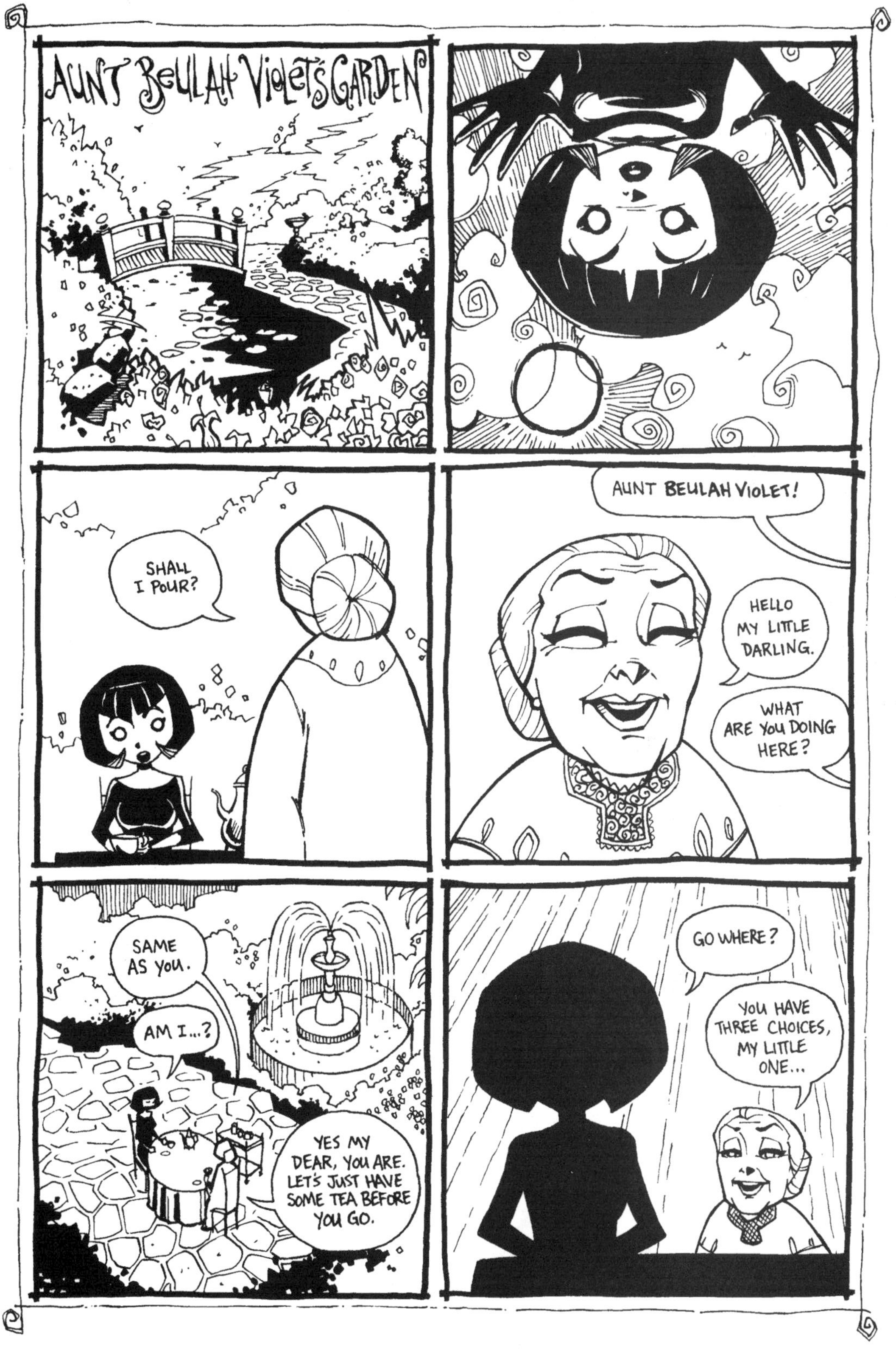
AUNT BEULAH VIOLET'S GARDEN
SHALL I POUR?
AUNT BEULAH VIOLET!
HELLO MY LITTLE DARLING.
WHAT ARE YOU DOING HERE?
SAME AS YOU.
AM I...?
YES MY DEAR, YOU ARE. LET'S JUST HAVE SOME TEA BEFORE YOU GO.
GO WHERE?
YOU HAVE THREE CHOICES, MY LITTLE ONE...

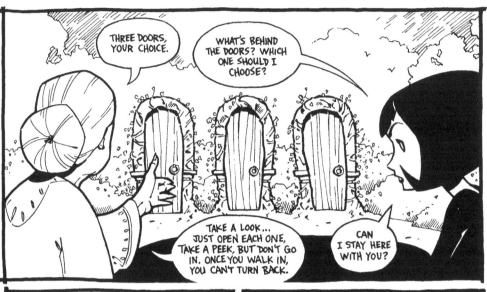

THREE DOORS, YOUR CHOICE.

WHAT'S BEHIND THE DOORS? WHICH ONE SHOULD I CHOOSE?

TAKE A LOOK... JUST OPEN EACH ONE, TAKE A PEEK, BUT DON'T GO IN. ONCE YOU WALK IN, YOU CAN'T TURN BACK.

CAN I STAY HERE WITH YOU?

AFRAID NOT, MY DEAR HEART. I CHOSE MY PATH LONG AGO AND MY TIME HERE IS SHORT.

IF YOU CHOOSE TO STAY HERE, YOU WILL BE ALONE.

I WAS ALONE BEFORE...

NOT TRULY. SWEETHEART, HAVE SOME TEA, THEN DECIDE. I SO MUCH WANT TO HEAR ABOUT YOUR LIFE. I HAVE MISSED YOU THESE PAST FEW YEARS.

DO YOU KNOW HOW IT CAME TO BE THAT YOU DIED SO YOUNG?

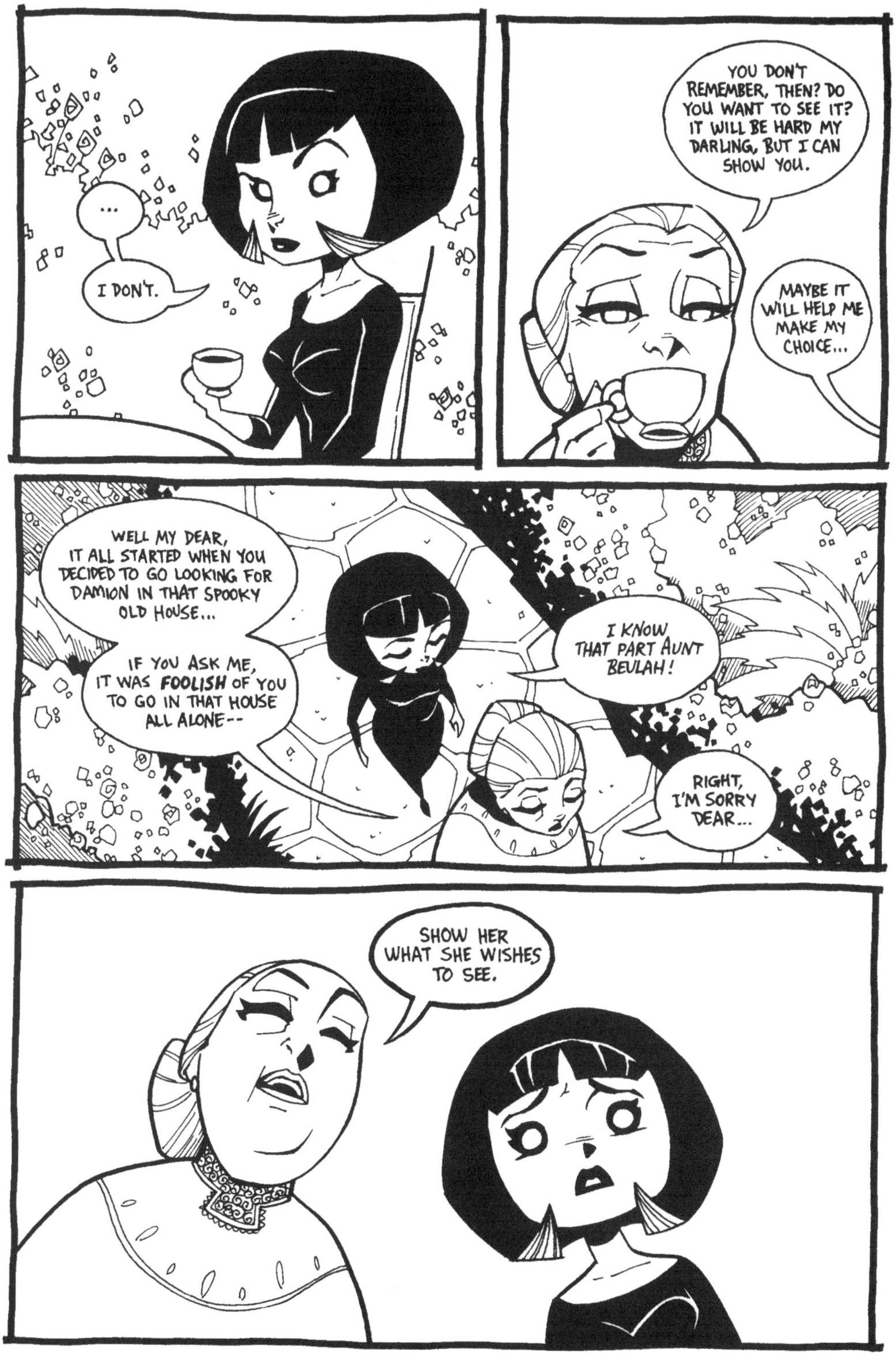
...
I DON'T.
YOU DON'T REMEMBER, THEN? DO YOU WANT TO SEE IT? IT WILL BE HARD MY DARLING, BUT I CAN SHOW YOU.
MAYBE IT WILL HELP ME MAKE MY CHOICE...
WELL MY DEAR, IT ALL STARTED WHEN YOU DECIDED TO GO LOOKING FOR DAMION IN THAT SPOOKY OLD HOUSE...
IF YOU ASK ME, IT WAS FOOLISH OF YOU TO GO IN THAT HOUSE ALL ALONE--
I KNOW THAT PART AUNT BEULAH!
RIGHT, I'M SORRY DEAR...
SHOW HER WHAT SHE WISHES TO SEE.

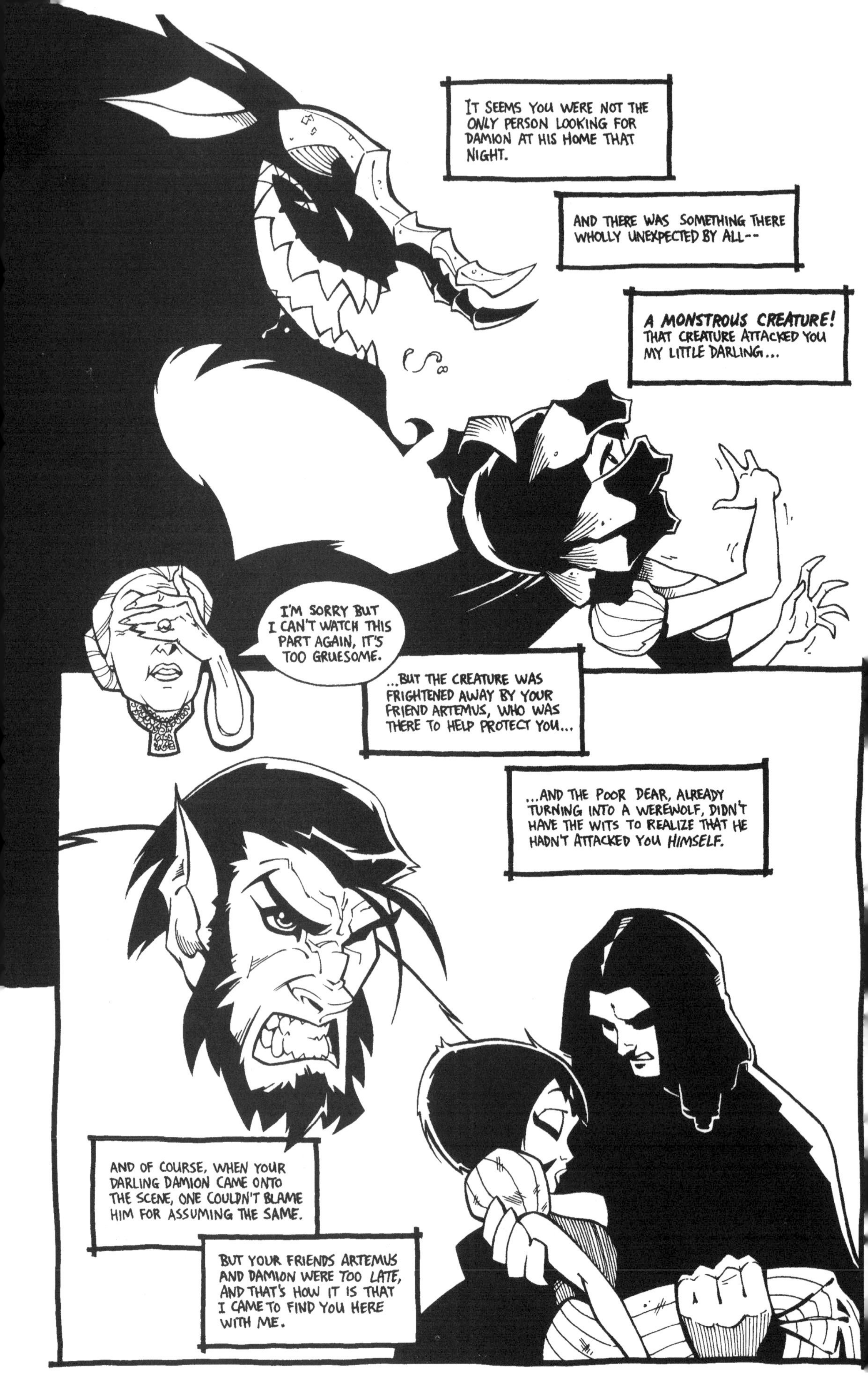
IT SEEMS YOU WERE NOT THE ONLY PERSON LOOKING FOR DAMION AT HIS HOME THAT NIGHT.
AND THERE WAS SOMETHING THERE WHOLLY UNEXPECTED BY ALL--
A MONSTROUS CREATURE! THAT CREATURE ATTACKED YOU MY LITTLE DARLING...
I'M SORRY BUT I CAN'T WATCH THIS PART AGAIN, IT'S TOO GRUESOME.
...BUT THE CREATURE WAS FRIGHTENED AWAY BY YOUR FRIEND ARTEMUS, WHO WAS THERE TO HELP PROTECT YOU...
...AND THE POOR DEAR, ALREADY TURNING INTO A WEREWOLF, DIDN'T HAVE THE WITS TO REALIZE THAT HE HADN'T ATTACKED YOU HIMSELF.
AND OF COURSE, WHEN YOUR DARLING DAMION CAME ONTO THE SCENE, ONE COULDN'T BLAME HIM FOR ASSUMING THE SAME.
BUT YOUR FRIENDS ARTEMUS AND DAMION WERE TOO LATE, AND THAT'S HOW IT IS THAT I CAME TO FIND YOU HERE WITH ME.

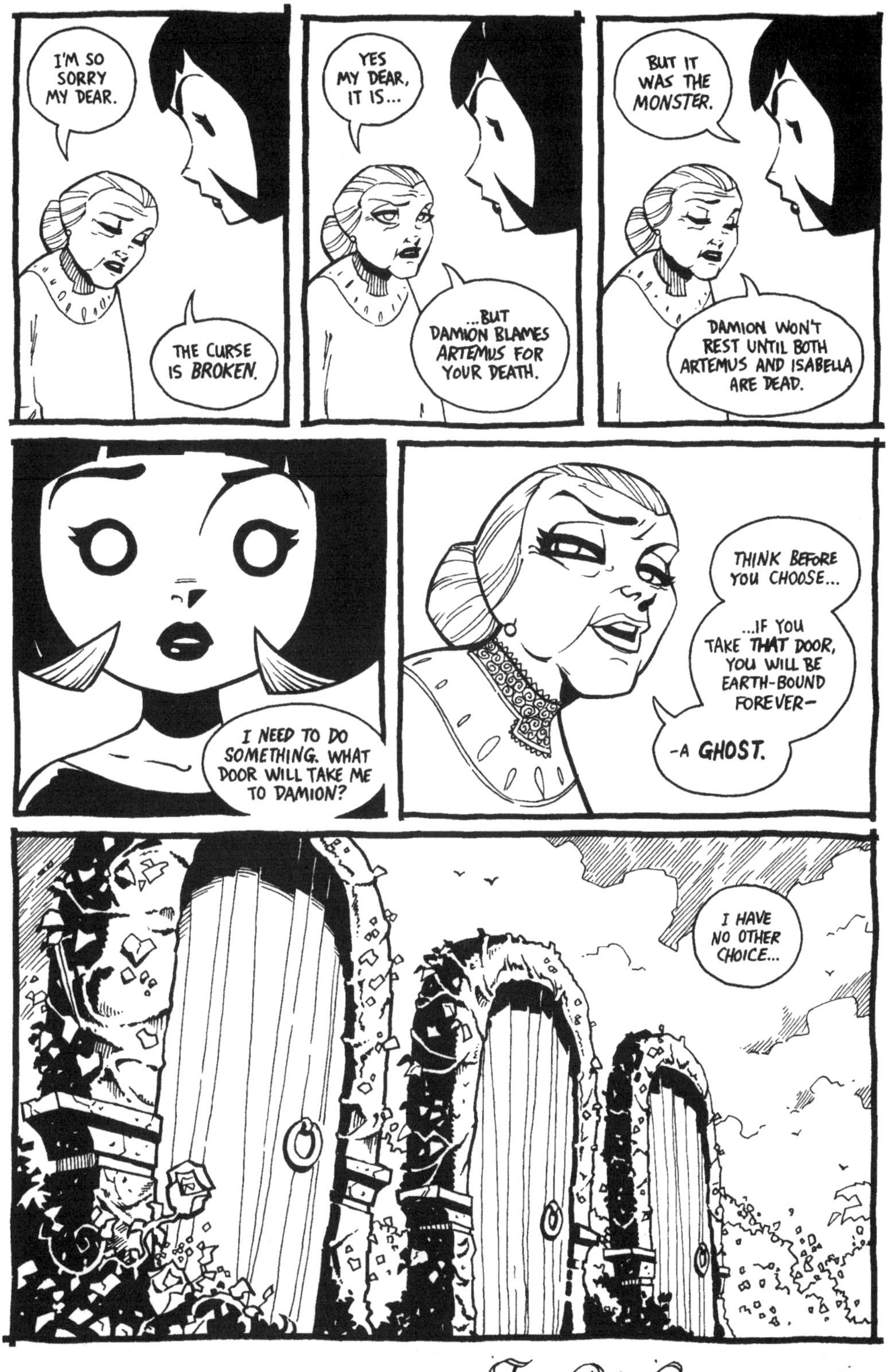
I'M SO SORRY MY DEAR.
THE CURSE IS BROKEN.
YES MY DEAR, IT IS...
...BUT DAMION BLAMES ARTEMUS FOR YOUR DEATH.
BUT IT WAS THE MONSTER.
DAMION WON'T REST UNTIL BOTH ARTEMUS AND ISABELLA ARE DEAD.
I NEED TO DO SOMETHING. WHAT DOOR WILL TAKE ME TO DAMION?
THINK BEFORE YOU CHOOSE...
...IF YOU TAKE THAT DOOR, YOU WILL BE EARTH-BOUND FOREVER-
-A GHOST.
I HAVE NO OTHER CHOICE...

To Be Continued...

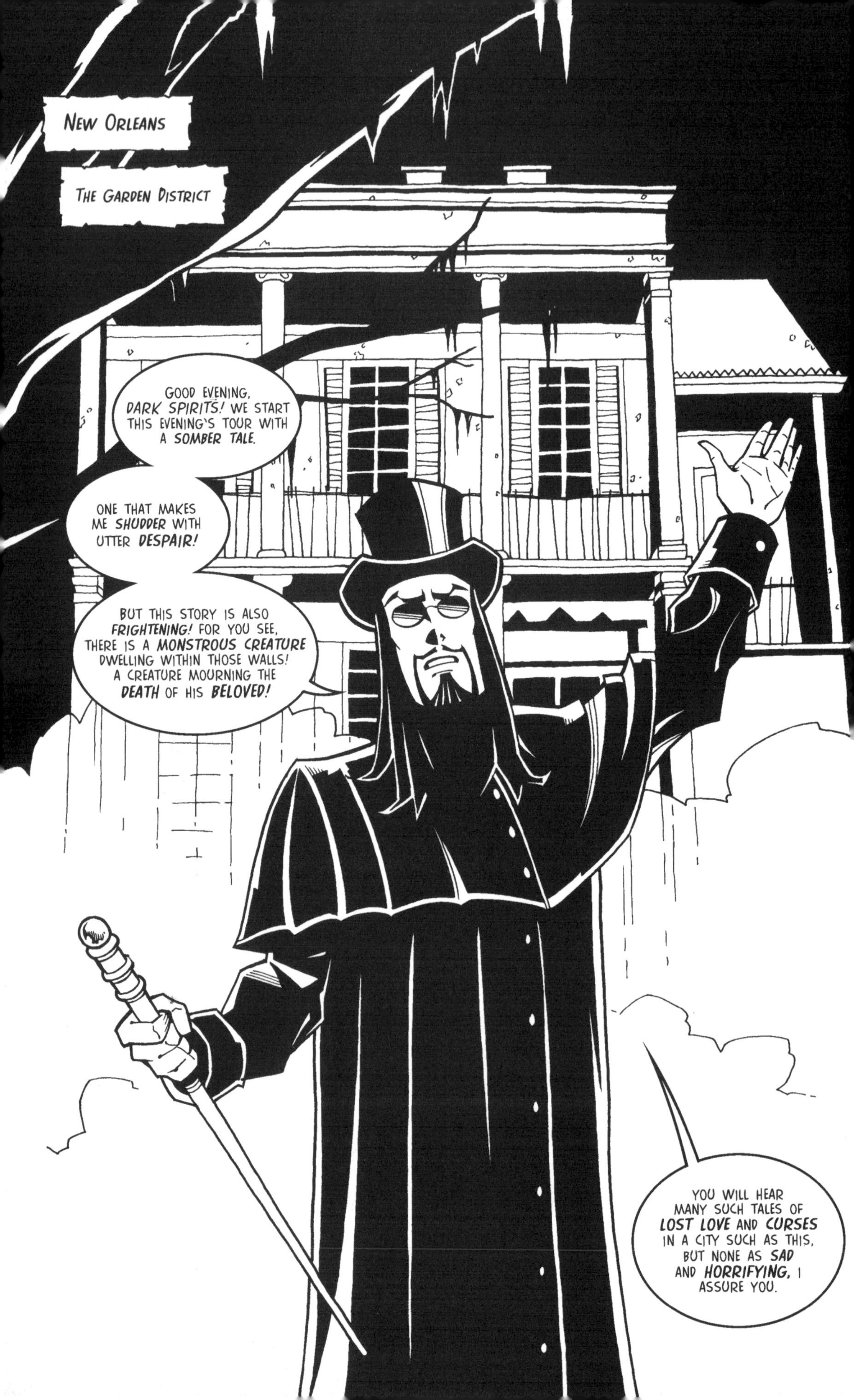
NEW ORLEANS
THE GARDEN DISTRICT
GOOD EVENING, DARK SPIRITS! WE START THIS EVENING'S TOUR WITH A SOMBER TALE.
ONE THAT MAKES ME SHUDDER WITH UTTER DESPAIR!
BUT THIS STORY IS ALSO FRIGHTENING! FOR YOU SEE, THERE IS A MONSTROUS CREATURE DWELLING WITHIN THOSE WALLS! A CREATURE MOURNING THE DEATH OF HIS BELOVED!
YOU WILL HEAR MANY SUCH TALES OF LOST LOVE AND CURSES IN A CITY SUCH AS THIS, BUT NONE AS SAD AND HORRIFYING, I ASSURE YOU.

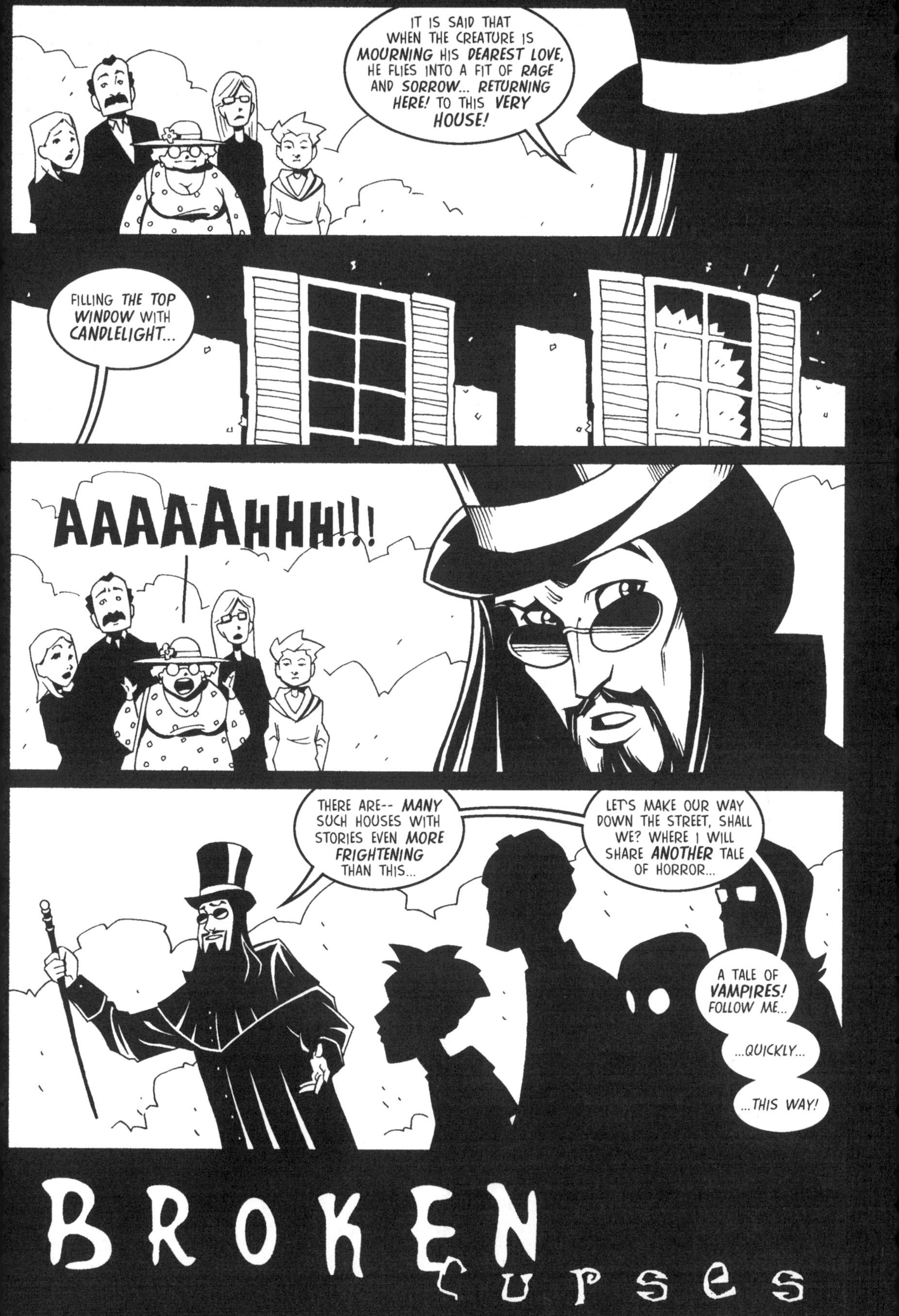
IT IS SAID THAT WHEN THE CREATURE IS MOURNING HIS DEAREST LOVE, HE FLIES INTO A FIT OF RAGE AND SORROW... RETURNING HERE! TO THIS VERY HOUSE!
FILLING THE TOP WINDOW WITH CANDLELIGHT...
AAAAAHHHH!!!
THERE ARE-- MANY SUCH HOUSES WITH STORIES EVEN MORE FRIGHTENING THAN THIS...
LET'S MAKE OUR WAY DOWN THE STREET, SHALL WE? WHERE I WILL SHARE ANOTHER TALE OF HORROR...
A TALE OF VAMPIRES! FOLLOW ME...
...QUICKLY...
...THIS WAY!
BROKEN
Curses

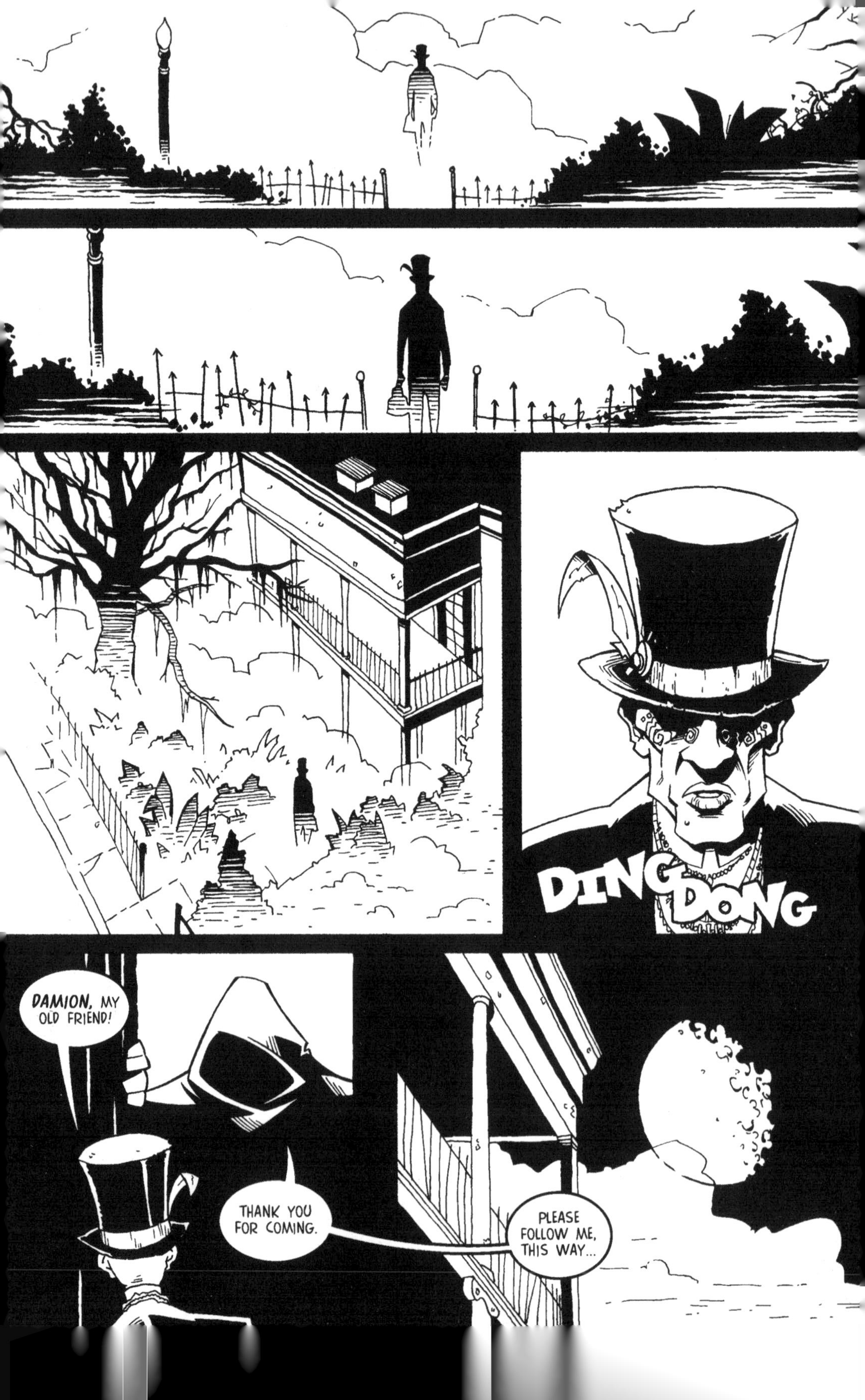
DING DONG
DAMION, MY OLD FRIEND!
THANK YOU FOR COMING.
PLEASE FOLLOW ME, THIS WAY...

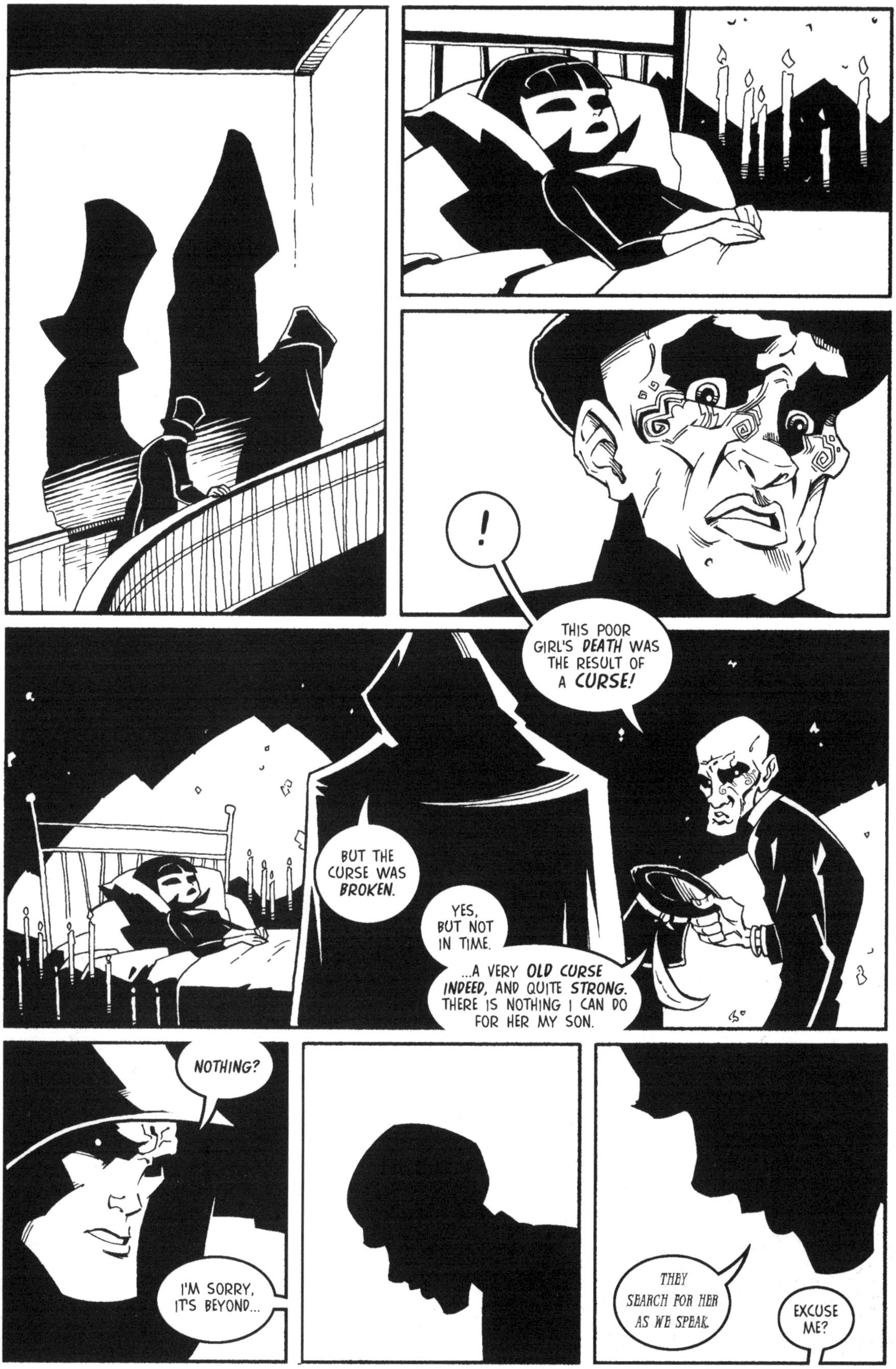
!
THIS POOR GIRL'S DEATH WAS THE RESULT OF A CURSE!
BUT THE CURSE WAS BROKEN.
YES, BUT NOT IN TIME.
...A VERY OLD CURSE INDEED, AND QUITE STRONG. THERE IS NOTHING I CAN DO FOR HER MY SON.
NOTHING?
I'M SORRY, IT'S BEYOND...
THEY SEARCH FOR HER AS WE SPEAK.
EXCUSE ME?

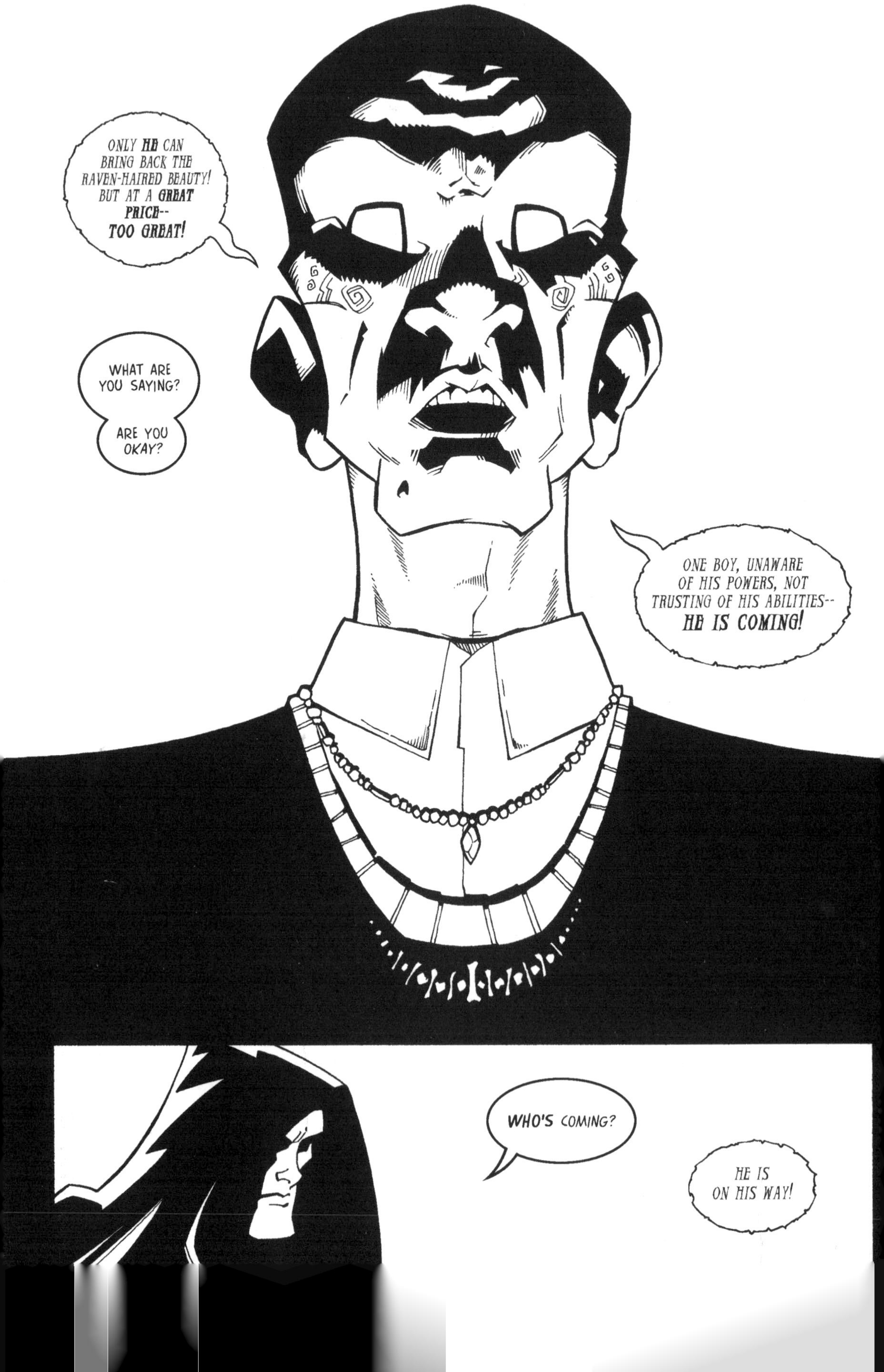
ONLY HE CAN BRING BACK THE RAVEN-HAIRED BEAUTY! BUT AT A GREAT PRICE-- TOO GREAT!
WHAT ARE YOU SAYING?
ARE YOU OKAY?
ONE BOY, UNAWARE OF HIS POWERS, NOT TRUSTING OF HIS ABILITIES-- HE IS COMING!
WHO'S COMING?
HE IS ON HIS WAY!

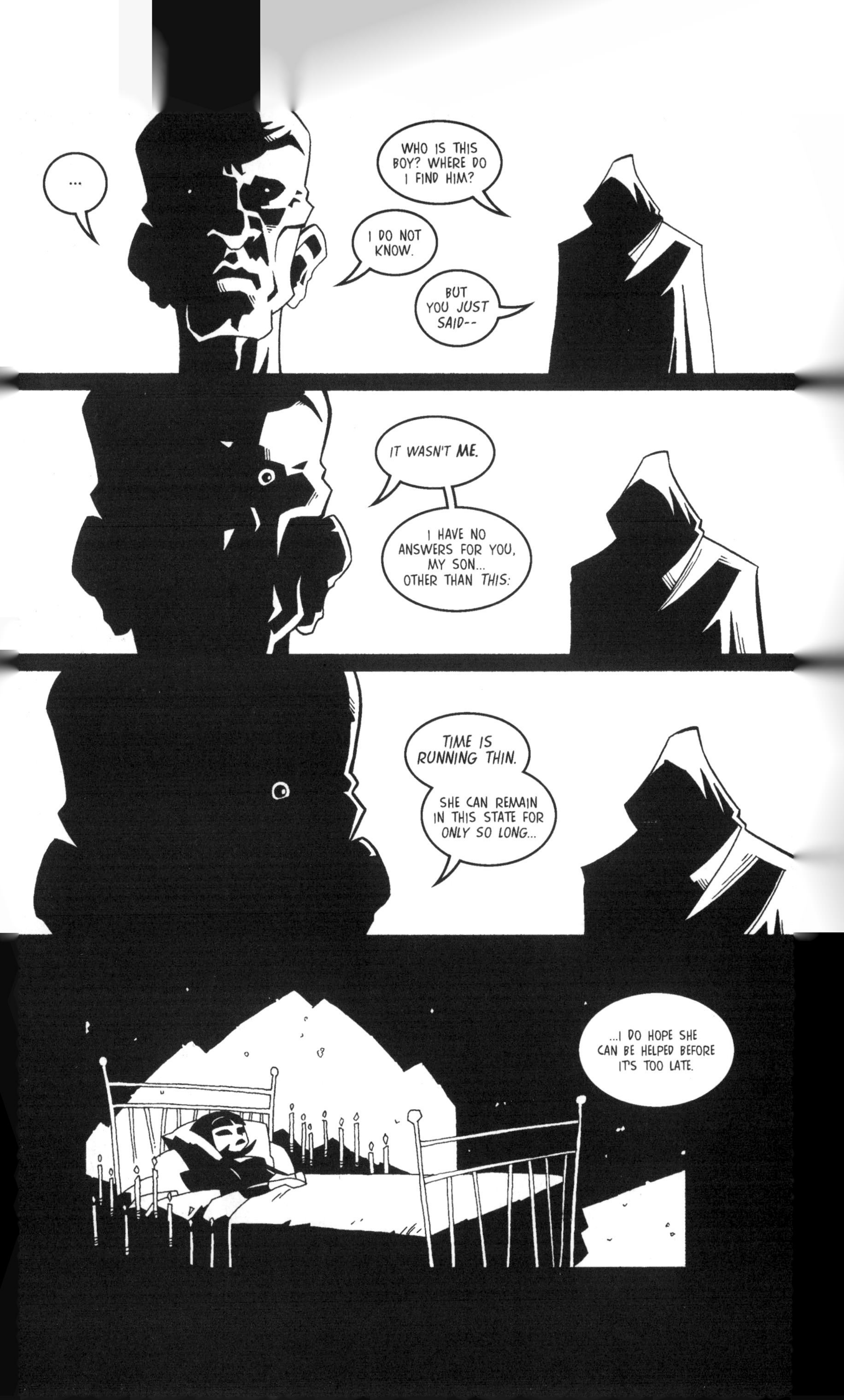
...
WHO IS THIS BOY? WHERE DO I FIND HIM?
I DO NOT KNOW.
BUT YOU JUST SAID--
IT WASN'T *ME.*
I HAVE NO ANSWERS FOR YOU, MY SON... OTHER THAN *THIS:*
TIME IS RUNNING THIN.
SHE CAN REMAIN IN THIS STATE FOR *ONLY* SO LONG...
...I DO HOPE SHE CAN BE HELPED BEFORE IT'S TOO LATE.

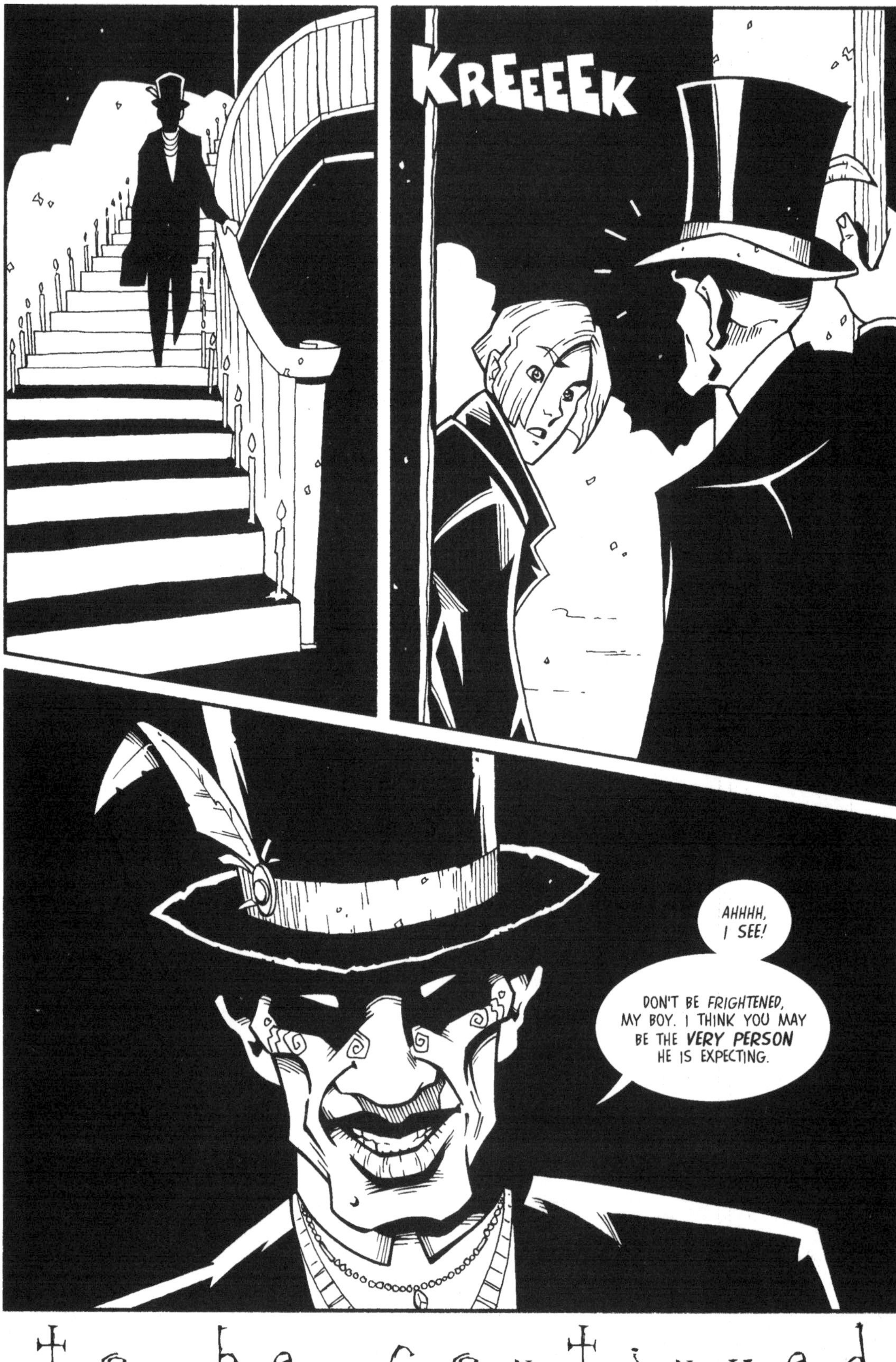
KREEEEK
AHHHH, I SEE!
DON'T BE FRIGHTENED, MY BOY. I THINK YOU MAY BE THE VERY PERSON HE IS EXPECTING.

to be continued

CHAPTER 17

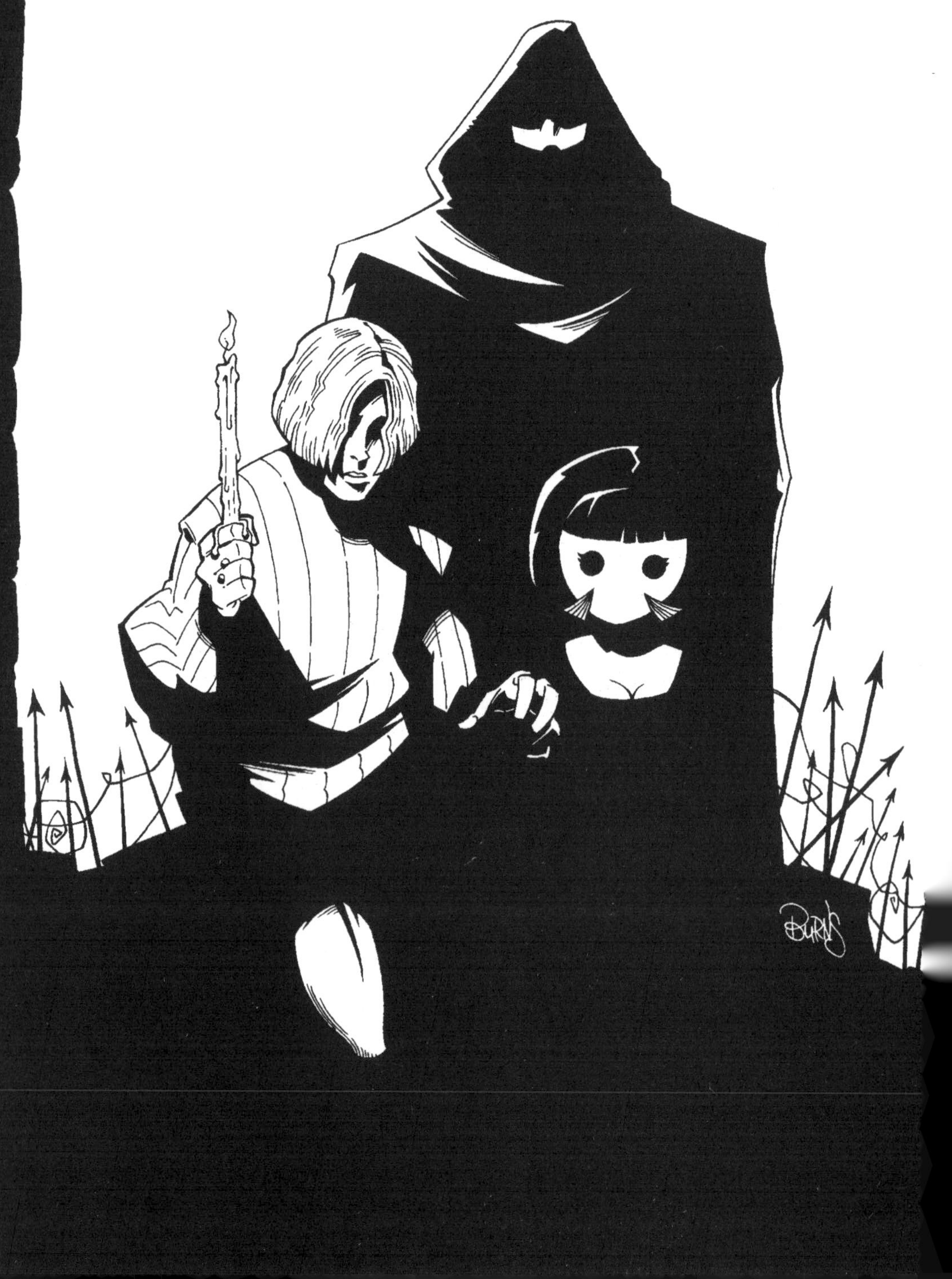
BURNS

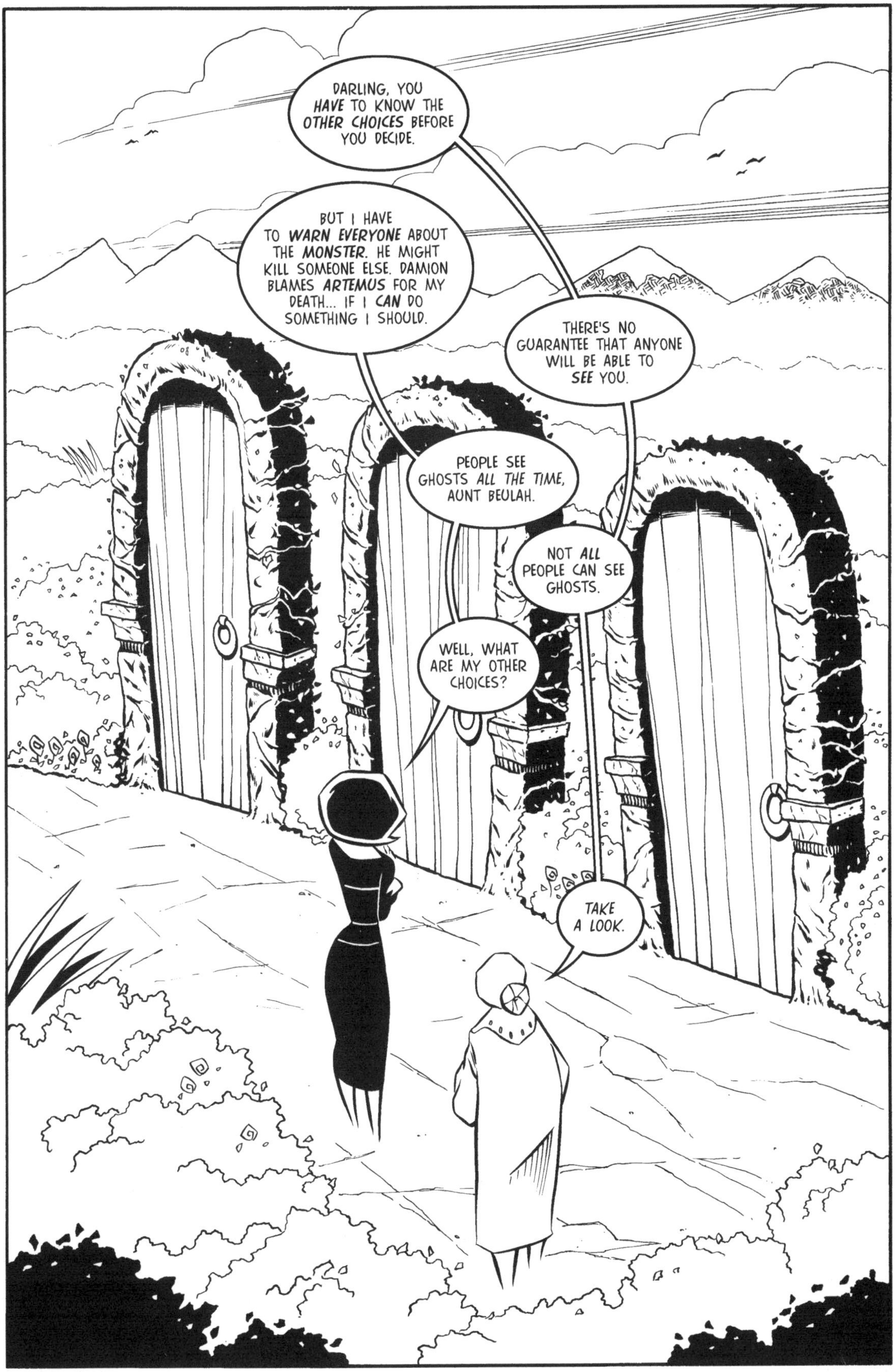
DARLING, YOU HAVE TO KNOW THE OTHER CHOICES BEFORE YOU DECIDE.
BUT I HAVE TO WARN EVERYONE ABOUT THE MONSTER. HE MIGHT KILL SOMEONE ELSE. DAMION BLAMES ARTEMUS FOR MY DEATH... IF I CAN DO SOMETHING I SHOULD.
THERE'S NO GUARANTEE THAT ANYONE WILL BE ABLE TO SEE YOU.
PEOPLE SEE GHOSTS ALL THE TIME, AUNT BEULAH.
NOT ALL PEOPLE CAN SEE GHOSTS.
WELL, WHAT ARE MY OTHER CHOICES?
TAKE A LOOK.

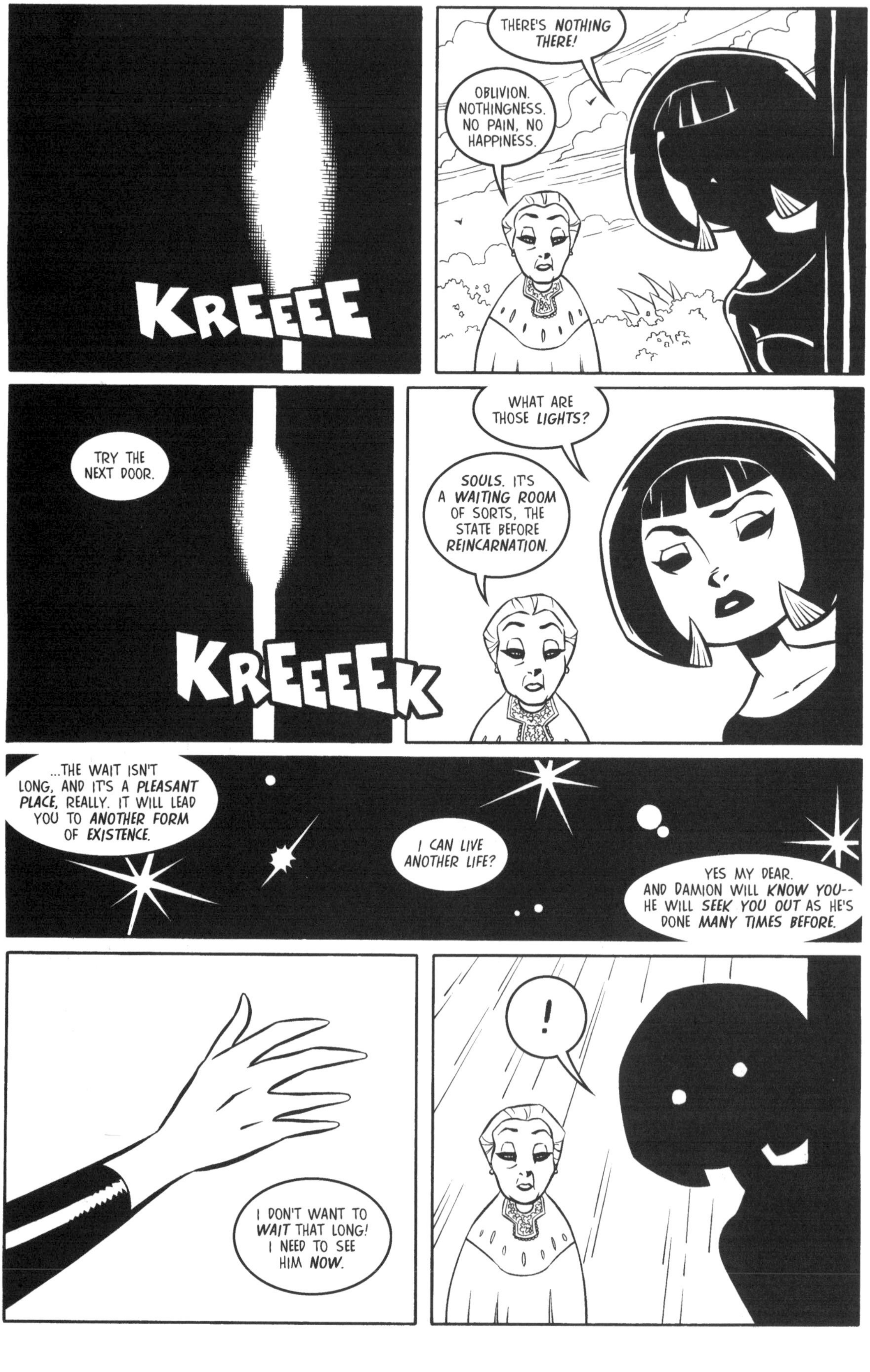
KREEEE
THERE'S NOTHING THERE!
OBLIVION. NOTHINGNESS. NO PAIN, NO HAPPINESS.
TRY THE NEXT DOOR.
KREEEEK
WHAT ARE THOSE LIGHTS?
SOULS. IT'S A WAITING ROOM OF SORTS, THE STATE BEFORE REINCARNATION.
...THE WAIT ISN'T LONG, AND IT'S A PLEASANT PLACE, REALLY. IT WILL LEAD YOU TO ANOTHER FORM OF EXISTENCE.
I CAN LIVE ANOTHER LIFE?
YES MY DEAR. AND DAMION WILL KNOW YOU-- HE WILL SEEK YOU OUT AS HE'S DONE MANY TIMES BEFORE.
I DON'T WANT TO WAIT THAT LONG! I NEED TO SEE HIM NOW.
!

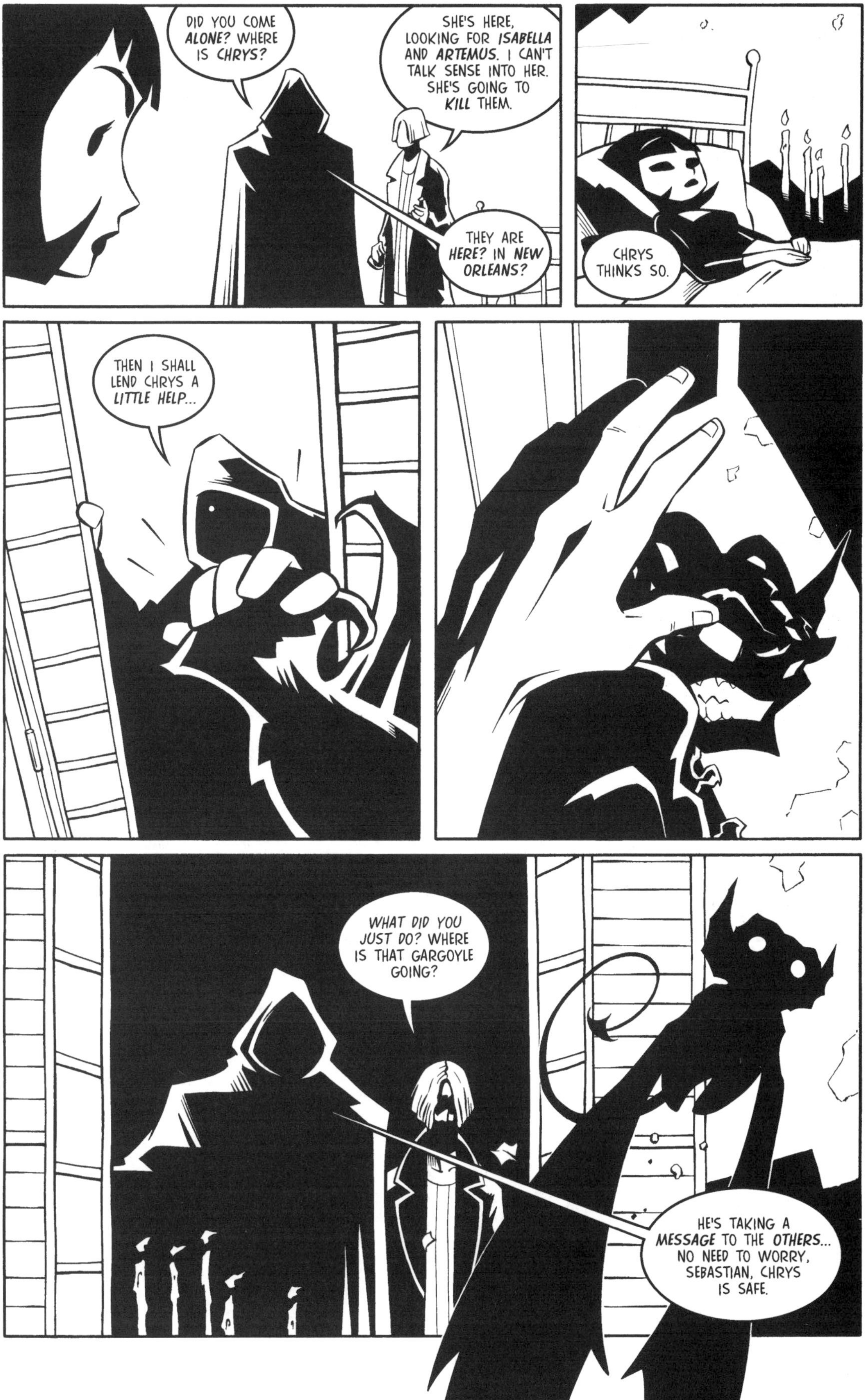
DID YOU COME ALONE? WHERE IS CHRYS?
SHE'S HERE, LOOKING FOR ISABELLA AND ARTEMUS. I CAN'T TALK SENSE INTO HER. SHE'S GOING TO KILL THEM.
THEY ARE HERE? IN NEW ORLEANS?
CHRYS THINKS SO.
THEN I SHALL LEND CHRYS A LITTLE HELP...
WHAT DID YOU JUST DO? WHERE IS THAT GARGOYLE GOING?
HE'S TAKING A MESSAGE TO THE OTHERS... NO NEED TO WORRY, SEBASTIAN, CHRYS IS SAFE.

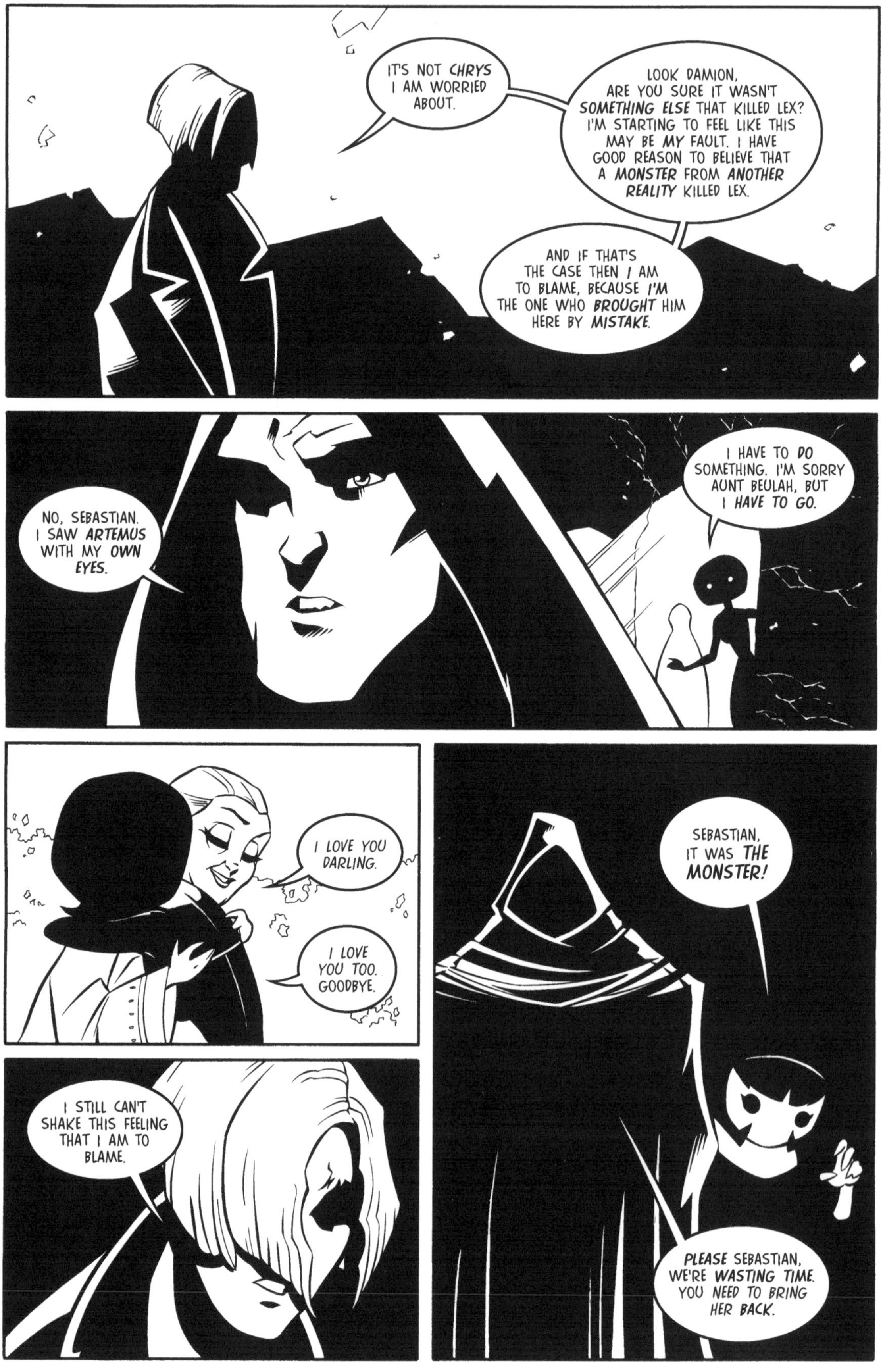
IT'S NOT CHRYS I AM WORRIED ABOUT.
LOOK DAMION, ARE YOU SURE IT WASN'T SOMETHING ELSE THAT KILLED LEX? I'M STARTING TO FEEL LIKE THIS MAY BE MY FAULT. I HAVE GOOD REASON TO BELIEVE THAT A MONSTER FROM ANOTHER REALITY KILLED LEX.
AND IF THAT'S THE CASE THEN I AM TO BLAME, BECAUSE I'M THE ONE WHO BROUGHT HIM HERE BY MISTAKE.
NO, SEBASTIAN. I SAW ARTEMUS WITH MY OWN EYES.
I HAVE TO DO SOMETHING. I'M SORRY AUNT BEULAH, BUT I HAVE TO GO.
I LOVE YOU DARLING.
I LOVE YOU TOO. GOODBYE.
I STILL CAN'T SHAKE THIS FEELING THAT I AM TO BLAME.
SEBASTIAN, IT WAS THE MONSTER!
PLEASE SEBASTIAN, WE'RE WASTING TIME. YOU NEED TO BRING HER BACK.

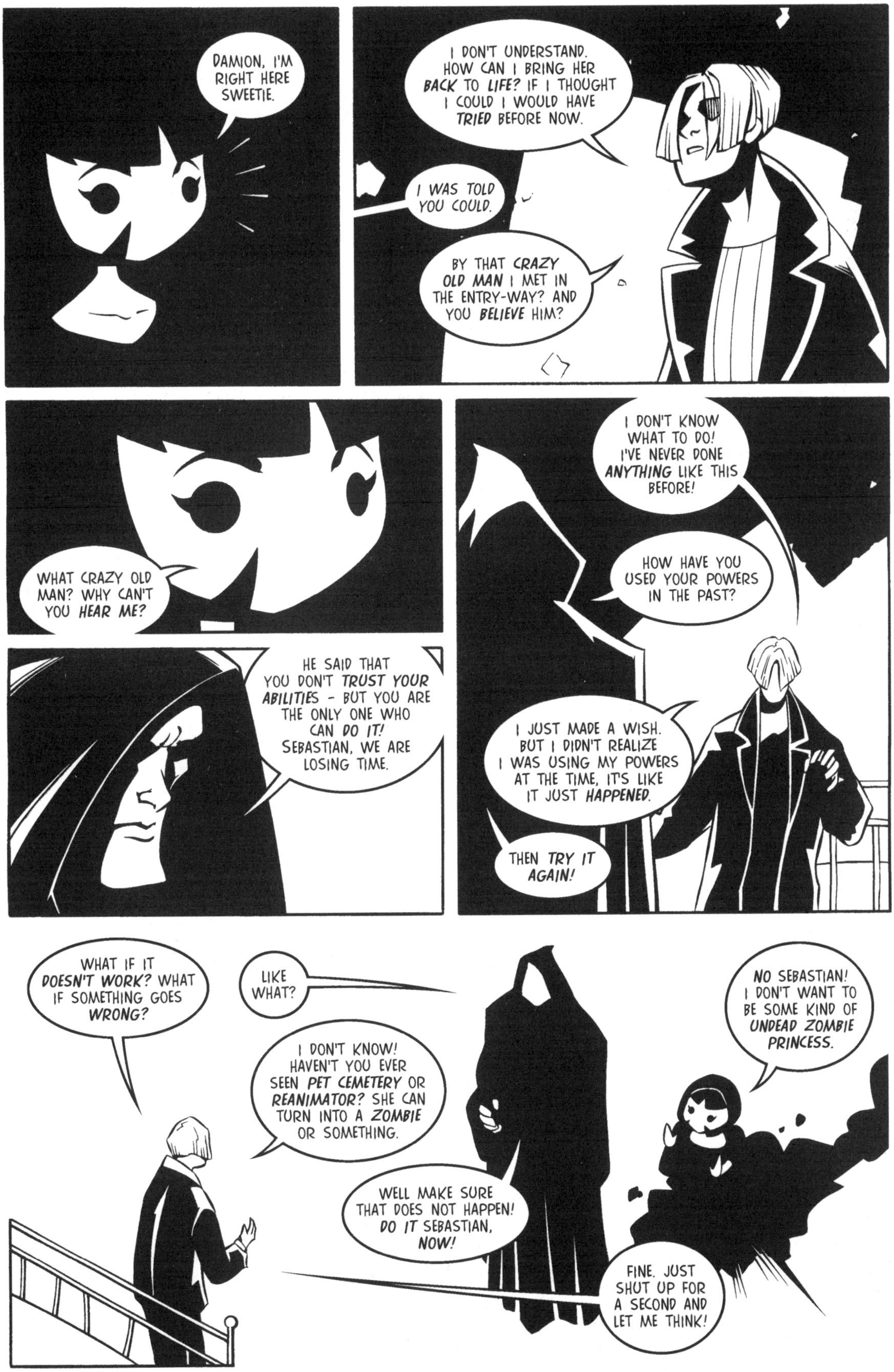
DAMION, I'M RIGHT HERE SWEETIE.
I DON'T UNDERSTAND. HOW CAN I BRING HER BACK TO LIFE? IF I THOUGHT I COULD I WOULD HAVE TRIED BEFORE NOW.
I WAS TOLD YOU COULD.
BY THAT CRAZY OLD MAN I MET IN THE ENTRY-WAY? AND YOU BELIEVE HIM?
WHAT CRAZY OLD MAN? WHY CAN'T YOU HEAR ME?
HE SAID THAT YOU DON'T TRUST YOUR ABILITIES - BUT YOU ARE THE ONLY ONE WHO CAN DO IT! SEBASTIAN, WE ARE LOSING TIME.
I DON'T KNOW WHAT TO DO! I'VE NEVER DONE ANYTHING LIKE THIS BEFORE!
HOW HAVE YOU USED YOUR POWERS IN THE PAST?
I JUST MADE A WISH. BUT I DIDN'T REALIZE I WAS USING MY POWERS AT THE TIME, IT'S LIKE IT JUST HAPPENED.
THEN TRY IT AGAIN!
WHAT IF IT DOESN'T WORK? WHAT IF SOMETHING GOES WRONG?
LIKE WHAT?
I DON'T KNOW! HAVEN'T YOU EVER SEEN PET CEMETERY OR REANIMATOR? SHE CAN TURN INTO A ZOMBIE OR SOMETHING.
NO SEBASTIAN! I DON'T WANT TO BE SOME KIND OF UNDEAD ZOMBIE PRINCESS.
WELL MAKE SURE THAT DOES NOT HAPPEN! DO IT SEBASTIAN, NOW!
FINE. JUST SHUT UP FOR A SECOND AND LET ME THINK!

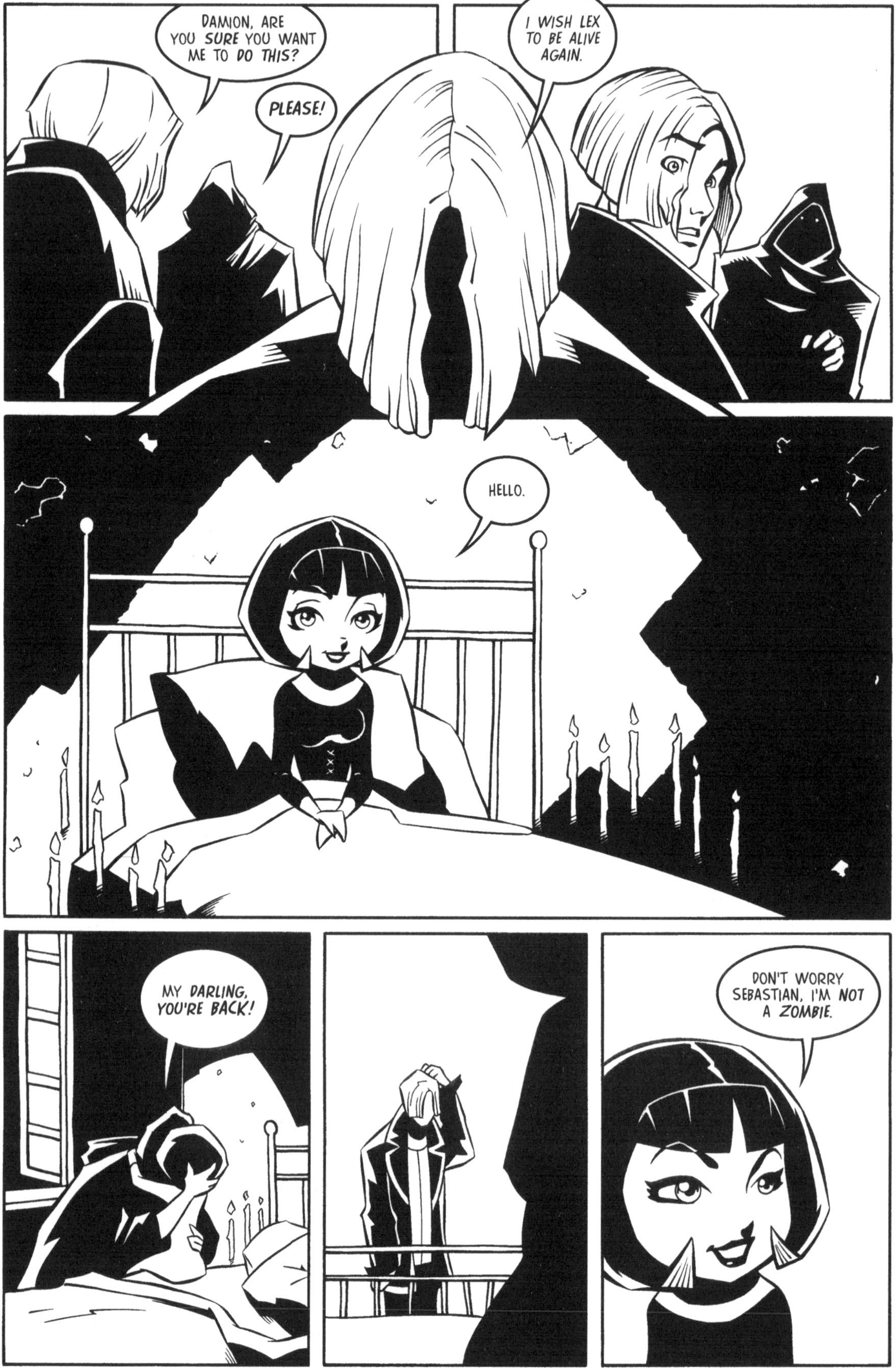
DAMION, ARE YOU SURE YOU WANT ME TO DO THIS?
PLEASE!
I WISH LEX TO BE ALIVE AGAIN.
HELLO.
MY DARLING, YOU'RE BACK!
DON'T WORRY SEBASTIAN, I'M NOT A ZOMBIE.

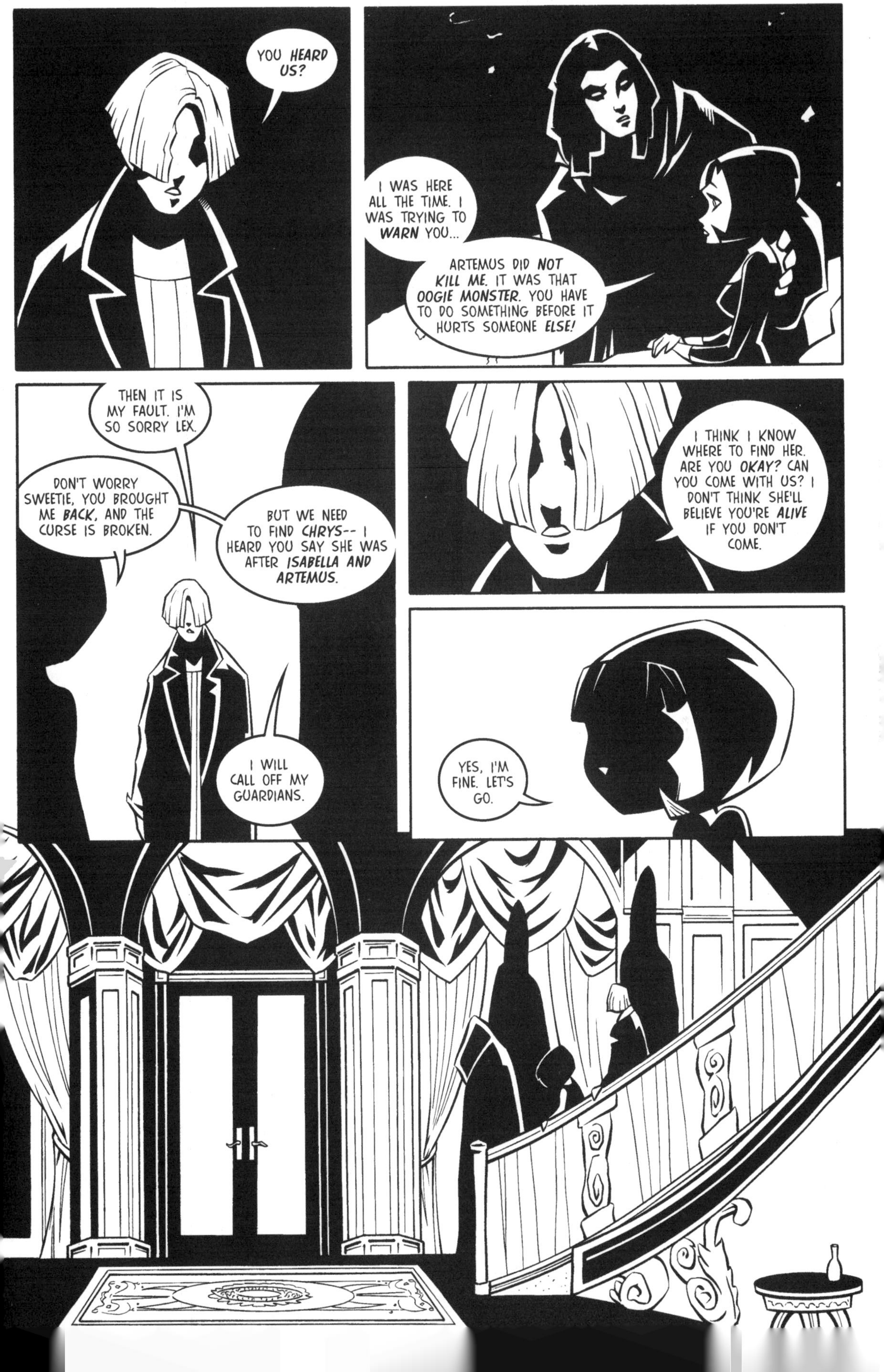
YOU HEARD US?
I WAS HERE ALL THE TIME. I WAS TRYING TO WARN YOU...
ARTEMUS DID NOT KILL ME. IT WAS THAT OOGIE MONSTER. YOU HAVE TO DO SOMETHING BEFORE IT HURTS SOMEONE ELSE!
THEN IT IS MY FAULT. I'M SO SORRY LEX.
DON'T WORRY SWEETIE, YOU BROUGHT ME BACK, AND THE CURSE IS BROKEN.
BUT WE NEED TO FIND CHRYS-- I HEARD YOU SAY SHE WAS AFTER ISABELLA AND ARTEMUS.
I WILL CALL OFF MY GUARDIANS.
I THINK I KNOW WHERE TO FIND HER. ARE YOU OKAY? CAN YOU COME WITH US? I DON'T THINK SHE'LL BELIEVE YOU'RE ALIVE IF YOU DON'T COME.
YES, I'M FINE. LET'S GO.

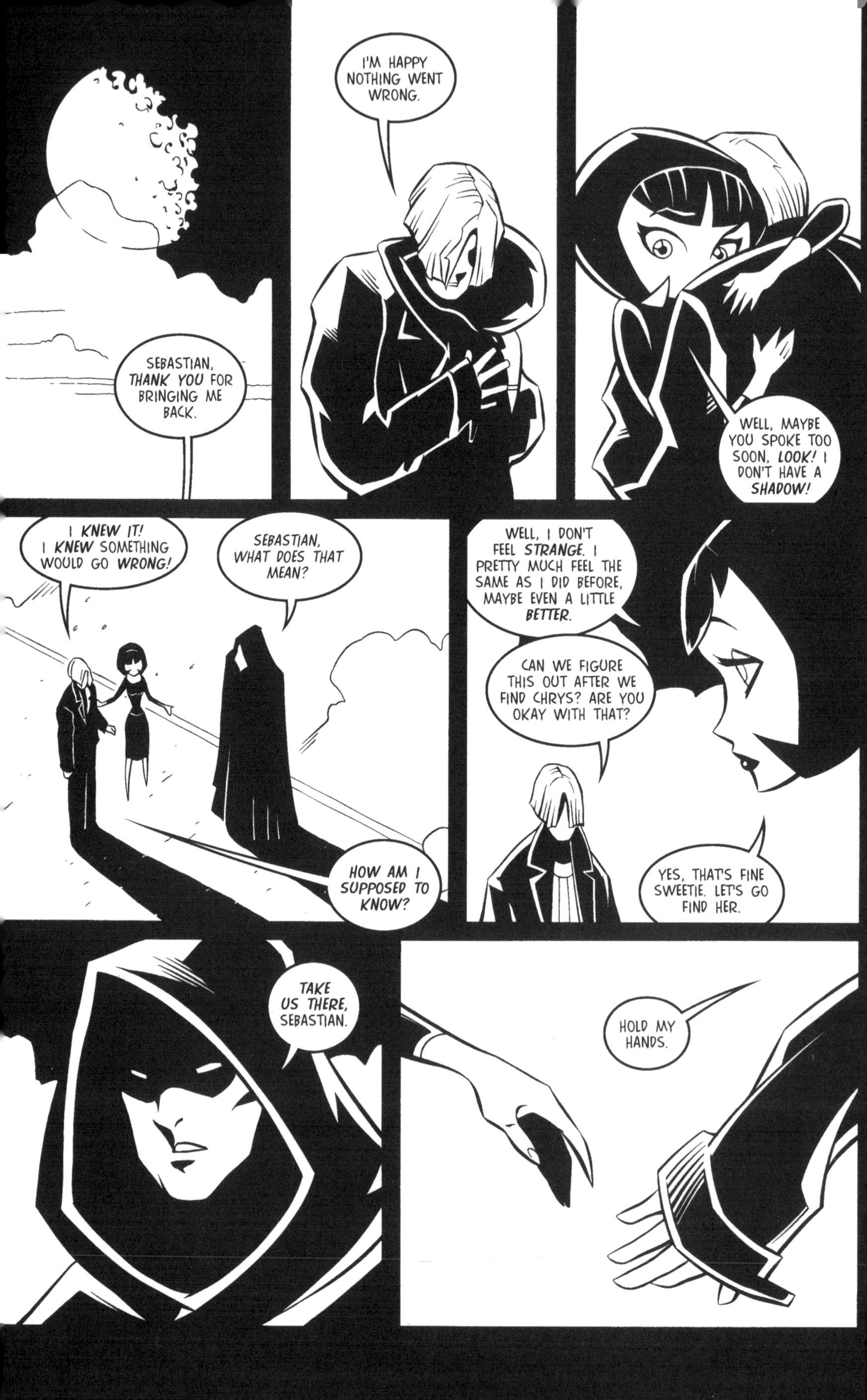
SEBASTIAN, THANK YOU FOR BRINGING ME BACK.
I'M HAPPY NOTHING WENT WRONG.
WELL, MAYBE YOU SPOKE TOO SOON, LOOK! I DON'T HAVE A SHADOW!
I KNEW IT! I KNEW SOMETHING WOULD GO WRONG!
SEBASTIAN, WHAT DOES THAT MEAN?
HOW AM I SUPPOSED TO KNOW?
WELL, I DON'T FEEL STRANGE. I PRETTY MUCH FEEL THE SAME AS I DID BEFORE, MAYBE EVEN A LITTLE BETTER.
CAN WE FIGURE THIS OUT AFTER WE FIND CHRYS? ARE YOU OKAY WITH THAT?
YES, THAT'S FINE SWEETIE. LET'S GO FIND HER.
TAKE US THERE, SEBASTIAN.
HOLD MY HANDS.

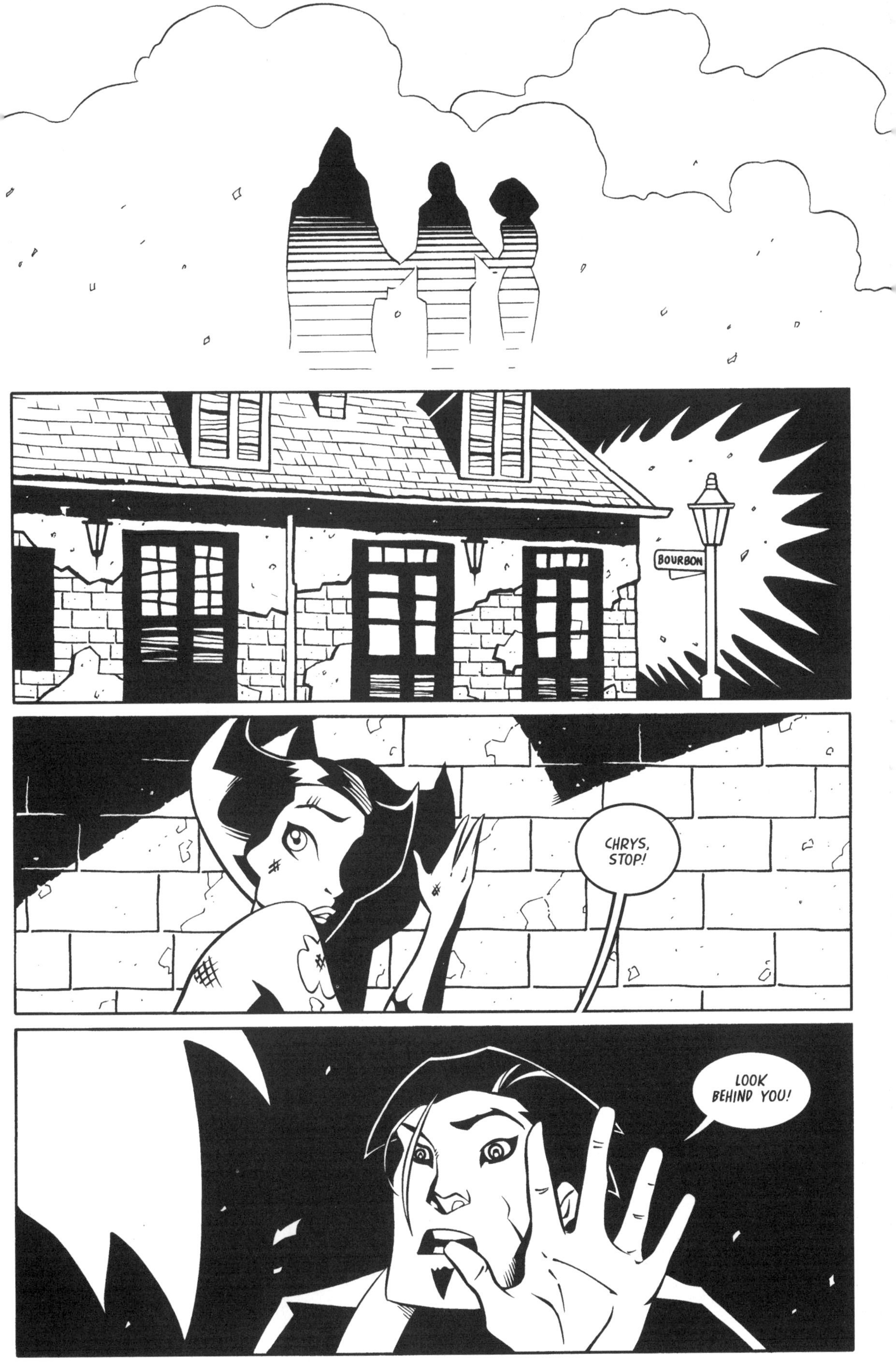
BOURBON
CHRYS, STOP!
LOOK BEHIND YOU!

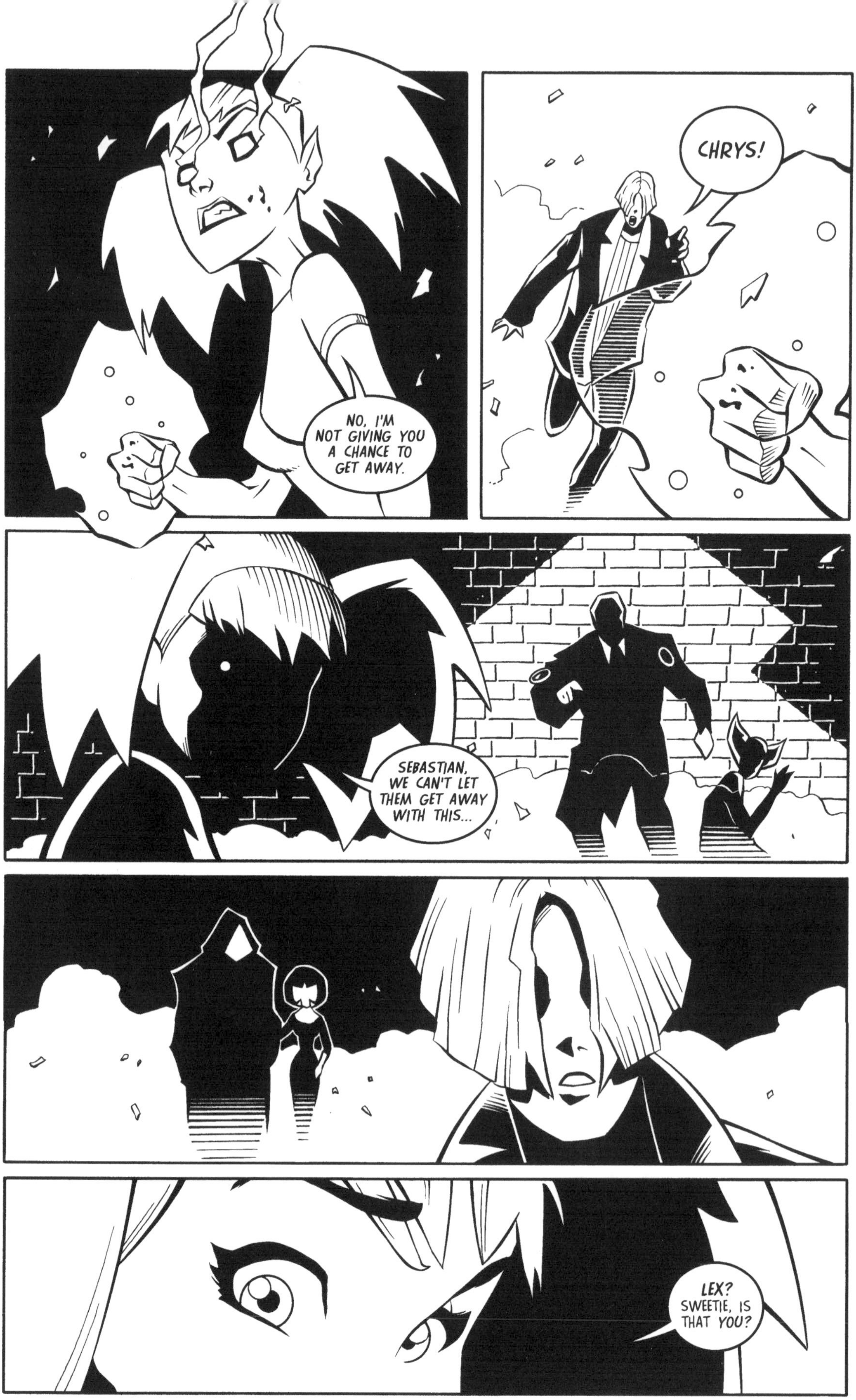
NO, I'M NOT GIVING YOU A CHANCE TO GET AWAY.
CHRYS!
SEBASTIAN, WE CAN'T LET THEM GET AWAY WITH THIS...
LEX? SWEETIE, IS THAT YOU?

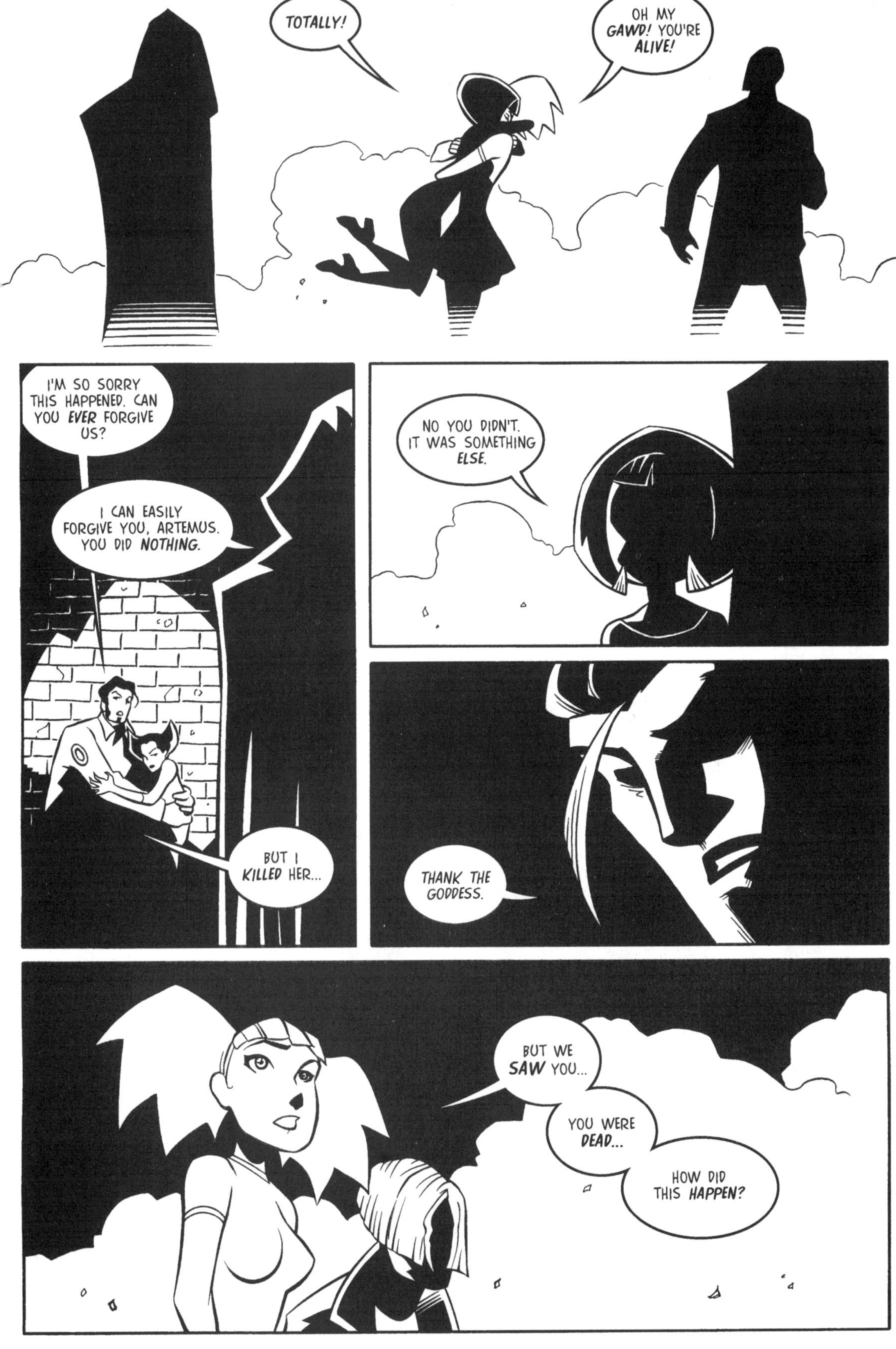
TOTALLY!
OH MY GAWD! YOU'RE ALIVE!
I'M SO SORRY THIS HAPPENED. CAN YOU EVER FORGIVE US?
I CAN EASILY FORGIVE YOU, ARTEMUS. YOU DID NOTHING.
BUT I KILLED HER...
NO YOU DIDN'T. IT WAS SOMETHING ELSE.
THANK THE GODDESS.
BUT WE SAW YOU...
YOU WERE DEAD...
HOW DID THIS HAPPEN?

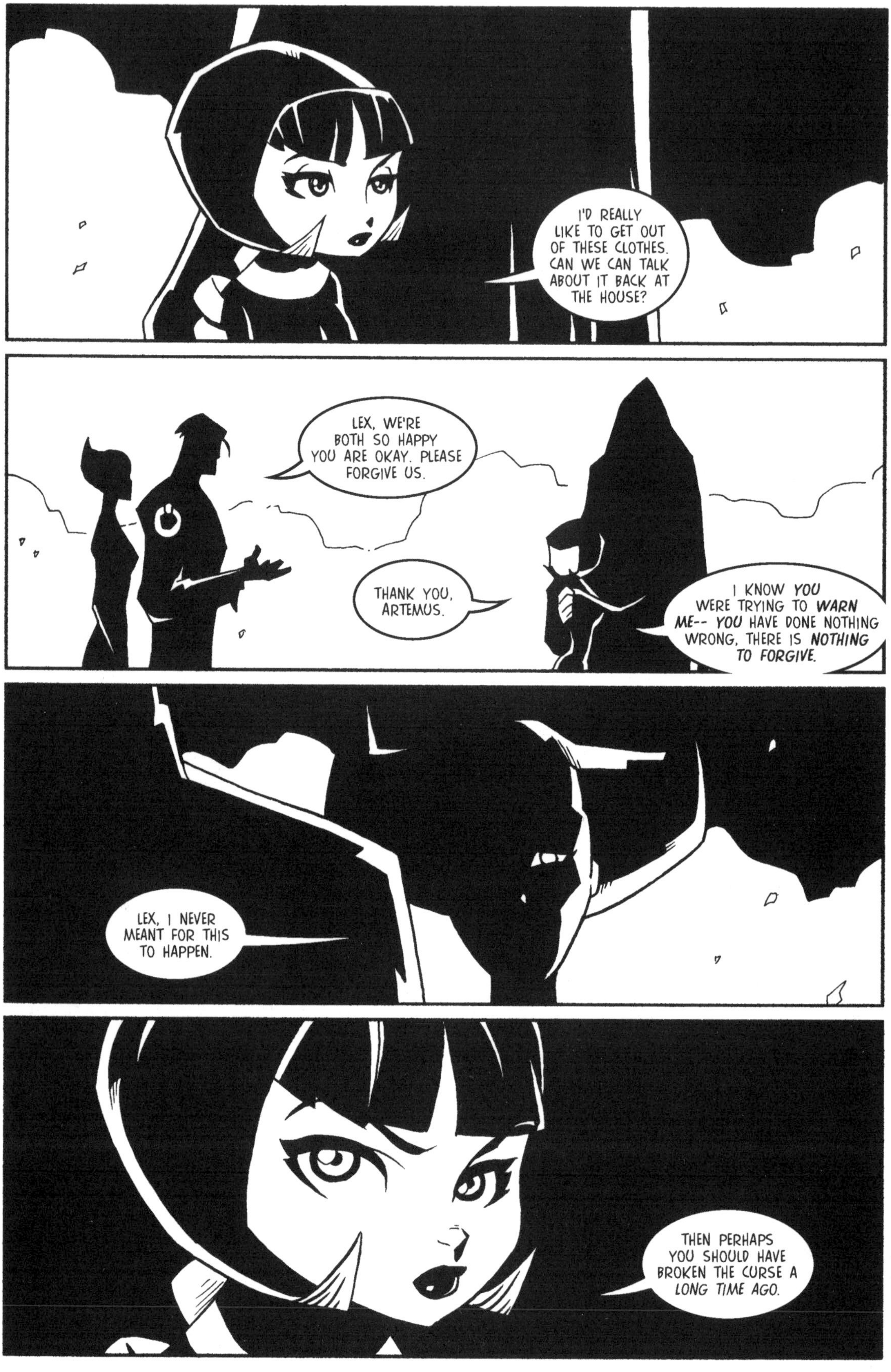
I'D REALLY LIKE TO GET OUT OF THESE CLOTHES. CAN WE CAN TALK ABOUT IT BACK AT THE HOUSE?
LEX, WE'RE BOTH SO HAPPY YOU ARE OKAY. PLEASE FORGIVE US.
THANK YOU, ARTEMUS.
I KNOW *YOU* WERE TRYING TO *WARN ME-- YOU* HAVE DONE NOTHING WRONG, THERE IS *NOTHING TO FORGIVE.*
LEX, I NEVER MEANT FOR THIS TO HAPPEN.
THEN PERHAPS YOU SHOULD HAVE BROKEN THE CURSE A *LONG TIME* AGO.

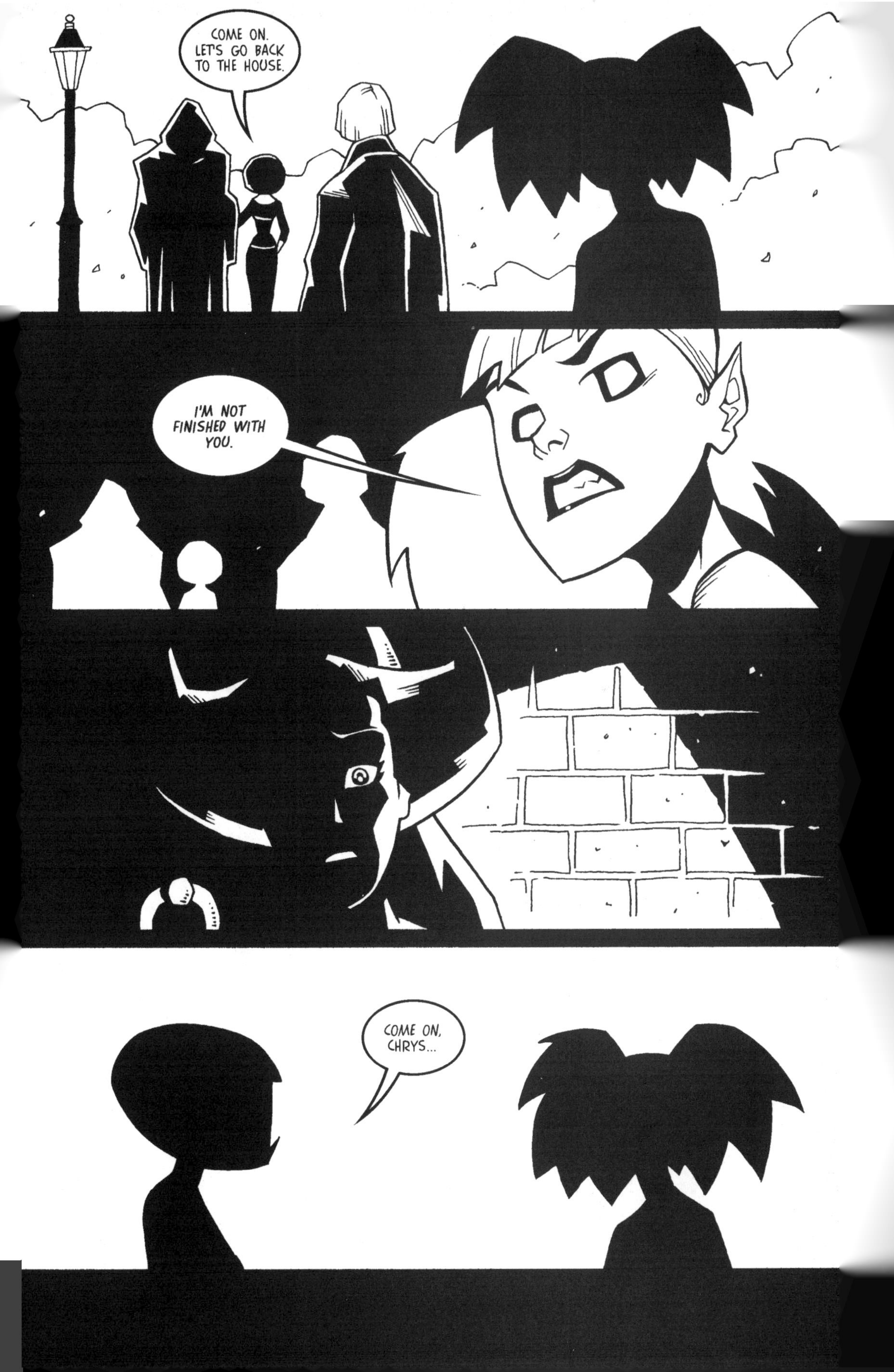
COME ON. LET'S GO BACK TO THE HOUSE.
I'M NOT FINISHED WITH YOU.
COME ON, CHRYS...

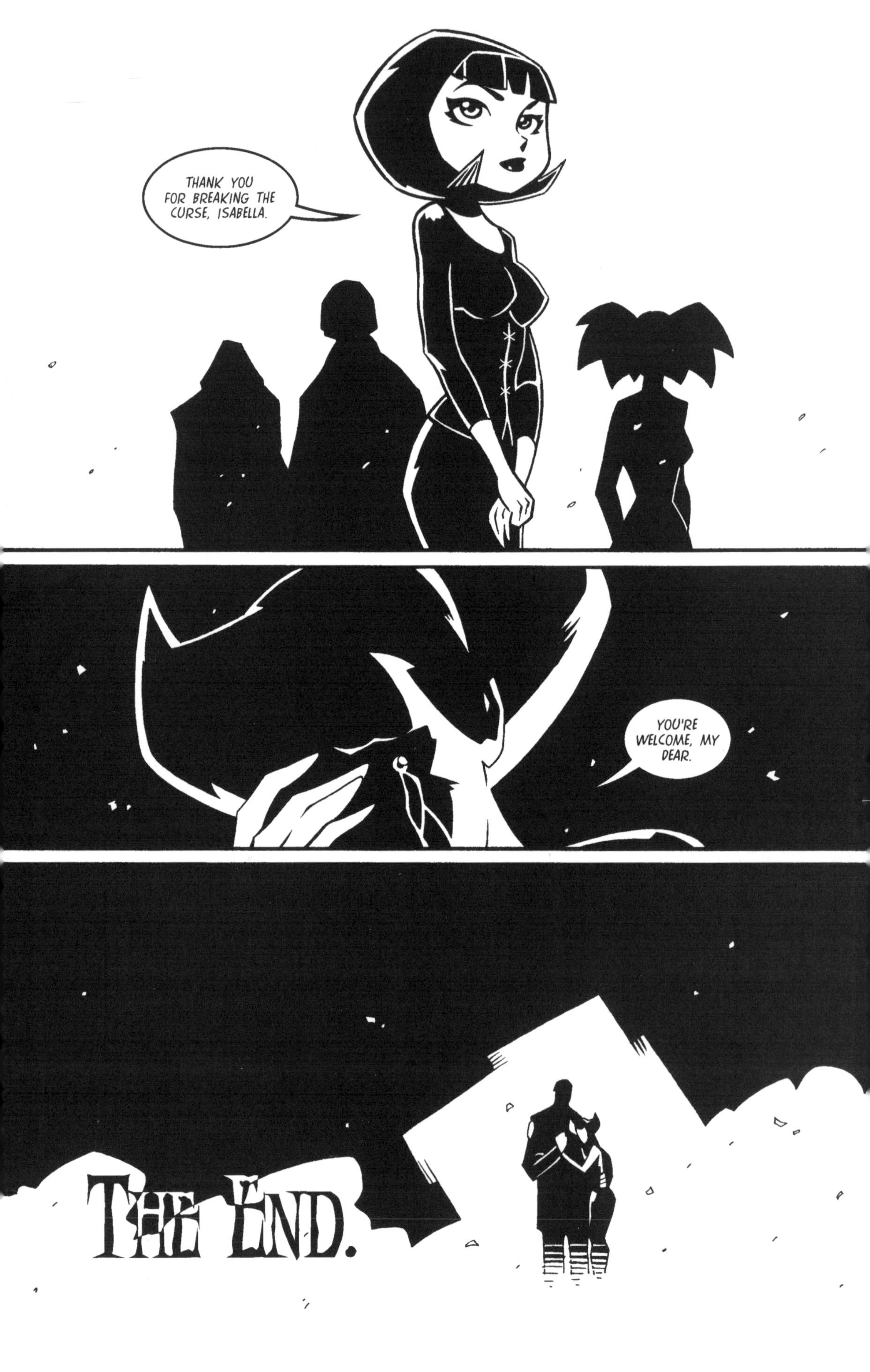
THANK YOU FOR BREAKING THE CURSE, ISABELLA.
YOU'RE WELCOME, MY DEAR.
THE END.

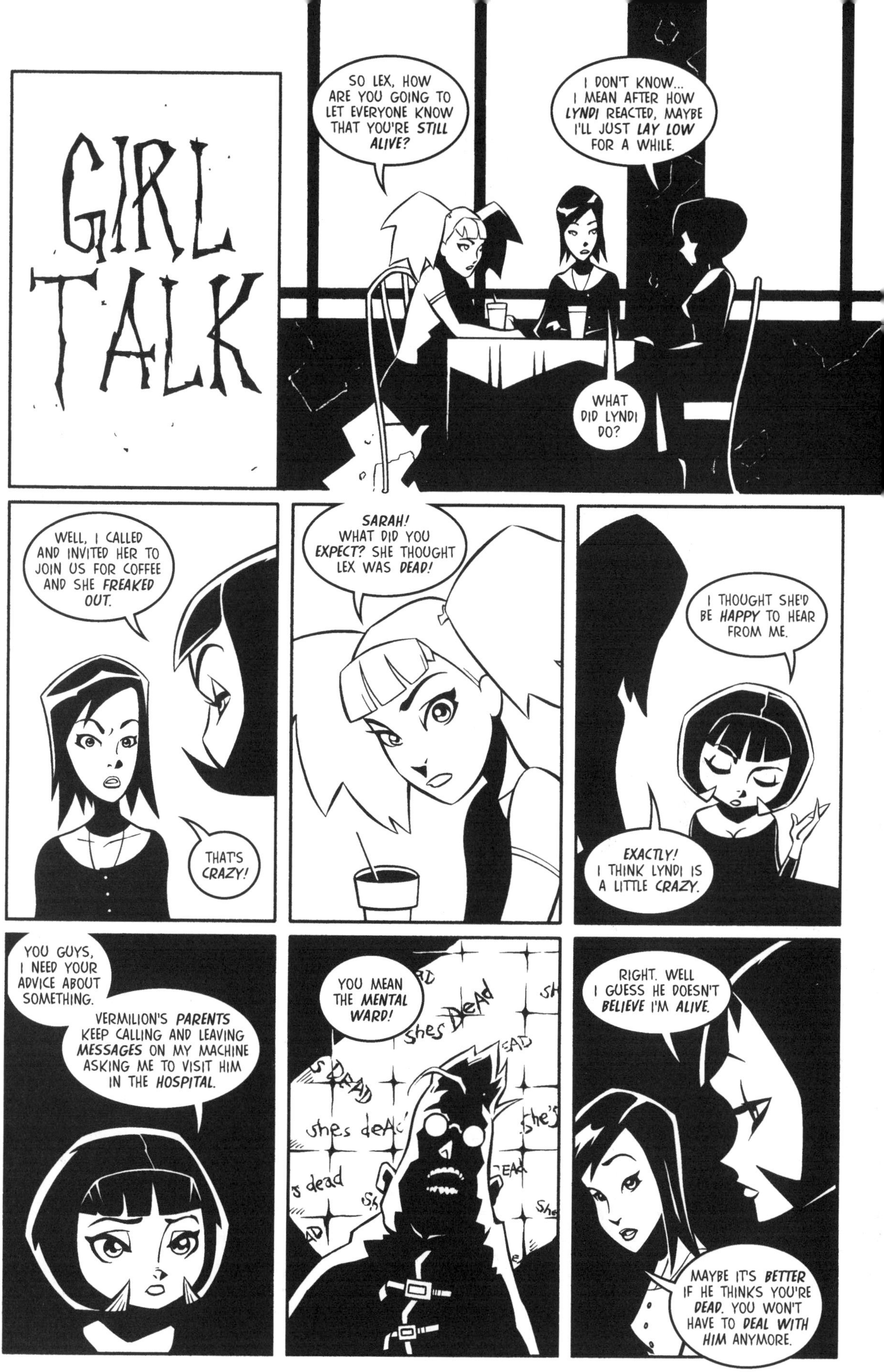
GIRL TALK
SO LEX, HOW ARE YOU GOING TO LET EVERYONE KNOW THAT YOU'RE STILL ALIVE?
I DON'T KNOW... I MEAN AFTER HOW LYNDI REACTED, MAYBE I'LL JUST LAY LOW FOR A WHILE.
WHAT DID LYNDI DO?
WELL, I CALLED AND INVITED HER TO JOIN US FOR COFFEE AND SHE FREAKED OUT.
THAT'S CRAZY!
SARAH! WHAT DID YOU EXPECT? SHE THOUGHT LEX WAS DEAD!
I THOUGHT SHE'D BE HAPPY TO HEAR FROM ME.
EXACTLY! I THINK LYNDI IS A LITTLE CRAZY.
YOU GUYS, I NEED YOUR ADVICE ABOUT SOMETHING.
VERMILION'S PARENTS KEEP CALLING AND LEAVING MESSAGES ON MY MACHINE ASKING ME TO VISIT HIM IN THE HOSPITAL.
YOU MEAN THE MENTAL WARD!
shes Dead
shes dead
RIGHT. WELL I GUESS HE DOESN'T BELIEVE I'M ALIVE.
MAYBE IT'S BETTER IF HE THINKS YOU'RE DEAD. YOU WON'T HAVE TO DEAL WITH HIM ANYMORE.

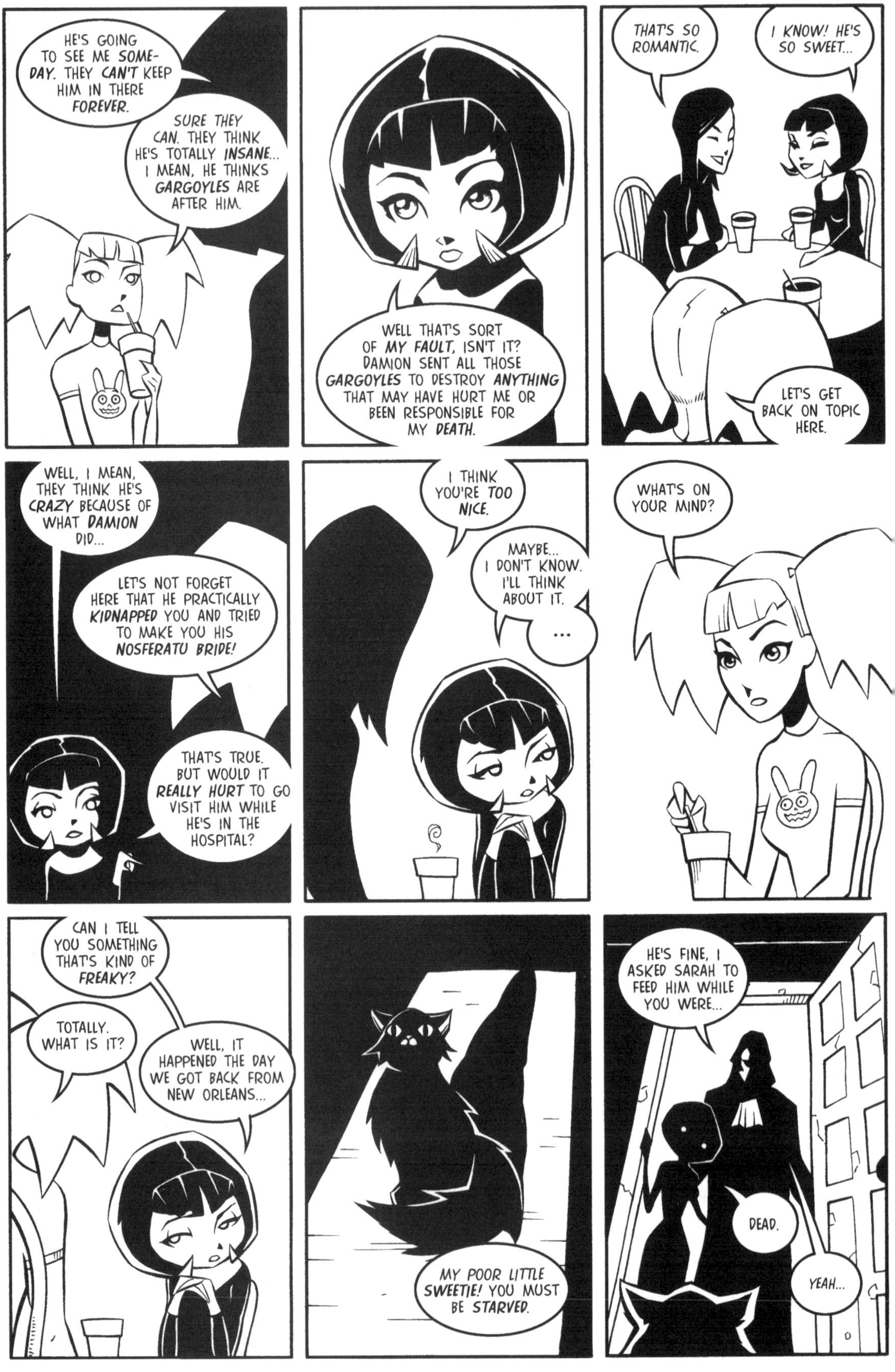
HE'S GOING TO SEE ME SOME-DAY. THEY CAN'T KEEP HIM IN THERE FOREVER.
SURE THEY CAN. THEY THINK HE'S TOTALLY INSANE... I MEAN, HE THINKS GARGOYLES ARE AFTER HIM.
WELL THAT'S SORT OF MY FAULT, ISN'T IT? DAMION SENT ALL THOSE GARGOYLES TO DESTROY ANYTHING THAT MAY HAVE HURT ME OR BEEN RESPONSIBLE FOR MY DEATH.
THAT'S SO ROMANTIC.
I KNOW! HE'S SO SWEET...
LET'S GET BACK ON TOPIC HERE.
WELL, I MEAN, THEY THINK HE'S CRAZY BECAUSE OF WHAT DAMION DID...
LET'S NOT FORGET HERE THAT HE PRACTICALLY KIDNAPPED YOU AND TRIED TO MAKE YOU HIS NOSFERATU BRIDE!
THAT'S TRUE. BUT WOULD IT REALLY HURT TO GO VISIT HIM WHILE HE'S IN THE HOSPITAL?
I THINK YOU'RE TOO NICE.
MAYBE... I DON'T KNOW. I'LL THINK ABOUT IT.
...
WHAT'S ON YOUR MIND?
CAN I TELL YOU SOMETHING THAT'S KIND OF FREAKY?
TOTALLY. WHAT IS IT?
WELL, IT HAPPENED THE DAY WE GOT BACK FROM NEW ORLEANS...
MY POOR LITTLE SWEETIE! YOU MUST BE STARVED.
HE'S FINE, I ASKED SARAH TO FEED HIM WHILE YOU WERE...
DEAD.
YEAH...

IT'S OKAY TO TALK ABOUT IT, DAMION.

I'M SURE IT WAS *HORRIBLE*.

I DIDN'T EVEN KNOW WHAT HAPPENED UNTIL MY *AUNT* SHOWED ME. I DON'T REMEMBER FEELING ANY *PAIN*. I WAS JUST WORRIED ABOUT *YOU*, REALLY.

SWEETIE, I THINK I JUST WANT TO GET OUT OF THESE *CLOTHES*, TAKE A *BATH* AND GO TO *BED*.

SOUNDS GOOD. I'LL GO RUN THE BATH FOR YOU. YOU GO GET INTO YOUR COMFY ROBE.

THANKS, DARLING...

AHHH, THAT'S SO MUCH BETTER.

I'M SURE I LOOK *AWFUL*.

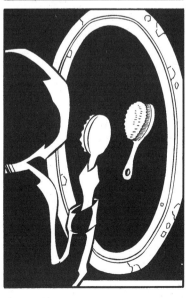

AAAAAAHH!

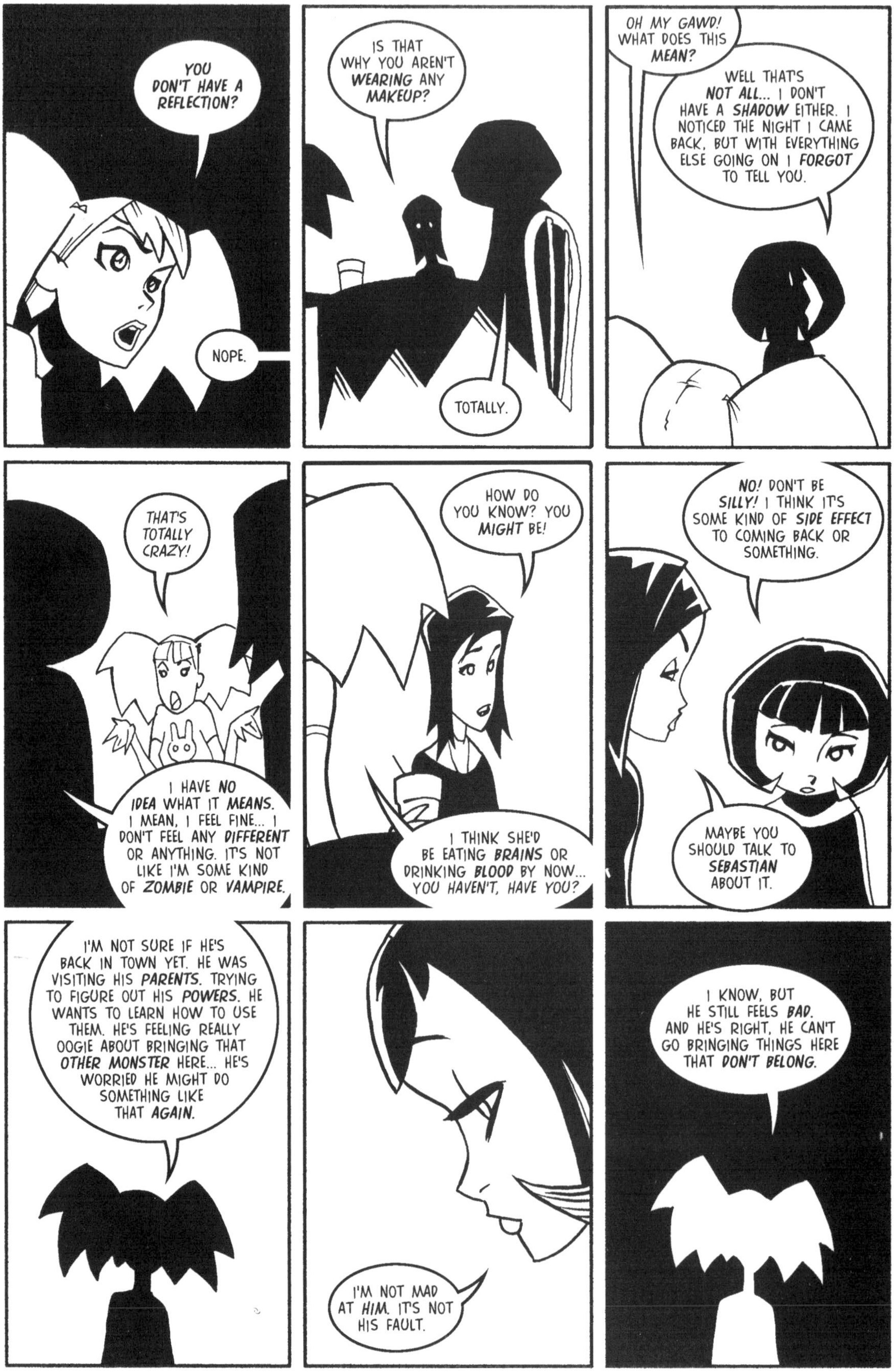
YOU DON'T HAVE A REFLECTION?
NOPE.
IS THAT WHY YOU AREN'T WEARING ANY MAKEUP?
TOTALLY.
OH MY GAWD! WHAT DOES THIS MEAN?
WELL THAT'S NOT ALL... I DON'T HAVE A SHADOW EITHER. I NOTICED THE NIGHT I CAME BACK, BUT WITH EVERYTHING ELSE GOING ON I FORGOT TO TELL YOU.
THAT'S TOTALLY CRAZY!
I HAVE NO IDEA WHAT IT MEANS. I MEAN, I FEEL FINE... I DON'T FEEL ANY DIFFERENT OR ANYTHING. IT'S NOT LIKE I'M SOME KIND OF ZOMBIE OR VAMPIRE.
HOW DO YOU KNOW? YOU MIGHT BE!
I THINK SHE'D BE EATING BRAINS OR DRINKING BLOOD BY NOW... YOU HAVEN'T, HAVE YOU?
NO! DON'T BE SILLY! I THINK IT'S SOME KIND OF SIDE EFFECT TO COMING BACK OR SOMETHING.
MAYBE YOU SHOULD TALK TO SEBASTIAN ABOUT IT.
I'M NOT SURE IF HE'S BACK IN TOWN YET. HE WAS VISITING HIS PARENTS. TRYING TO FIGURE OUT HIS POWERS. HE WANTS TO LEARN HOW TO USE THEM. HE'S FEELING REALLY OOGIE ABOUT BRINGING THAT OTHER MONSTER HERE... HE'S WORRIED HE MIGHT DO SOMETHING LIKE THAT AGAIN.
I'M NOT MAD AT HIM. IT'S NOT HIS FAULT.
I KNOW, BUT HE STILL FEELS BAD. AND HE'S RIGHT, HE CAN'T GO BRINGING THINGS HERE THAT DON'T BELONG.

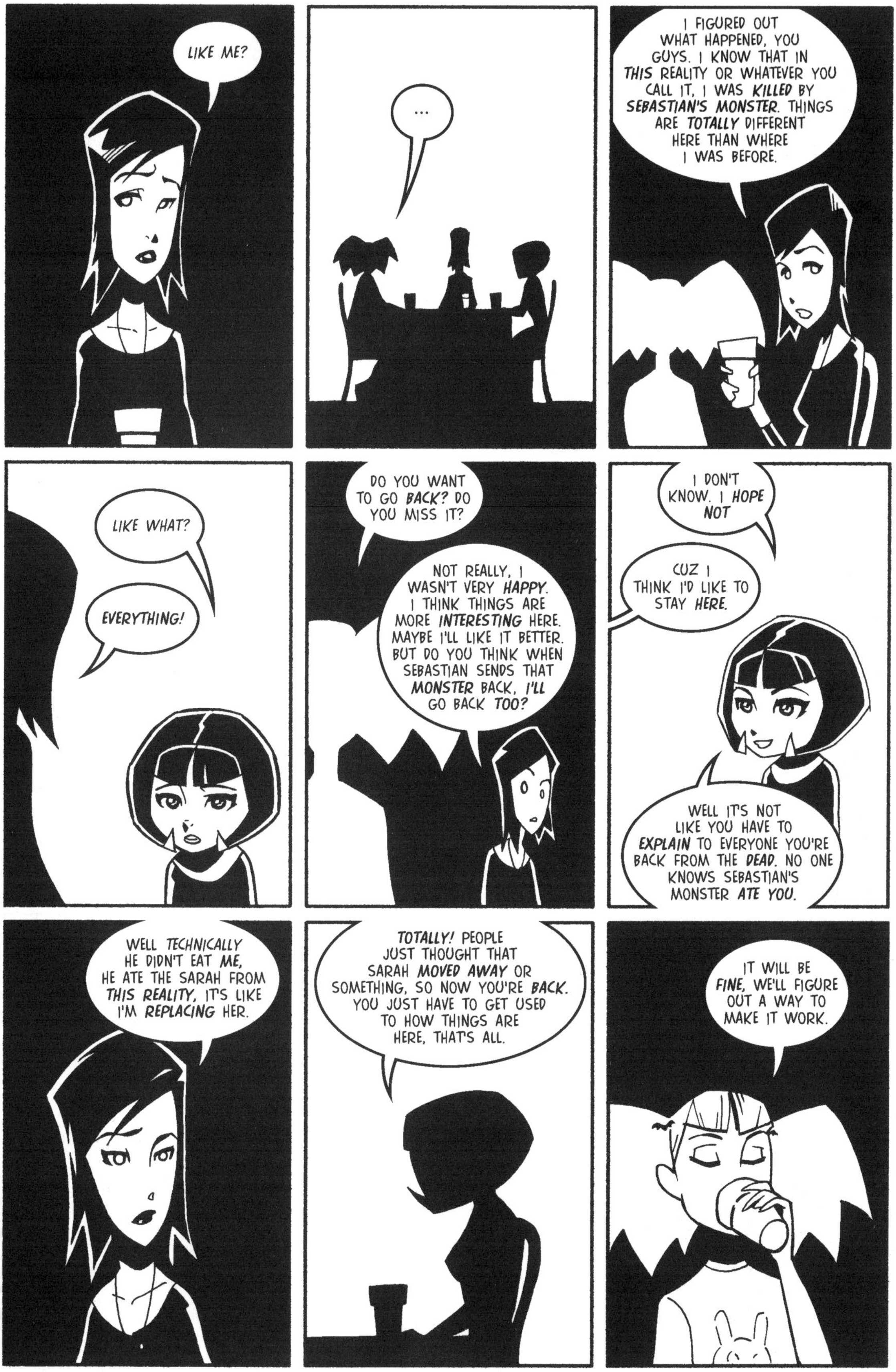
LIKE ME?
...
I FIGURED OUT WHAT HAPPENED, YOU GUYS. I KNOW THAT IN THIS REALITY OR WHATEVER YOU CALL IT, I WAS KILLED BY SEBASTIAN'S MONSTER. THINGS ARE TOTALLY DIFFERENT HERE THAN WHERE I WAS BEFORE.
LIKE WHAT?
EVERYTHING!
DO YOU WANT TO GO BACK? DO YOU MISS IT?
NOT REALLY, I WASN'T VERY HAPPY. I THINK THINGS ARE MORE INTERESTING HERE. MAYBE I'LL LIKE IT BETTER. BUT DO YOU THINK WHEN SEBASTIAN SENDS THAT MONSTER BACK, I'LL GO BACK TOO?
I DON'T KNOW. I HOPE NOT
CUZ I THINK I'D LIKE TO STAY HERE.
WELL IT'S NOT LIKE YOU HAVE TO EXPLAIN TO EVERYONE YOU'RE BACK FROM THE DEAD. NO ONE KNOWS SEBASTIAN'S MONSTER ATE YOU.
WELL TECHNICALLY HE DIDN'T EAT ME, HE ATE THE SARAH FROM THIS REALITY, IT'S LIKE I'M REPLACING HER.
TOTALLY! PEOPLE JUST THOUGHT THAT SARAH MOVED AWAY OR SOMETHING, SO NOW YOU'RE BACK. YOU JUST HAVE TO GET USED TO HOW THINGS ARE HERE, THAT'S ALL.
IT WILL BE FINE, WE'LL FIGURE OUT A WAY TO MAKE IT WORK.

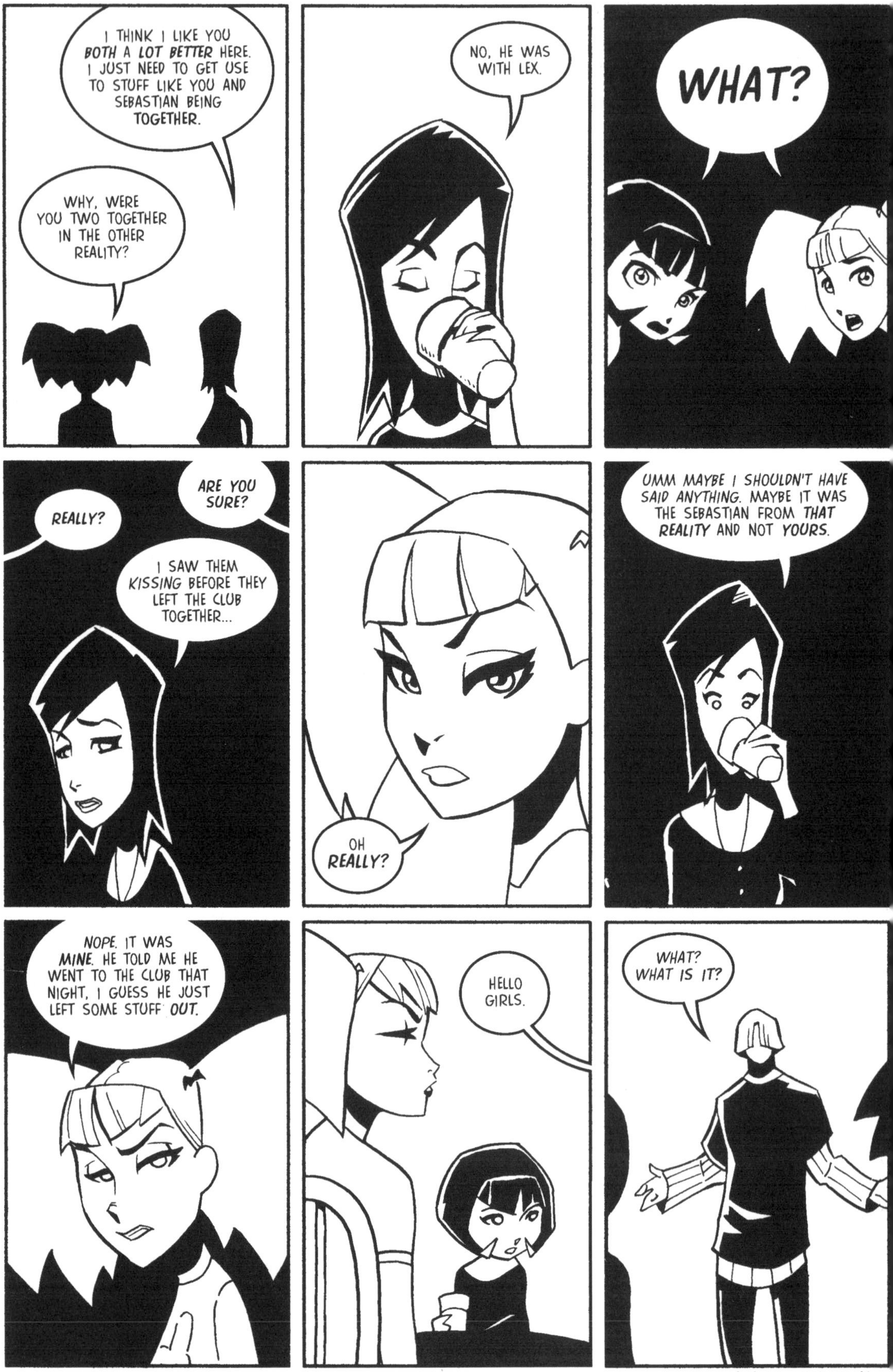
I THINK I LIKE YOU BOTH A LOT BETTER HERE. I JUST NEED TO GET USE TO STUFF LIKE YOU AND SEBASTIAN BEING TOGETHER.
WHY, WERE YOU TWO TOGETHER IN THE OTHER REALITY?
NO, HE WAS WITH LEX.
WHAT?
ARE YOU SURE?
REALLY?
I SAW THEM KISSING BEFORE THEY LEFT THE CLUB TOGETHER...
OH REALLY?
UMM MAYBE I SHOULDN'T HAVE SAID ANYTHING. MAYBE IT WAS THE SEBASTIAN FROM THAT REALITY AND NOT YOURS.
NOPE. IT WAS MINE. HE TOLD ME HE WENT TO THE CLUB THAT NIGHT, I GUESS HE JUST LEFT SOME STUFF OUT.
HELLO GIRLS.
WHAT? WHAT IS IT?

TO BE CONTINUED.

GUEST ART

Paul Chien

Rick Cortez

Anthony Guarisco

Billy Martinez

Crab Scrambly

Jill Thompson

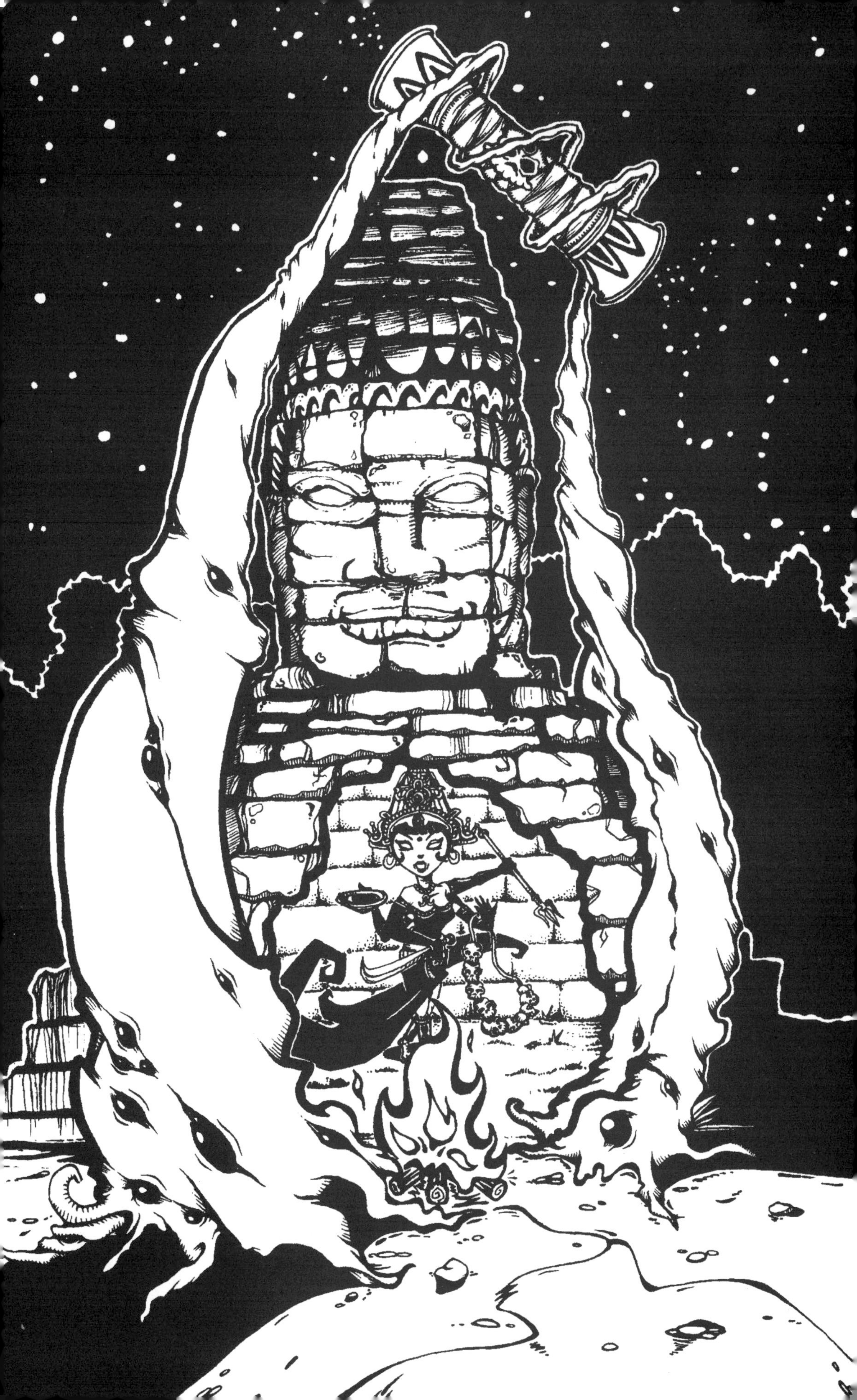

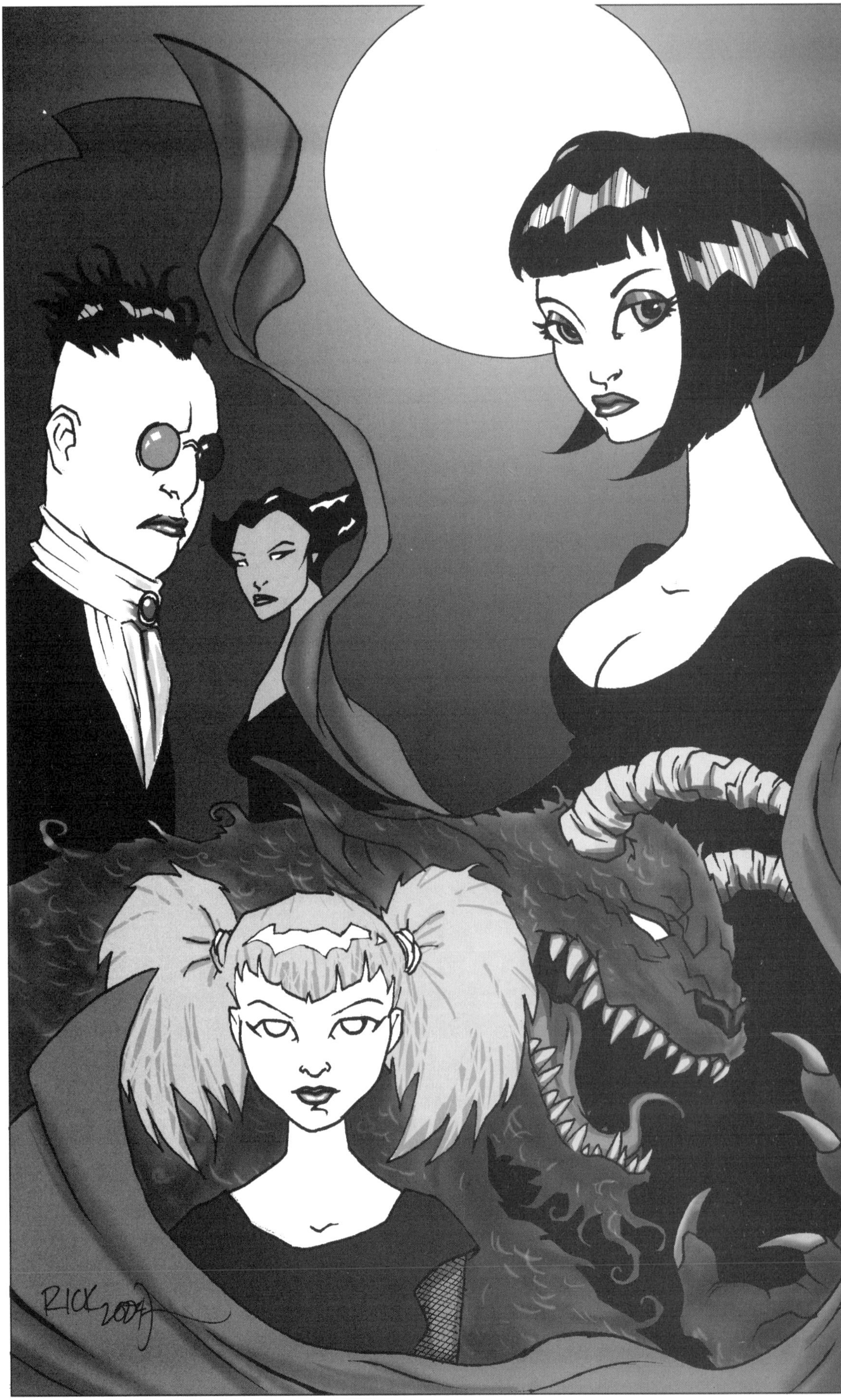
RICK 2004

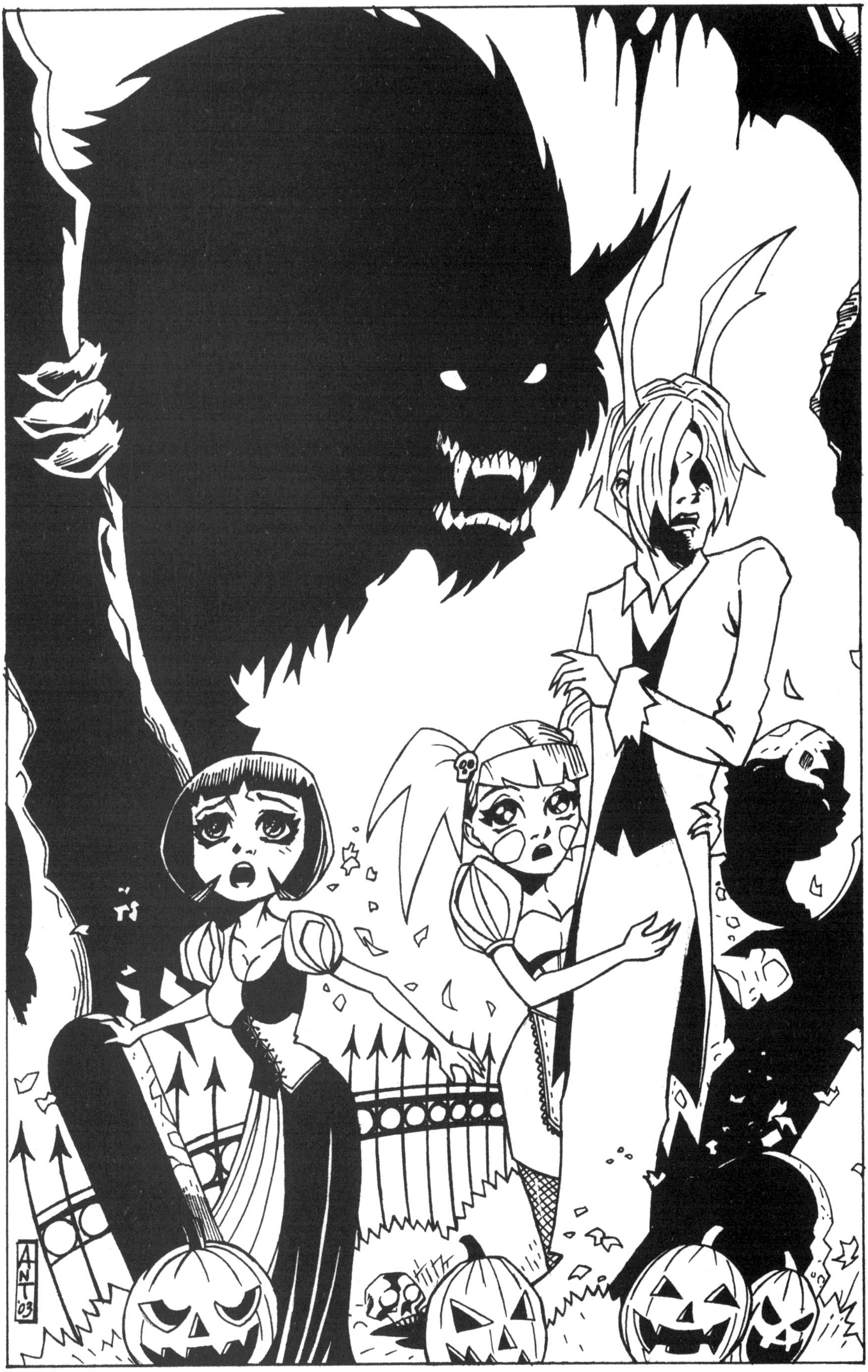
ANT '03

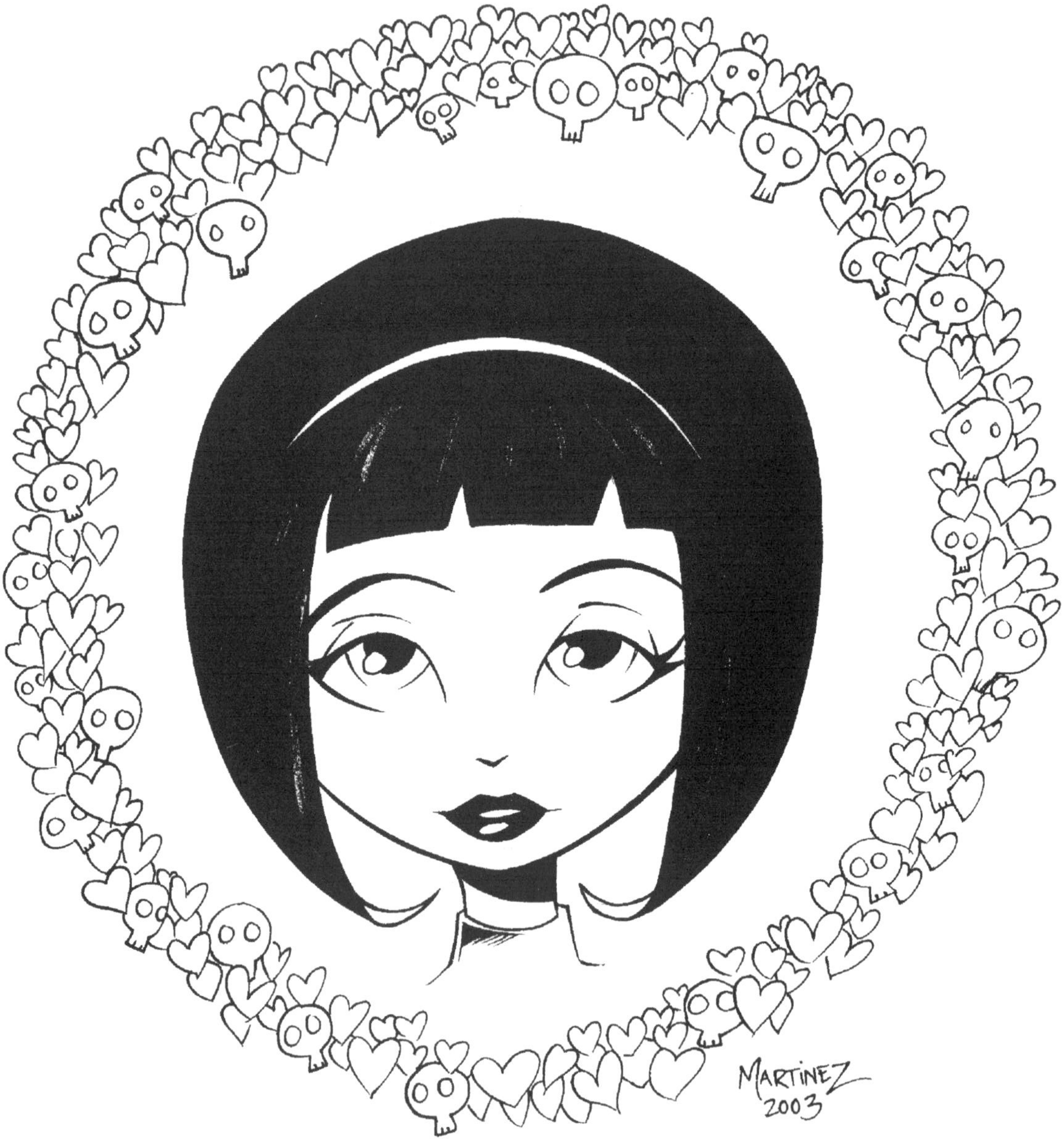
MARTINEZ
2003

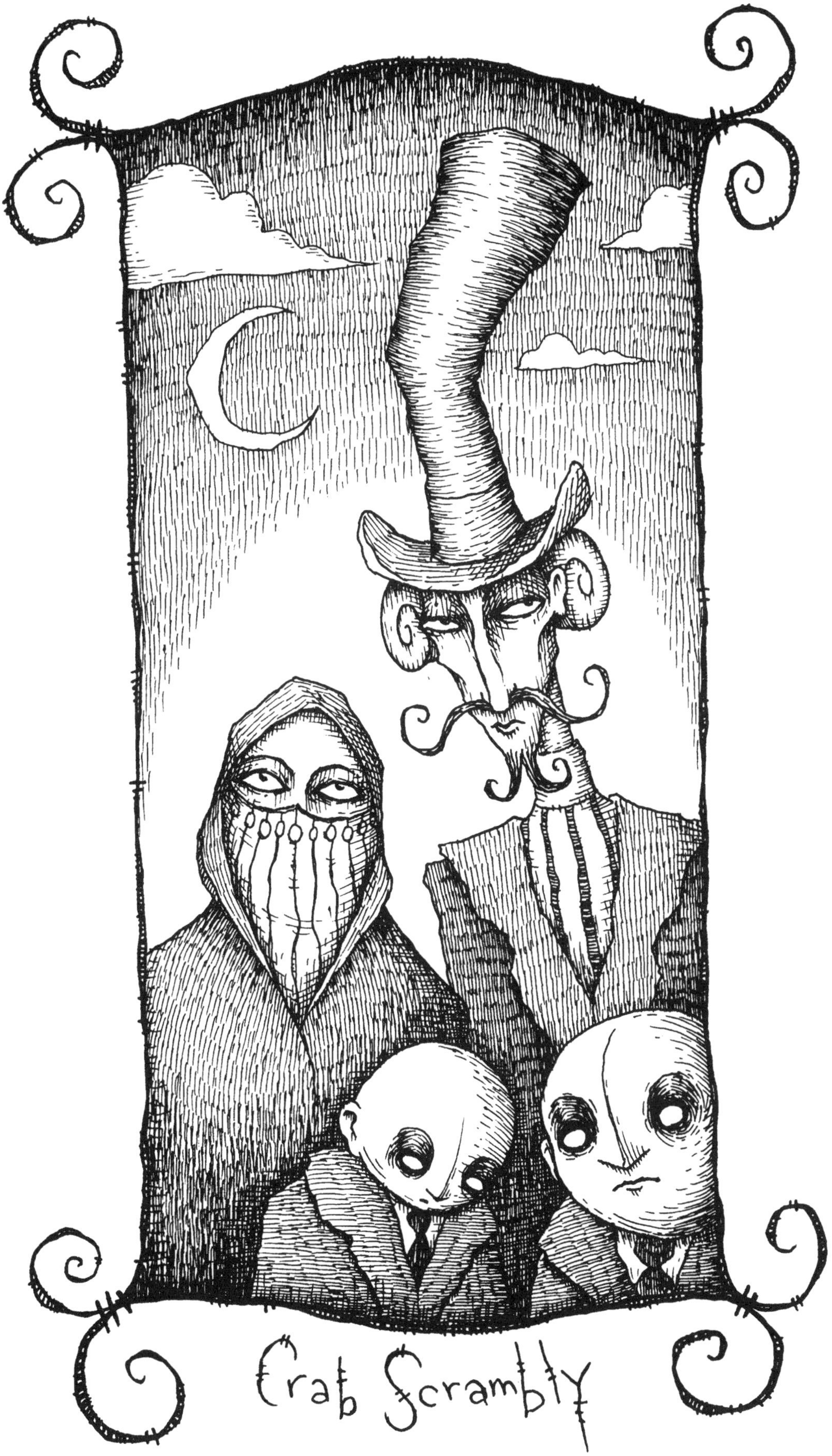

Crab Scrambly

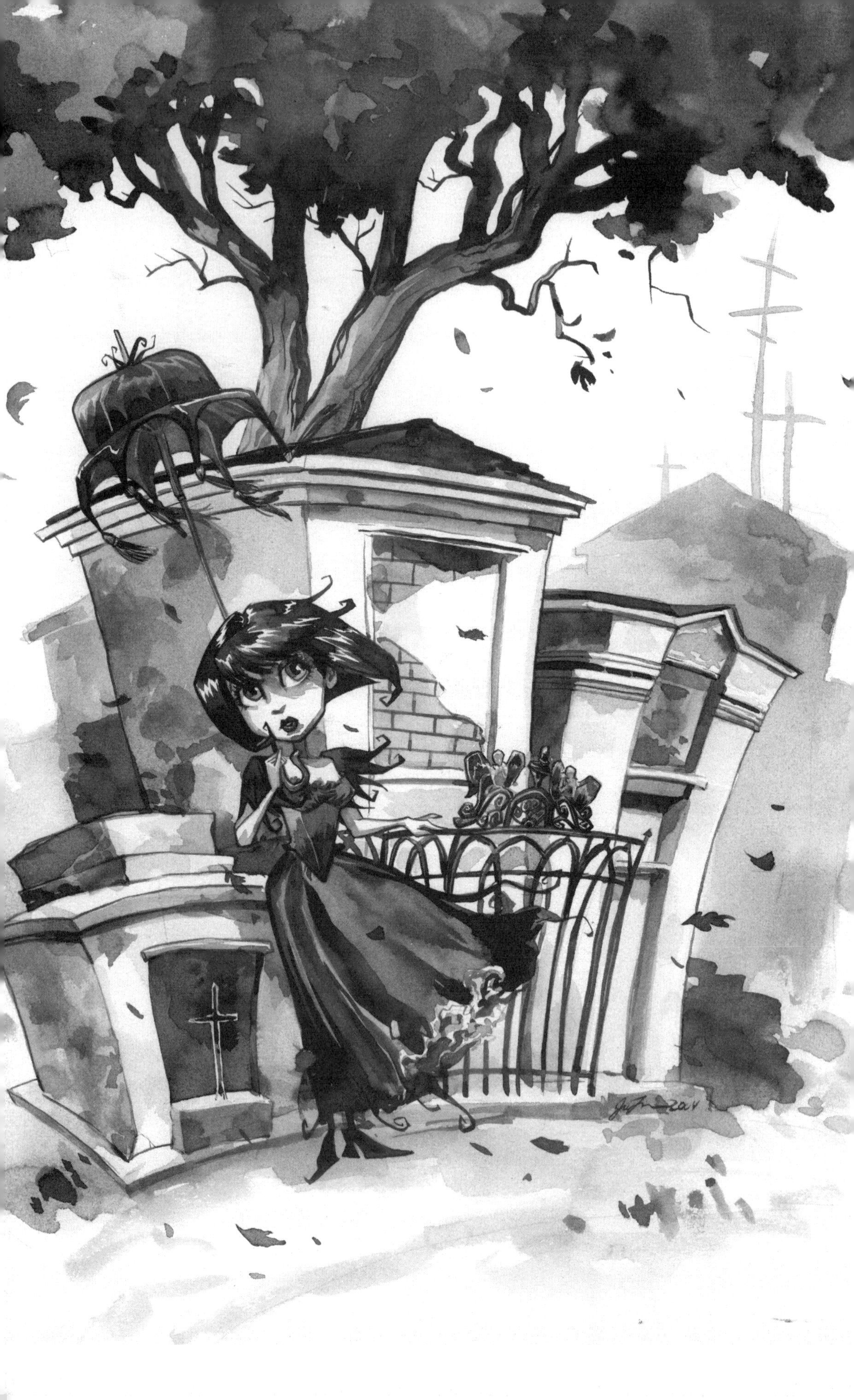

BROKEN curses

An Excerpt from Serena's Script for *GloomCookie* #16

BROKEN curses

–Our story starts out with a tour group in the Garden District of New Orleans. It's dark, hazy, foggy. The old-fashioned street lamps glow in the haze.

Notes on the neighborhood:

 The Garden District is an old neighborhood in New Orleans. The houses are grand old affairs ranging from Greek Revival to Antebellum style (period) and everything in between — and hybrids thereof. All the houses have porches, most wrap around.

 Most all the house have balconies or galleries. Galleries are like balconies but they have fluted columns or poles that support them.

 It's called the Garden District because of the lush gardens, full of tress, flowers, ivy and vines that surround the houses.

 The streets and sidewalks have areas that are cracked from the roots of the massive tress that line the streets. It is not unusual to see crumbling sidewalks or walls in this part of town.

–The sky is always in a haze of purple light at twilight and the stars are somehow still visible.

–The moon shines brightly through the canopy of trees that line the street our house is on.

"Our House":

 A large grand three story affair that takes up all of the corner. It's overgrown with flowers, plants, tress and vines. The house itself is quite wondrous, crumbling and in disrepair but nonetheless beautiful.

 It has an ornate ironwork gallery with fluted columns that support it, and an ornate wrought iron fence that surround the garden and house.

Our story starts with Chaz, a spooky tour guide. Please reference the New Orleans issue Ted and I did, where Lex and Damion go to on that tour. Please dress Chaz exactly like he appears in that issue.

–Chaz is standing in front of "our house." He is talking to his tour group, who are gathered listening to his story.

Notes on Chaz:

 He is very animated, dramatic; he moves his arms about for effect with sweeping arm movements. He uses his face very well when telling a story and his eyes get big.

He's a "Classy Vampiric Southern Gentlemen."

–Chaz's back is to our house as he speaks to the group.

–The group is facing the house and him.

–Chaz tells his story:
   Chaz: Good evening, dark spirits! We start this evening's tour with a somber tale. One that makes me shudder with utter despair!

   But this story is also frightening! For you see, there is a monstrous creature dwelling within those walls!

   A creature mourning the death of his beloved!

–People in the group look a little frightened.
   C: You will hear many such tales of lost love and curses in a city such as this, but none as sad and horrifying as this, I assure you.

   It is said that when the creature is mourning his dearest love he flies into a fit of rage and sorrow... returning here! To this very house! Filling the top window with candlelight...

NOTE TO BREEHN:
   If you find drawing Chaz over and over telling his story rather unexciting, then feel free to include a montage sort of thing to go a long with the story he's telling.
   Personally I think just showing him tell the story will be fine... but I will leave it up to you if you are having problems with this scene.

–Just then the window is filled with light. A few people in the tour scream! One points at the window.

–Chaz turns around and he looks at the window. He's totally shocked and frightened. But he composes himself quite nicely before he turns around and faces the group.
   C: There are many such houses with stories even more frightening than this... Let's make our way down the street, shall we? Where I will share another tale of horror... a tale of vampires! Follow me... quickly... this way!

–They disappear into the night as they quickly walk off. We stay with our house.
   There is someone standing at the gate.
   He is a thin, old, dark-skinned man with tattoos around his eyes. He has a slightly shabby tails coat and an untucked white shirt with black pants that are slightly too short for him, showing his skinny tattooed ankles.
   He has a dusty top hat with feather plumes coming off the side of the hat.

He has lots of rings, a necklace, and many bangles on his arms. He has a doctor's bag with him.

—He rings the bell.

—Damion answers.

    Man: Damion, my old friend!
    Damion: Thank you for coming.

—The man looks grave, but kindly. He puts both his hands out in welcome, clasping Damion's hands with a sad yet warm smile.
    D: Please follow me, this way...

—They go up a long curling staircase that is lined with candles. The light is casting spooky shadows on the walls.

—They finally reach Lex's room, where she is lying on the bed, seemingly sleeping.

There is no light in the room other than candlelight. Her bed is surrounded with candles — as well as her dresser, nightstand — pretty much everywhere you look there are candles.

—The man takes one look at her and is unquestionably sad and frightened.
    M: This poor girl has died as a result of a curse!
    D: But the curse was broken.
    M: Yes, but not in time.

—The man is thinking.
    M: A very old curse indeed, and quite strong. There is nothing I can do for her, my son.
    D: Nothing?
    M: I'm sorry. It's beyond...

—The man suddenly looks like he is getting a vision. He becomes rigid, blank-faced; his eyes roll back into his head, and he says...
    M: They search for her as we speak.
    D: Excuse me?

—But the man does not seem to hear Damion, he is in a trance, possessed by another.

—The man continues...
    M: Only he can bring back the raven-haired beauty! But at a great price — too

great!

D: What are you saying?

–The man does not respond — he just looks freaky in his trance and his eyes all rolled back in his head.

D: Are you okay?

M: One boy, unaware of his powers, not trusting his abilities — he is coming!

D: Who's coming?

–The man does not answer.

M: He is on his way!

–Note on the lettering: I think we should make the lettering a little bit different for the man when he is possessed — to make it clear he is not using his own voice — something spooky looking but not cheesy!

–The man comes back to himself, unaware of the words he just spoke.

D: Who is this boy? Where do I find him?

M: I do not know.

D: But you just said...

M: It wasn't me. I have no answers for you, my son... other than this:

–The man looks at Lex again.

M: Time is running thin.

–He looks at her again; he looks sad.

M: She can remain in this state for only so long. I do hope she can be helped before it's too late.

–Damion looks sad.

–They hug and the man leaves the room -- leaving Damion alone with Lex.

–We follow the man down the stairs, he lets himself out... he opens the door and finds a frightened looking Sebastian standing there. The doctor addresses Sebastian, then leaves.

M: Ahhh, I see!

S: (Sebastian says nothing, he looks too freaked out to talk)

M: Don't be frightened, my boy. I think you may be the very person he is expecting.

TO BE CONTINUED...

◉

SEBASTIAN   ISABELLA   CHRYS   LEX   VERMILION   ARTEMUS   DAMION